英美概况

A Brief Introduction to Britain and America

温洪瑞 李学珍 主编

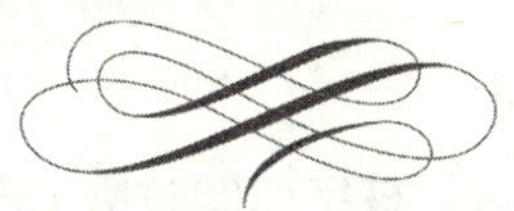

第 3 版

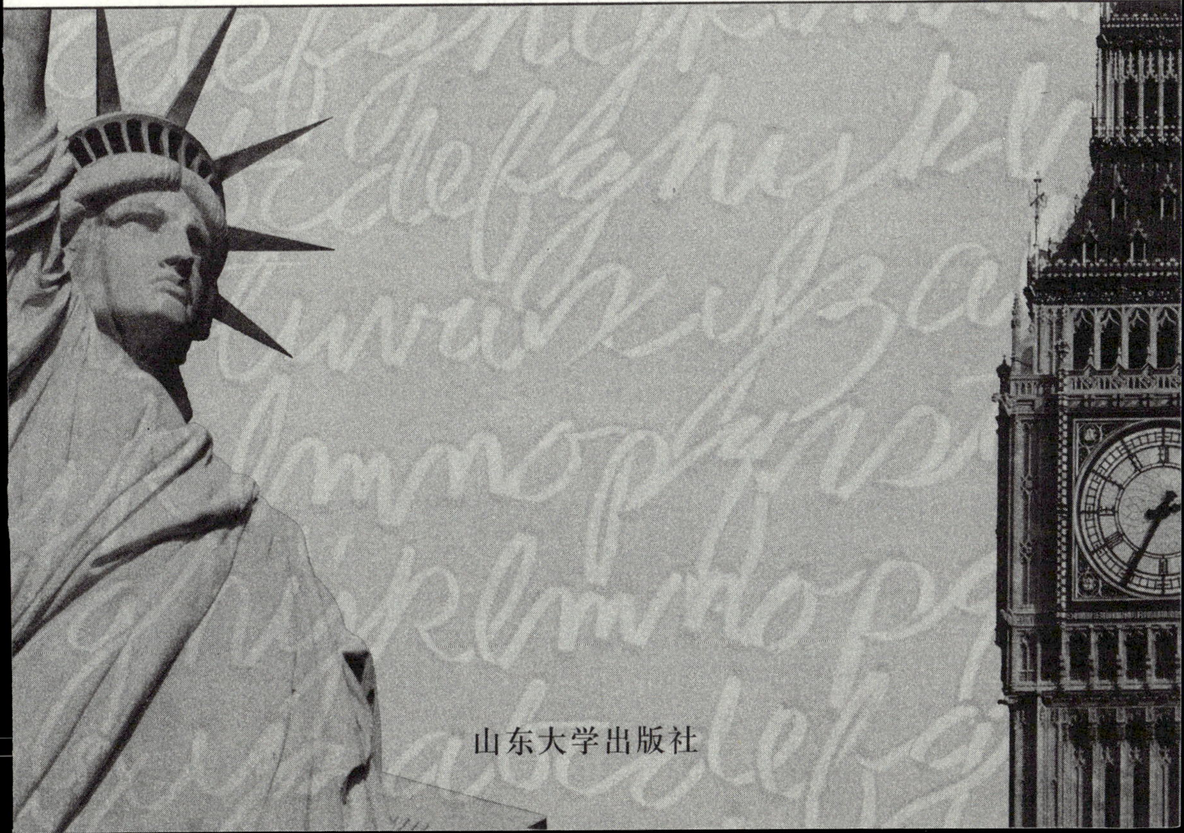

山东大学出版社

图书在版编目(CIP)数据

英美概况/温洪瑞,李学珍主编. —3 版. —济南:
山东大学出版社,2008. 6(2018. 8 重印)
ISBN 978-7-5607-1833-0

Ⅰ. 英…
Ⅱ. ①温…②李…
Ⅲ. ①英语—高等学校—教材
②英国—概况—英文
③美国—概况—英文
Ⅳ. H319. 4:K

中国版本图书馆 CIP 数据核字(2006)第 165298 号

山东大学出版社出版发行
(山东省济南市山大南路 27 号　邮政编码:250100)
山 东 省 新 华 书 店 经 销
泰安金彩印务有限公司印刷
720 毫米×1000 毫米　1/16　22 印张　406 千字
2008 年 6 月第 3 版　2018 年 8 月第 21 次印刷
定价:28.00 元

序

《英美概况》即将付梓，应邀为其作序，我欣然从命，缘起如下：

一、该书成稿已久，作为使用教材，历经十余春秋。作者孜孜不倦，默默耕耘，精益求精，几番更新，倾注无尽心血，使其终于问世，当是幸事，为此致贺。

二、两位作者先后赴沪参加美籍专家执教的中美文化研讨班，史料例证有根基；一道参与翻译《英汉对照实用中医文库》，语言文字有功底；同为硕士生导师，联袂开设“英美文化专题”学位课，学术理论有水平；联名申请出版基金，携手推出《英美概况》英文教材，合作共事创新绩，可谓佳话，借此介绍。

三、编写原则针对性强。具有自己的特色。选材难易得当，注重实用；内容充实、新颖、适合教学；语言通顺、地道，便于自学。《英美概况》实属应社会之需，补教学之缺，并带有创新性的一部好的教材，质量应属上乘，特此推荐。

是为序。

李延福

1997 年 4 月于山东大学

三版前言

承蒙广大读者对《英美概况》教材的厚爱与关心，使其第三版有机会得以付梓。为了不辜负广大读者的期望，我们本着有错必纠、精益求精、与时俱进和方便读者的原则，在保持原教材基本框架结构不变的情况下，对教材进行了认真的修订，主要是更改、充实或补充某些新的内容，以便读者能够从中更多地了解近年来英美两国发展变化的最新情况。

此次修订正值2008年北京奥运会即将来临之际，我们衷心希望教材的修订本能够以新的面目，客观地、简明扼要地、更好地为读者提供有关这两个主要英语国家有用的文化背景知识，为使用英语进行中外交流奠定背景知识基础，清除因文化差异而造成的交流障碍，帮助读者打开对外交流的方便之门。若能如此，该教材的修订也算是我们语言文化工作者对北京奥运所尽的一点微薄之力吧！我们期待着以更高的质量、更新的品味，向北京奥运会献礼！

时间有限，错漏难免。在此，对广大读者、教材使用者和出版社领导以及所有关注和帮助过本教材发展的专家学者表示衷心的谢意！殷切希望听到更多关于进一步修订的宝贵建议。

编　者

2008年6月于烟台南山学院

修订版前言

本教材自1997年出版以来受到许多专家读者的热情关注，通过各种方式肯定了其优点并不吝赐教，指出其错误、缺陷与不足。专家、读者的宝贵意见是此次修订的主要依据。

本着创新求实、与时俱进的精神，作者在多年使用和征求读者意见的基础上，决定对本教材进行修订。此次修订的原则是在保持原书内容、难易程度和篇幅基本不变的情况下，修改原书中的错误，更换过时的内容和数据；删去书后词汇附录，增补课后汉语注释，以便于读者查阅与自学、理解与翻译；文中需要加以注释的疑难或专有名词均使用黑体字，并在课后用汉语注出。根据概况课知识性强和难以记忆的特点，适当修改、补充课后练习，使其更加灵活多变、更好地覆盖教材的基本内容，以达到反复接触、强化理解与记忆的目的。

此次修订由温洪瑞负责执行并完成。在此过程中，得到山东大学出版社领导和外语学院的专家、学者的热情支持。没有他们的支持和无私的帮助，修订是不可能达到如期效果的。对于他们的支持与帮助，特此致以衷心的谢意。

书中不足之处，仍希望专家读者不吝赐教。

编　者

2003年10月于济南

前言

本书应当前教学需要，在参阅大量国内外文献资料的基础上，以马列主义立场、观点为指导进行取舍、整理和编排而成，并经过多年课堂试用和反复修改。

本教材的宗旨是密切结合教学实际，为英语语言文学专业的专、本科学生简明扼要地提供学习英语必须掌握的英美两国的地理、政治、经济和历史知识，为学好本专业奠定坚实的文化背景知识基础，为培养外向型外语人才，为改革开放、建设有中国特色的社会主义服务。

本教材的编写原则如下：

一、密切联系时代与本专业其他课程教学的实际需求精选材料，力求做到繁简得当，学以致用。

二、充分考虑到本课程知识性强的特点，教材的编排力求内容丰富、新颖，编排合理，便于教学，易于记忆。

三、用英语编写，力求语言通顺、地道，便于学生在学习知识的同时提高英语的理解与应用水平。

本教材共20课，每一课都附有知识性练习、讨论与思考题，每一课开头部分有内容提要，便于学生自学、理解和记忆。书后附有英美历史大事记、英王朝历代国王名表及任期、美国50州、美国历任总统名表及任期等，以便查阅。

本教材可用作英语专业专、本科生教材，自学考试教材和英语爱好者的业余读物。经多年课堂试用，证明使用效果良好。

本书在编写过程中得到了山东大学教务处、外语学院和出版社领导的大力支持。山东大学外语学院的李延福教授、丁原骥教授在百忙之中审阅了本书的全部文稿，提出了许多宝贵的修改意见。在此，对上述各位的支持与帮助表示衷心的谢意，并向在本书编写过程中参考的有关文献的作者致谢。

由于作者水平有限，错漏之处在所难免，衷心希望专家读者批评指正。

编　者

1997年2月

Contents

Part One An Introduction to Great Britain

Part Two An Introduction to the United States

APPENDIX Ⅰ

APPENDIX Ⅱ

Part One
An Introduction to Great Britain

Lesson 1 Geography: The Land

Major Points

Britain

is officially called the United Kingdom of Great Britain and Northern Ireland.

is situated in Western Europe, a country of islands off the northwestern coast of Europe.

is rather small, with a total area of some 244,019 square kilometers.

has played a major role in shaping the modern world.

is made up of England, Wales, Scotland and Northern Ireland.

is divided into the lowland area and the highland area.

has large mountain ranges: the Pennine Chains, the Cumbrian Mountain Range, the Grampian Mountains, and the Cambrian Mountain range.

has such important rivers as the Thames, the Severn, the Mersey, the Humber, the Clyde and the Forth.

has a temperate, maritime climate.

is rich in coal, petroleum, natural gas deposits, but rather poor in other natural resources.

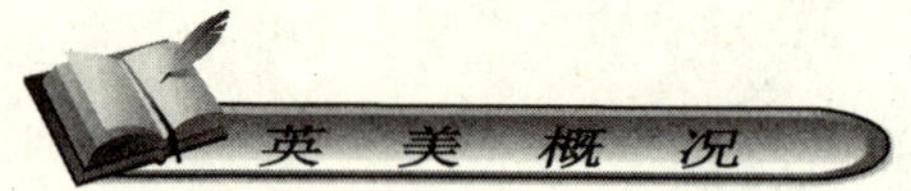

Main Contents

1. The Name of the Country

The full and official name of the Union formed by England, Scotland, Wales and Northern Ireland is **the United Kingdom of Great Britain and Northern Ireland**, usually abbreviated to the United Kingdom or UK, Great Britain, or simply Britain, or sometimes informally England.

People in England, Wales, Scotland and Northern Ireland were once separate nations; England has controlled the other nations over a period of several centuries. The name "Britain" comes from the **Brythons** (**Britons**) who migrated from the European Continent before 300 B. C. The name "England" comes from the Anglo-Saxon conquerors; it means "Angla-land," the land of the Anglo-Saxons, collectively known as Angles who migrated from the northwest of the European Continent in the 5th century A. D. The name for the Union that once existed in the period between 1800 and the early 1920's was "the United Kingdom of Great Britain and Ireland," which changed to its present form in 1927 after the 26 Irish Free States achieved their independence in the early 1920's.

2. Location and Size

Britain is situated in Western Europe and is separated from the European continent by **the North Sea**, **the Strait of Dover** and **the English Channel.** It lies between 50° and 60° north latitude, and roughly between 2° east and 8° west longitude. The prime meridian of 0° just passes through the old observatory at **Greenwich**.

The neighboring countries of Britain include France, Holland, Germany, Denmark, Norway, Belgium, the Irish Republic, and Iceland.

Britain is a rather small country, with a total area of some 244,019 square kilometers, accounting for less than 2% of the land area of the world and ranking about the 75th in size among countries in the world. It is just under 966 kilometers in a straight line from the south coast to the extreme north of mainland Britain, and about 483 kilometers across the widest part. No point in the country is as far as 121 kilometers away from tidal waters.

Small as it is in both size and population, Britain has played an important role in shaping the modern world. It was once one of the oldest and strongest colonial powers in the world and ruled a vast empire, as boasted to be, "an empire on which the sun never sets." Beginning with the Age of Exploration (about 1450—1600), English ships carried explorers, traders, and colonists to every corner of the globe. The English eventually ruled wherever they settled. Thus the British have spread their way of life around the globe through conquest and colonization. Many nations have laws and governments modeled on the British system. Millions of people speak English, probably the world's most widely spoken language. The works of British greatest authors and thinkers—**Geoffrey Chaucer**, William Shakespeare, **Isaac Newton**, **John Locke**, **John Keats**, and **William Wordsworth**, to name only a few—are known and read in every corner of the world. The British inventions, such as the spinning Jenny, the steam engine and the railroads during the Industrial Revolution helped make modern life possible. In the 20th century, British scientists and engineers have helped develop the jet aircraft, radar and penicillin, the miracle drug that has saved millions of lives. As a member country in **the Security Council of the United Nations**, Britain plays an important part in international and European affairs.

3. Landforms

Of the four nations of Britain—England, Scotland, Wales and Northern Ireland, England is the largest and occupies most of **the British Isles.** Scotland occupies the northern part and Wales the western part of the British Isles. Northern Ireland occupies the northern part of Ireland.

The island of Great Britain can be roughly divided into the lowland area and the highland area in terms of landform. The former comprises Midland, southern and eastern England, and the latter the broad central upland known as **the Pennines**, **the Lake District**, most of Wales and Scotland. In the British Isles there are hundreds of smaller islands, including **the Channel Islands**, **the Scilly Isles**, **the Isles of Wight and Man**, **Anglesey**, **the Inner and Outer Hebrides**, **the Orkneys and Shetlands.**

England, with a total area of more than 130,000 square kilometers, may be divided into three landform regions: the east and the southeast are made up of rolling downs and low-lying plains; middle England is a region of mountains formed by the Pennines, which, with the average altitude between 200 and 500 meters, form the "backbone" of England, extending south from the Scottish border to Derbyshire. Cross Fell, 893 meters high, is the highest peak of the Pennines. The north and west of England are hilly, partly formed by the **Cumbrian Mountain Range**, the highest mountain peak of which is **Scafell** (977 m), the highest in England but the third highest mountain throughout the country.

Scotland has an area of 78,760 square kilometers. About two thirds of Scotland is covered by the Highlands. The chief range in the Highlands is **the Grampian Mountains**, which contain **Ben Nevis** (1344 m), the highest mountain on the island of Great Britain. The central lowlands of Scotland include the valleys of the **Clyde**, **Tay** and **Forth** rivers. This is the most important area in Scotland, which contains most of the industry and population. **Edinburgh**, the capital of Scotland, and Glasgow, the largest city in Scotland, are both located in this area. The Southern Uplands are a region of rolling moorlands cut by some small fertile river valleys. The Southern Uplands reach their highest point in **Merrick**.

Wales covers an area of about 20,700 square kilometers. It is geographically divided into the industrial south, the central plateaus and lakes and the mountainous north of the farmers and tourists. Most of Wales is mountainous, mainly formed by **the Cambrian Mountain Range**. Its highest peak **Snowdon** (1085 m) is the second highest mountain in Britain. In Wales, only 12% of the land is arable, 6% is covered with forest, and much of the land is pastureland for sheep and cattle. The most fertile land in Wales is found near the coast and in the interior valleys. Coal has been mined in the area between **Cardiff** and Swansea.

The central part of Northern Ireland is composed of plains surrounded by such highlands and mountains as **Antrim**, **Sperrin** and **Mourne**. On the central plain lies **Lough Neagh**, the largest lake in the whole country. Northern Ireland is mainly agricultural, with industry concentrated in the two ports of **Belfast** and Londonderry.

4. Rivers and Lakes

Being short and swift, few rivers in Britain are navigable.

The most important river in Britain is **the Thames River** (338 kilometers long), which rises in Cotswold Hills and flows through the capital city London

and empties into the English Channel. The river is navigable for large ships to London.

The longest river in Britain is **the Severn River** (354 kilometers in length), which rises in the mountains of Wales and empties into the Bristol Channel, where the ports of Cardiff and Bristol are located.

The Mersey River (110 kilometers in length) flows between Lancashire and Cheshire into the Irish Sea. Its estuary, navigable for ocean vessels, is linked to Manchester by a ship canal, with the port Liverpool on its mouth.

The Humber River in Humberside is also navigable for large ships to **Hull.**

The Clyde and the Forth are the most important rivers in Scotland. The former flows through Glasgow, and the latter passes by Edinburgh, with the port Leith on its mouth.

Since Britain was subjected to considerable glaciations, the highlands, especially in northern Scotland, the Cumbrian Mountains, and the North Wales, contain many deep valleys filled with long, ribbon-shaped lakes. These regions constitute great attractions for tourists. Lakes in Britain are chiefly found in the English Lake District, the Scottish Highlands, the Welsh mountains and Northern Ireland. The largest Lake in England is **Lake Windermere.** It covers an area of 16 square kilometers and is located in the Lake District, in the northwest of England. Lake District is one of the popular touring sports in England, where there are 15 lakes radiating like the spokes of a wheel from a central hub. It is commonly accounted the most beautiful part of England, where William Wordsworth and the other Lake Poets were born and lived, who were inspired by the perfection of water, trees and heather-covered slopes.

Lake Neagh in Northern Ireland is the largest of all throughout the country and covers an area of some 396 square kilometers.

5. The Coast

For a small country of islands Britain has a great length of coastline (about 11,450 kilometers). The coast is very varied, with perhaps the best parts in the southwest of England and in the west of Scotland. The coast of Devon and **Cornwall**, in the southwest, is much indented, with many sheltered bays and coves and fine rocky headlands. With so large a population on so small an island the best parts of the coast are inevitably rather crowded during the summer. In the parts nearest to great centers of population big seaside resort towns have grown up. Four of these—**Brighton**, **Bournemouth**, **Southend** in the south, and **Blackpool** in the northwest—have become important towns, remarkable for the great number of visitors they receive.

6. Climate

Britain has a **temperate maritime climate**, which is damp and warm all the year round and generally does not run to extremes. As the prevailing southwesterly winds are warmed by **the Gulf Stream** and made moist by the Atlantic Ocean, the climate in Britain is much milder than that of many places in the same latitude. During a normal summer, the temperature occasionally rises about 27℃ in the south; winter temperatures below −7℃ are rare. The annual air temperature is about 10℃, varying from around 5℃ in the coldest month (January) to 17℃ in the warmest month (July) on average. The British Isles as a whole have an annual average rainfall of over 1,020 millimeters, while England has about 860 millimeters. The mountainous areas of the west and the north have far more rain than the plains of the east and the south.

The climate in Britain has three features. The first one is that there are more fogs or smog in winter, for which London is famous. The second one is that there are more rainy days but less sunny days. The rainfall is not very heavy and there is not often any very violent storm or wind. In some places there are over 260 rainy days a year. The third one is its instability or changeability. All the seasons are very variable; there is no part of the year at which it is possible to expect, with any degree of assurance, that weather will be dry or wet, clear or dull, and a bad day in July can be as cold as a mild day in January.

7. Natural Resources

The main natural resources in Britain are coal, petroleum, natural gas, iron ore, limestone, clay, shale, chalk and tin. Coal and petroleum are the most important.

Coal. Many of the coalfields in the United Kingdom have been in continuous production since the beginning of the 17th century. The coal industry was brought under the national ownership by the Labor government in 1947, and since then many of the poor coalfields have been closed down and more profitable mines modernized.

The **Ayrshire** field in Scotland and the deposits of the Lowlands continue

to supply Scottish industry. South Wale has valuable coal deposits, which are used for industry and as fuel for heating homes. The leading anthracite fields in Britain are in Wales. The coal mining area of central England, including York, Birmingham and **Nottingham, Leicester and Derby**, is the largest one of the country, which constitutes about 40% of the total output. There are also coalmines in the northeast and southeast of England, in **Durham, Northumberland** and **Canterbury**. The annual coal production output in Britain is over 120 million tons.

Petroleum. Only small quantities of oil had been found in Britain before big oil fields were discovered under the North Sea, east of the British Isles in 1965. The oil deposit is estimated as 3,000—4,500 million tons. Britain began to put oil into production in the 1970's and by 1980 the annual output of oil had reached 100 million tons. Britain is now not only self-sufficient in oil supply, but has become the fifth largest oil exporter in the world.

Forestry. With its mild climate and varied soils, Britain has a diverse pattern of natural vegetation. Originally, one third of the country was covered with forests, but now woodlands only covers 8.6% of its surface and some 85% of the country's timber needs are supplied by import as a result of long years of denudation.

Fresh Water. With too much rain and many short and rapid rivers, Britain is rich in water resources. However, it still cannot meet the needs of the growing industry and agriculture irrigation. Water pollution affects on many English and Scottish rivers. The fresh water problems, including inland water pollution, are far from being solved.

Wild Life. There are no longer any really dangerous wild animals in Britain, except the wild cat, occasionally found in the depths of Scottish forests. The wolf died out several centuries ago and there are no bears or wild boars. The largest wild animal is the stag, for wild deer are found in Scotland and in Southwest England. Foxes are found all over Britain, though chiefly in England. The other animals found in Britain are rabbits, stoat, weasel and hedgehogs.

Birds are numerous and law protects many of them, especially the rare species, such as the eagle and the osprey. The chief songbirds are the nightingale and the blackbird. Of sea birds the most common are the various kinds of gulls.

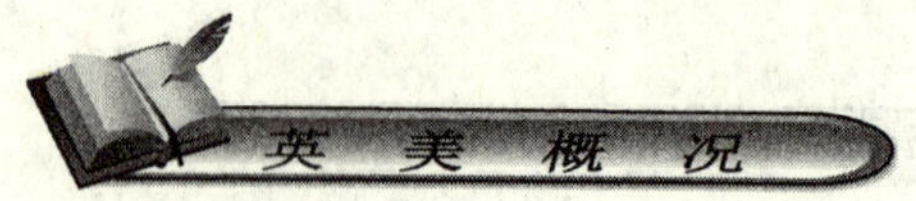

There are various species of fresh-water fishes and angling is a nationwide pastime, whether in lakes and rivers or in the sea, where there are also many kinds of fishes.

Notes

1. the United Kingdom of Great Britain and Northern Ireland 大不列颠及北爱尔兰联合王国
2. Brythons (Britons) 布立吞人
3. the North Sea 北海
4. the Strait of Dover 多佛尔海峡
5. the English Channel 英吉利海峡
6. Greenwich 格林尼治
7. Geoffrey Chaucer 杰奥弗里·乔叟(1340?～1400),第一位伟大的英国诗人。
8. Isaac Newton 艾萨克·牛顿(1642～1727),英国科学家。
9. John Locke 约翰·洛克(1632～11704),英国哲学家。
10. John Keats 约翰·济慈(795～1812),英国诗人。
11. William Wordsworth 华兹华斯(1770～1850),英国诗人,于1843年被封为桂冠诗人。
12. the Security Council of the United Nations 联合国安理会
13. the British Isles 大不列颠群岛
14. the Pennines 奔宁山脉,地处英格兰北部。
15. the Lake District 湖区,地处英格兰西北部。
16. the Channel Islands 海峡群岛,地处英吉利海峡。
17. the Scilly Isles 夕利群岛,位于英格兰西南端。
18. the Isle of Wight 怀特岛,位于英格兰南部海岸外。
19. the Isle of Man 马恩岛,位于爱尔兰海。
20. Anglesey 位于威尔士西北部岛屿。
21. the Inner Hebrides 内赫布里底群岛,位于苏格兰西北部。
22. the Outer Hebrides 外赫布里底群岛,位于苏格兰西北部。
23. the Orkneys 澳克尼群岛,位于苏格兰之北。
24. the Shetlands 设特兰群岛,位于苏格兰之北。
25. Cumbrian Mountain Range 康布里安山脉,地处英格兰西北部湖区。
26. Scafell 斯科费尔峰,英国第三高峰。
27. the Grampian Mountains 格兰扁山脉,地处苏格兰高地。

28. Ben Nevis 尼维斯峰，格兰扁山脉的最高峰，英国第一高峰。
29. Clyde 克莱德河，流经格拉斯哥，河两岸有有名的船坞与造船厂。
30. Tay 泰河，起源于苏格兰高地，注入北海，苏格兰最长的河流。
31. Forth 福斯河，苏格兰重要河流，流经爱丁堡以北约两公里处。
32. Edinburgh 爱丁堡，苏格兰首府。
33. Merrick 梅里克，位于苏格兰南部台地。
34. the Cambrian Mountain Range 坎布里安山脉，威尔士山地。
35. Snowdon 斯诺登峰，威尔士山地的最高峰，英国第二高峰。
36. Cardiff 加的夫，威尔士首府。
37. Antrim 安特里姆高原
38. Sperrin 斯别林山
39. Mourne 莫恩山
40. Lough Neagh /Lake Neagh 讷湖，英国第一大湖，地处北爱尔兰中央平原。
41. Belfast 贝尔法斯特，北爱尔兰首府。
42. the Thames River 泰晤士河，流经英格兰南部，英国最重要的河流。
43. the Severn River 塞文河，英国最长的河流。
44. the Mersey River 默西河，英格兰河流。
45. the Humber river 亨伯河，英格兰河流。
46. Hull 赫尔(港)
47. Lake Windermere 温德米尔湖，英格兰湖区，英格兰第一大湖。
48. Cornwall 康沃尔半岛，英格兰西南端。
49. Brighton 布莱顿
50. Bournemouth 伯恩茅斯
51. Southend 绍森德
52. Blackpool 布莱克浦
53. temperate maritime climate 海洋性温带气候
54. the Gulf Stream 墨西哥湾暖流
55. Ayrshire 亚尔郡(苏格兰西南部之一郡)
56. Nottingham 诺丁汉
57. Leicester and Derby 莱斯特和德比
58. Durham 达勒姆
59. Northumberland 诺森伯兰郡
60. Canterbury 坎特伯雷

Questions for Discussion

1. Give a brief account of the location, size and geographic features of Britain.
2. What a role has Britain played in shaping the modern world?
3. Point out the large mountain ranges, rivers, lakes and big seaside-resort towns of Britain on the map and tell where they are located.
4. Describe the climate in Britain and point out its three features.
5. What natural resources is Britain blessed with? Of the resources, which two are the most important to Britain's economy? Point out their distribution respectively.
6. What animals and birds can still be found in Britain?

Exercises

Ⅰ. Choose the correct answer and circle the letter before it.

1. The full and official name of Great Britain changed into its present-day form in the year of ________.
   A. 1920 B. 1927 C. 1914 D. 1945
2. The highest mountain peak in Britain is in ________.
   A. England B. Scotland
   C. Wales D. Northern Ireland
3. The longest river in Britain is ________.
   A. River Severn B. River Thames
   C. River Mersey D. River Humber
4. The largest lake in Britain is located in ________.
   A. England B. Scotland
   C. Wales D. Northern Ireland
5. The highest mountain peak in Britain is called ________.
   A. Ben Nevis B. Cross Fell
   C. Snowdon D. Scafell

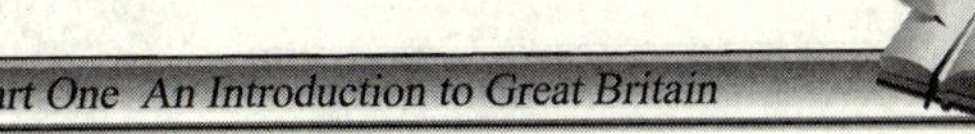

6. The Lake District is well-known for ________.
   A. its wild and beautiful scenery B. its varied lakes
   C. the lake Poets D. all of the above three
7. Which of the following is NOT the feature of British climate?
   A. coldness. B. more rainy days.
   C. changeability. D. more fogs.
8. The leading anthracite coalfields in Britain are in ______.
   A. Scotland B. England
   C. Wales D. the North Sea

Ⅱ. Fill in the following blanks with appropriate words or expressions.

1. Britain is separated from the European continent by ______, ________ and ________.
2. The total area of Britain is about ________ square kilometers.
3. The chief ranges in England are the ________ and the ________ Mountains.
4. The highest mountain on the island of Great Britain is ________ in ________ Mountains.
5. The Central Lowlands of Scotland include the valleys of the ________, ________ and ________ Rivers.
6. The highest point in Wales is __________ in the ________ Mountain range.
7. The most important rivers in Scotland are ________ and ____________.
8. Britain has a ________, maritime climate.
9. Britain's most important natural resources are ________ and ________.
10. In 1965, big oil fields were discovered under the ________.

Ⅲ. Match the names of the rivers in Column A with the names of their ports in Column B. Put the letter before the name of a city in the corresponding blank.

Column A	Column B
1. ____ The Thames River	a. Hull
2. ____ The Severn River	b. Liverpool
3. ____ The Humber River	c. London
4. ____ The Mersey River	d. Bristol

5. ____ The Clyde River e. Leith
6. ____ The Forth River f. Glasgow

Ⅳ. Translate the following into Chinese.

1. the United Kingdom of Great Britain and Northern Ireland
2. the Strait of Dover
3. the English Channel
4. Greenwich
5. the Channel Islands
6. the Orkney Isles
7. the Shetlands
8. the British Isles
9. the Pennines
10. the Cumbrian Mountain Range
11. The Cambrian Mountain Range
12. the Grampian Mountain Range
13. the Thames River
14. the Severn River
15. Lake Neigh
16. Lake District
17. the Isle of Man
18. Edinburgh
19. Glasgow
20. Cardiff

Ⅴ. Explain the following in English.

1. Lake District
2. Edinburgh
3. Cardiff
4. Glasgow
5. Lough Neagh

Lesson 2 Geography: The People

Major Points

Britain

has a population of over 60.2 million.

has one of the highest population densities in the world.

has seven conurbations that contain almost one third of its population.

has four nations: the English, the Scottish, the Welsh and the Irish. English is the official language and spoken by the majority of the population, but Celtic and Gaelic can still be heard in remote areas.

is a Christian country with a diversity of religious sects: the Church of England, the Free Churches and the Roman Catholic Church.

is full of conservatisms.

maintains regional differences politically, economically and culturally.

is dotted with a dozen of principal cities: London, Birmingham, Glasgow, Liverpool, Edinburgh, Cardiff, Belfast, Manchester, Sheffield, etc.

Main Contents

1. Populations and Population Density

According to the 2005 census, the total population of Britain is about 60.2 million. Compared with 56.488 million in 1984. Britain is the third largest country in population in Europe, only next to Russia and Germany. Britain has one of the highest **population densities** in the world, with some 248 persons living in every square kilometer, about ten times that of the United States.

2. Population Distribution

The population in Britain is predominantly urban and suburban; seven great conurbations contain almost a third of the population. The seven **conur-**

bations are **Greater London**, **W. Midlands**, **South Yorkshire**, **W. Yorkshire**, **Greater Manchester**, **Merseyside**, and **Tyne & Wear**. About one half of the population live within the area of an ellipse extending across England with South Lancashire and West Yorkshire at one end and the London area at the other and having the industrialized **Midland** at its center. Other main concentrations of population are the **Tyne and Tees Valleys** (including Newcastle upon Tyne) and the Clyde Valley in Scotland (including Glasgow). There are also considerable concentrations in Southeast Wales, round the cities Belfast, Bristol and Edinburgh, and along the eastern half of England's south coast.

3. Nations and the Languages Spoken

The main nations in Britain are the English, Scottish, Welsh and Irish.

The English people, descendants of **Anglo-Saxons**, who came to England in the middle of the fifth century after the Romans left Britain in 410 A. D. , make up about 80% of the total population. The Welsh and Irish are the descendants of the **Celts**, who came to England before the Romans.

The major languages spoken in Britain are English, **Gaelic** and **Welsh**. English is the official language of the country and is spoken by most of the population. About one fifth of the people in Wales still speak the ancient Welsh language. Gaelic, as well as English, is now spoken by some Scots and by a few people in Northern Ireland. Many dialects that once were heard in different parts of the country are heard less and less often as movies, radio, television, and travel have helped to promote the use of standardized English (also known as Received Pronunciation or RP English).

English is descended from the language of the Germanic people-the Anglo-Saxons who invaded the British Isles in the fifth and the early sixth centuries. Their language is called **Old English** (450—1150), which is quite different from Modern English in phonology, morphology and syntax. After the Norman Conquest of 1066, English as a language of a subjugated people underwent tremendous changes through contact with Danes and Norman French, the forwarding of stress brought about the loss of some of the old inflections (grammatical forms), and the English vocabulary was gradually enlarged by borrowing and assimilating thousands of French, Latin and Greek words and words from many other languages. Then English had entered the second stage by 1150—**Middle English** (1150—1450), in its evolution from Old English to

Modern English. Very late in this period, the pronunciation of most long vowels and diphthongs began to change in what is now called the Great Vowel Shift, and changes in grammar occurred as well. By the close of the Middle English period, English had triumphed in England and displaced both French and Latin as the written language of the people. The most memorable writing in the "New language" was that of Geoffrey Chaucer, whose ***Canterbury Tales*** is often read in its original, Middle English form. After **William Caxton** introduced the printing press to England in 1476, most books were printed in London and were written in the London dialect, as London had become the chief commercial center, the center of government, and near the great universities. The London dialect was thus disseminated throughout England. The introduction of the printing press, the establishment of the first English postal system by Henry Ⅷ in 1516 both promoted the spread of the London dialect, which in turn helped to establish the London dialect as the literary standard for the country. By 1500, English had entered the period called **Modern English** (1450—present), which is subdivided into **Early Modern English** (1450—1650), i. e. the language of Shakespeare, **Authoritarian English** (1650—1800), **Mature Modern English** (1800—1920) and **Late Modern English** (1920—present), the language we learn today.

4. Religion

Britain is a Christian country. Over half of the citizens there embrace Christianity. They are either **Protestants** or **Catholic.**

The Church of England is **the established church** of the English nation. The King or Queen is the head of the Church and is crowned by the Archbishop of Canterbury in **Westminster Abbey.**

The Church of England has a continuous history going back before **the Reformation** to the earliest days of English Christianity. It began its journey to independence from Rome over a question which had nothing to do with doctrine under Henry Ⅷ, who declared himself head of the English church in 1534 when the Pope would not let him divorce his first wife, **Catherine of Aragon.** Later the influence of the Reformation led the English Church to go its own way in forms of worship and in doctrine. Protestantism was introduced under Edward Ⅵ. Mary Ⅰ brought a Catholic reaction, but with **Elizabeth** Ⅰ the Church of England was established on a moderate Protestant basis.

Protestants not belonging to the Church of England suffered religious and political persecution in the 17th century, and were excluded from many offices and places until the early 19th century; in those days they were called "**dissenters**," but later the rather more polite term "**non-conformist**" came to be used instead. Today the still more polite term "members of the **Free Churches**" is more usual. Of the old dissenting sects the **Baptists** and **the United Reformed Church** (consisting of the Congregational and Presbyterian Churches, who merged in 1972) are perhaps the most important. **Quakers** have always been a very small and select group, but they are in general rather wealthy. **Methodists** are more important than any of those old sects in the matter of numbers. Now Methodism is probably the main religion of the people in many northern mining and industrial areas and also in Wales.

The Roman Catholic Church was much persecuted and very weak in England for a long time after the Reformation. Its English hierarchy was extinct from the 16th century until 1850. Now in England and Wales, the number of Roman Catholics seems to be growing.

Christian communities from overseas **Commonwealth** and foreign countries, which have established centers for worship, especially in London, include the **Orthodox**, **Lutheran** and the **Armenian Church**. The principal non-Christian communities in Britain are the **Jews**, the **Moslems** and the **Buddhists**.

Most of the British social customs are based on the Christian tradition, such as Christmas, Easter, **the Western Calendar** and Sunday. **Christmas** is kept on December 25th in memory of the birth of **Jesus Christ**. People exchange gifts with friends and relatives. Children believe that **Santa Claus** comes down from the North Pole to leave presents for them. **Easter** is kept on the first Sunday after the first full moon after the vernal equinox, commemorating Christ's resurrection. Parents color hard-boiled eggs before Easter. Late Saturday night or early Sunday morning the eggs are hidden, and the children have an Easter egg hunt Sunday. Little children believe the Easter rabbit comes and leaves the eggs for them. According to the Western Calendar, Year One is calculated from the birth of Jesus Christ. Christians acknowledge Sunday as the "**Sabbath Day**." To them the "Sabbath Day" is the holy day of the week, and is required to spend in rest and worship.

5. Conservatism of the English People

English people tend to be rather conservative. The conservative attitude consists of an acceptance of things that are familiar, and an inclination to be suspicious of anything that is strange and foreign. They did not adopt rational reforms such as the **metric system** until 1975, and the **monetary system** until 1971 though they had suffered inconvenience from adhering to the old ways. The conservatism may also be illustrated by the fact that they still keep the monarchy today.

Apart from the conservatism on a grand scale, England is full of small-scale and local conservatism. Regiments in the army, municipal corporations, schools and societies have their own private traditions that command strong loyalties. Such groups have customs of their own which they are very reluctant to change.

6. Differences Between Nations

There are discernible differences among different classes of the British society and differences between the four nations as they were once separated ones. These differences divide the United Kingdom. It is true to say that the class structure of UK society is relatively obvious. The culture of a factory worker whose father was a factory worker may be quite different from that of a stockbroker whose father was a stockbroker; they will tend to read different newspapers, watch different television programs, speak with a different accent, do different things in their free time, and have different expectations. Both in Wales and in Scotland there are strong demands for more recognition of their national distinctions through the system of government. Scotland has always had a separate educational system, and a separate legal system and distinct local administration. Northern Ireland has its own Parliament in normal circumstances. The majority of people there are Protestants, who are strongly attached to England and Scotland. Northern Ireland (often called **"Ulster"** after an ancient kingdom which once existed in that part of Ireland), the smallest of the four nations both in area and population, is tormented by differences between Protestants who are by far a majority and strongly attached to England and Scotland and the big Catholic minority whose sentimental links are with the Irish Republic. In Northern Ireland, after decades of violent conflict, the Good Friday Agreement of 1998 led to a new assembly with devolved powers, bringing hopes of lasting peace. The assembly was suspended in 2002 amid a row over alleged IRA activities. Its suspension was to lasting for three and a half years. In a bid to restart the political process and after consultations with Dublin, the UK passed legislation paving the way for the recall of the Northern Ireland Assembly in May 2006. But assembly elections in the following March led to the eventual swearing-in of the leaders of the power-sharing government on 8 May 2007, ending five years of direct rule from London.

Even within each of the four countries there are different regions: the difference between the "highland" and "lowland" Scots has a long historical significance, for example: north and south England are also considered to be culturally distinct, though the boundary between them is not marked on any map, and exists only as a rather unclear mental attitude. Nevertheless, there is some basis to the distinction in economic terms as the south is on average wealthier than the north.

7. Principal Cities

The population in Britain is predominantly urban and suburban. About three quarters of the population are living in cities and towns.

London, the capital of both England and the UK, has a population of about 7 million. Greater London was created in 1965, which includes the City of London and 32 boroughs and is governed by the Chairman of Greater London Council. **The City of London** is located at the center of the metropolitan area and covers an area of 1.6 square kilometers. The city of London, managed by the Lord Mayor, serves as the financial center of the country, where there is a concentration of banks, including the Bank of England, insurance companies and stock exchanges. The City of London and its 12 surrounding boroughs are referred to as **Inner London**, the remaining 20 boroughs, **Outer London**.

The Romans first built London as an advancing base and a trading center in the first century. London has developed from this small Roman town surrounded by walls with gates.

To the east of the City of London is the large area called the **East End**, which are the industrial area and the port of London. With houses for workers, this is the poorest quarter of London.

To the west are the fine shops and theatres of the area vaguely known as the **West End**. The southern part of this area is **the City of Westminster**, the political center of the country, where are located the **Buckingham Palace, the Palace of Westminster, White Hall, No. 10 Downing Street** and **Hyde Park.**

Westminster Abbey is an ancient church where kings and queens are crowned and where, particularly in Poets' Corner, many famous men and women are buried.

There are many museums and art galleries in London, among which the most famous one is the **British Museum.** The national library is kept at the Museum, where **Karl Marx** wrote his famous *Capital*.

Now London has become the great center of commerce, administration, culture and transportation of Britain, and one of the largest international ports in the world. As the biggest manufacturing center, London has such industries as printing, publishing, food processing, chemicals, clothing and electric and mechanical engineering.

Other Capitals

Edinburgh, the capital of Scotland, is a fine old city built partly in the valley of **River Leith** and partly on the rolling hills that surround it. It served as the capital of Scottish Kingdom from 1437 to 1707 before Scotland formed the union with England.

Edinburgh has now become one of the important financial and transportation centers in Britain. Its main industries are shipbuilding, chemicals, distilling and brewing.

Cardiff, the capital of Wales, has a population of 284,000. Close to the Welsh coal mining area, the city is one of the largest coal shipping ports in the world, and a center of iron and steel industry in Britain.

Belfast, the capital of Northern Ireland, has a population of about 400,000. It is an important industrial, commercial and cultural center in Northern Ireland. Its industries include shipbuilding, linen, man-made fibers and aircraft manufacture.

Other Big Cities

Birmingham, with a population of 1.1 million, is the second largest city in Britain. It is now a metropolitan district of West Midlands and one of the nation's leading industrial centers. Its industries include metal goods, hardware, cars, electrical equipment, machine tools, jewelry and plastics.

Glasgow is the largest city in Scotland, having a population of 734,000. It is a shipping, industrial and commercial center of Scotland. It leads the whole country in shipbuilding. The other industries are metal producing, oil refining, chemicals, electronics, textiles, clothing and whiskey making.

Liverpool is one of the large ports in Britain, having a population of 491,000. Now the city is a district of Merseyside metropolitan area.

Manchester is one of the oldest cities in Britain. It became important for the country only after the Industrial Revolution. The city of Manchester is now a metropolitan district of Greater Manchester. The city's best known newspaper, *the Guardian*, is read all over the world, as is Charles Dickens' novel *Hard Times*, which is set in the 19th century Manchester.

Newcastle upon Tyne, a port city in Tyne & Wear, is now a metropolitan district with city status. Its main industries are ship building, iron & steel and chemicals.

Sheffield, an industrial city in South Yorkshire, is famous for its production of high-grade steel, steel manufacturing, especially cutlery, celebrated silver plate.

Hull, located at the mouth of the Humber River, is an important fishing port in Britain.

Southampton is the main passenger port for crossing the Atlantic and one of the royal navy bases.

Plymouth is a seaport city with a fine harbor. It also serves as a naval base.

Notes

1. population density 人口密度
2. population distribution 人口分布
3. conurbation 由大城市及其周围的卫星城市组成的都市区
4. Greater London 大伦敦都市区
5. W. Midlands 西密德兰都市郡
6. South Yorkshire 南约克都市郡
7. W. Yorkshire 西约克都市郡
8. Greater Manchester 大曼彻斯特都市郡
9. Merseyside 默西赛德都市郡
10. Tyne & Wear 泰恩及威尔都市郡
11. Midland 密德兰(工业区)

12. Tyne and Tees Valleys 泰恩和提兹河流域
13. Anglo-Saxon 盎格鲁—撒克逊人
14. Celt 凯尔特人
15. Gaelic 盖尔语
16. Welsh 威尔士语
17. Old English 古英语,盎格鲁—撒克逊人的语言。
18. Middle English 中古英语
19. *Canterbury Tales* 坎特伯雷故事集
20. William Caxton 威廉·卡克斯顿
21. Modern English 现代英语
22. Early Modern English 早期现代英语(1450～1650)
23. Authoritarian English 权威期现代英语(1650～1800)
24. Mature Modern English 成熟期现代英语(1800～1920)
25. Late Modern English 晚期现代英语(1920 年至今)
26. Protestant 新教徒
27. Catholics 罗马天主教徒
28. the Church of England 英格兰圣公会
29. the established church 国教
30. Westminster abbey 西敏寺大教堂
31. the Reformation (新教脱离天主教的)宗教改革
32. Catherine of Aragon 亚拉岗的凯瑟琳,亚拉岗是西班牙东北部之一地区,从前曾为一个王国。
33. Mary Ⅰ 玛丽一世,亨利八世和凯瑟琳之女。
34. Elizabeth Ⅰ 伊丽莎白一世,亨利八世和安妮·博林之女。
35. dissenters/non-conformist 异教徒
36. Free Churches 自由教
37. Baptists 浸礼教
38. the United Reformed Church 联合改革教(1972 年由公理会与长老会合并而成)
39. Quakers 教友会,"贵格"派
40. Methodists 卫理会
41. Commonwealth (of Nations) 英联邦
42. Orthodox 正教
43. Lutheran 路德教派的,路德教徒

44. Armenian church 亚美尼亚教
45. Jews 犹太人
46. Moslems 回教徒;伊斯兰教徒
47. Buddhists 佛教徒
48. the Western Calendar 阳历
49. Christmas (Day) 圣诞节
50. Jesus Christ 耶稣基督
51. Santa Claus 圣诞老人
52. Easter 复活节
53. Sabbath Day 安息日
54. metric system 长度度量体制
55. monetary system 货币体制
56. Ulster 阿尔斯特,昔日爱尔兰之一省,后为爱尔兰共和国和北爱尔兰所分割,常用来意指北爱尔兰。
57. the City of London 伦敦城,大伦敦都市郡的一个区,位于伦敦市中心,是英格兰银行及各大银行、股票交易市场的集结地,那里有伦敦市长官邸,是英国的金融中心。
58. Inner London 内伦敦(由伦敦城及其周围的12个市区组成)
59. Outer London 外伦敦(由内伦敦周围的20个市区组成)
60. East End 伦敦东区
61. West End 伦敦西区
62. the City of Westminster 威斯敏斯特城
63. Buckingham Palace 白金汉宫
64. the Palace of Westminster 威斯敏斯特宫
65. White Hall 白厅,原来确有其厅,后被大火焚毁,现为伦敦一街道名,街的两侧为政府各部,故常指英国政府。
66. No. 10 Downing Street 唐宁街10号,英国首相官邸。
67. Hyde Park 海德公园
68. Westminster Abbey 西敏寺大教堂
69. British Museum 大不列颠博物馆
70. Karl Marx 卡尔·马克思
71. River Leith 利斯河,流经爱丁堡北部的利斯港。
72. Birmingham 伯明翰,英格兰中部城市
73. Glasgow 格拉斯哥,苏格兰第一大城市

74. Liverpool　利物浦，英格兰西部港口城市，位于默西塞德河口。
75. Manchester　曼彻斯特，英国工业革命时期的棉纺织业中心。
76. Newcastle upon Tyne 泰恩河畔纽卡斯尔，英格兰东北部城市。
77. Sheffield　设菲尔德，英格兰中部城市，以优质钢而闻名于世。
78. Hull　赫尔，英格兰东部港口，是英国著名的深水渔港。
79. Southampton　南安普敦，英格兰南部港口。
80. Plymouth　普利茅斯，英格兰南部港口。

Questions for Discussion

1. Point out the major concentrations of population in Britain.
2. Give a brief account of the three stages in the evolution of the English language.
3. Tell what you know about the history of the Church of England and the Roman Catholic Church in Britain.
4. Relate briefly the history of the Church of England and the Roman Catholic Church in Britain.
5. Name the non-Christian religious denominations you know in Britain.
6. Why is it said that English people tend to be rather conservative? Give some examples to show their conservative attitude.
7. Are there any differences among the nations in Britain? If any, what are they?
8. Tell what you know about the British Museum, Buckingham Palace, the Palace of Westminster, White Hall, and Hyde Park.

Exercises

Ⅰ. Choose the correct answer and circle the letter before it.

1. The seven Conurbations in Britain contain ________ of the population of the country.

   A. one-fourth　　B. one-third

   C. half　　D. one-fifth

2. The English people are descendants of ________.
   A. Celts　　B. Romans
   C. Anglo-Saxons　　D. Danes
3. Middle English took shape about a century after the ______ Conquest.
   A. Roman　　B. Anglo-Saxon
   C. Norman　　D. Danish
4. London dialect was once disseminated throughout the country NOT because London was ________.
   A. a commercial center　　B. a political center
   C. a printing center　　D. a linguistic center
5. In the Great Vowel Shift, the pronunciation of the English ________ changed completely.
   A. short vowels and diphthongs
   B. long vowels and diphthongs
   C. short vowels
   D. all vowels
6. The established church of Britain is ________.
   A. The Church of England
   B. The Church of Scotland
   C. Free churches
   D. The United Reformed Church
7. Which of the following religious sect does not belong to Free Churches?
   A. The Roman Catholic church.
   B. Quakers.
   C. Methodists.
   D. Baptists.
8. Easter is kept, commemorating the ________ of Jesus Christ.
   A. coming　　B. birth
   C. death　　D. resurrection
9. Scotland has had a separate ________ system.
   A. legal　　B. monetary
   C. parliamentary　　D. postal
10. Northern Ireland is tormented by differences between ________.
   A. the Irish minority and the Welsh majority

B. the Protestant majority and the Catholic minority
C. the Protestant minority and the Catholic majority
D. the Scottish majority and the Irish minority

Ⅱ. Fill in the following blanks with appropriate words or expressions.

1. Britain has a total population of about ________ million, with some ________ persons living in every square kilometer.
2. The English people are the descendants of ________, while the Scots, Welsh and Irish are the descendants of the ________.
3. The major languages spoken in Britain are ________, ________ and ________.
4. The Church of England is the ________ church of the English nation.
5. Protestant churches not belonging to the Church of England are called ________ Churches, including such sects as ________, ________, ________ and ________.
6. The Roman Catholic Church was much persecuted in England for a long time after the ________.
7. The principal non-Christian communities in Britain are the ________, the ________ and the ________.
8. Most of the British social customs are based on the ________ tradition.
9. Sunday is acknowledged as the "________ Day" by Christians.
10. The British did not adopt rational reforms such as ________ system until 1975, and the ________ system until 1971.

Ⅲ. Explain the following in English.

1. Old English
2. Middle English
3. Modern English
4. The Church of England
5. Free Churches
6. Christmas
7. Easter
8. Westminster Abby
9. Reformation
10. Protestants
11. City of London
12. Outer London
13. Poets' Corner
14. Birmingham
15. Glasgow

Ⅳ. Match the names of the cities in Column A with the descriptions in Column B. Put each of the letters before the descriptions in the corresponding blank in Column A.

		Column A	Column B
1.	____	Liverpool	a. the steel manufacturing center of Britain
2.	____	Hull	b. the former center of textile industry of Britain
3.	____	Sheffield	c. the fishing port in Humberside
4.	____	Manchester	d. the largest city in Britain
5.	____	Glasgow	e. the second largest city in Britain
6.	____	London	f. the district of Merseyside
7.	____	Birmingham	g. the largest city in Scotland
8.	____	Belfast	h. the capital of Wales
9.	____	Edinburgh	i. The capital of Northern Ireland
10.	____	Cardiff	j. the capital of Scotland

Lesson 3 British Economy

Major Points

British Economy has undergone a considerable decline ever since the end of the 19th century and early the 20th century due to the great loss Britain suffered in the two World Wars, the collapse of the British Empire, very high military expenditure and its insufficiency in industrial investment.

The British economic decline is a relative rather than absolute one.

The British economy went through a particularly bad period in the 1970s when there was a stagflation.

The 1980s saw the recovery of British economy owing to the reforms by Margaret Thatcher.

The negative aspect of Thatcher's reform was a rapid increase in unemployment.

Britain is second only to the US as a destination for international direct investment and the second biggest international investor in the world.

The national economy of Britain can be broken down into three main areas: primary industries, secondary industries and tertiary industries.

British agriculture is highly efficient, producing 58% of the food needed by the nation with only 2% of the labor force.

Britain's chief agricultural products are wheat, barley, oats, potatoes, sugar beets and beef and dairy.

The fishing industry provides 55% of the UK demand for fish.

Since oil and gas were discovered under the North Sea, Britain has become one of the major producers of oil and gas and the fifth largest exporter of oil in the world.

British companies are particularly strong in pharmaceuticals, chemicals, aerospace and food and drink.

The British tertiary industries, including retailing, tourism, insurance, banking, shipping, etc. produce 65% of the national wealth.

Britain exports about one-sixth of the total world exports of the manufactured goods and buys about one-fifth of the raw materials exported in the world.

Britain's traditional customers in trade were the Commonwealth countries and its colonies. Its new customers in trade are members of EU, the United States and Canada.

The invisible trade makes a great contribution to Britain's balance of payment problems.

London is one of the top three financial centers in the world.

Britain adopted the new decimal currency system in 1971.

Britain's central bank is the Bank of England.

The so-called Big Four refers to Lloyds, Barclays, Midland and the National Westminster Bank group.

Main Contents

1. The Relative Decline of British Economy

By the1880's the British economy was dominant in the world, producing one third of the world's manufactured goods, half its coal and iron, half its cotton. But by 1890s this was no longer the case, Britain having been overtaken by both the United States and Germany. From the end of World War Ⅱ until the present, the story of the British economy is usually thought of as one of decline, though Britain still remains a member of **the Group of Seven large industrial economies** (the US, Britain, Germany, France, Japan, Italy and Canada). The causes of the decline are as follows.

Firstly, the country suffered a great loss in the two World Wars. It had gone heavily to debt to finance the war, selling many of its accumulated overseas assets, and borrowing large amounts from the United States and Canada. These debts meant that Britain entered the post-war period with a major economic problem.

Secondly, the era of **the British Empire** was over. The British Empire collapsed immediately after the end of the Second World War. India gained its in-

dependence in 1947, quickly followed by the rest of the Empire, leaving Britain as just a medium-size European country.

Thirdly, despite the relatively rapid and trouble-free process of de-colonization, Britain was still forced to maintain a substantial and expensive military presence in many overseas locations until the end of 1960's when the process was completed. Britain had to spend a higher proportion of its national wealth on the military than most of its competitors because its position as one of the shapers of the post-war world required substantial military contributions both as one of **NATO**'s major partners and as a member of the UN Security Council.

Fourthly, during the war, British industry was badly damaged but survived comparatively unaffected, unlike that of its competitors, that of Germany and Japan, which had to start from nothing. This disadvantage for them may have worked in their favor in that as they had to invest, they could invest in the most modern equipment and new products. However, British economy continued with its older factories and pre-war products. Its output was very low compared with the two potentially large economies, so the catching-up with the UK was inevitable as they recovered.

The failure to invest sufficiently in industry also reflects a long-standing and continuing problem in the British economy. Relatively low rates of investment (the amount of money businesses put aside from profits to reinvest in the business in new products and production methods) were characteristic of the British economy in relation to other developed economies.

It should be remembered that the decline of British economy was not an absolute decline: Britain is not poorer, or producing less than it was in 1945, in fact, it is a lot wealthier and more productive than it was then. The problem is that though it has improved, other countries have improved more rapidly, hence the slide from being the 2nd largest economy (after the United States) to being the sixth, as it is at present. So Britain has experienced economic decline, but this decline is relative to some other economies rather than absolute.

2. Recent History of British Economy

The British economy went through a particularly bad period in the 1970s when rates of inflation reached up to 25% with the rises of oil price. Workers went on strikes for more pay. **Stagflation** (stagnation and inflation) led to a change of government at the general election of 1979, when the British people voted in the Conservative party under Margaret Thatcher, with the promise of a radical program of reform. Under **Margaret Thatcher**, government expenditure was reduced, taxation reformed, foreign exchange controls lifted, rules governing banks loosened and worker strikes restricted. Throughout the 1980s an extensive program of privatization was carried out, with many state-owned businesses (such as steel, telecom, gas, aerospace) joining the private sector. It seemed in some ways to be successful in that inflation came under control, and businesses made profits. The 1980s saw the recovery of the British economy. However, the negative aspect of Thatcher's reform was a rapid increase in unemployment. While companies were more efficient, producing the same amount with less workers, and therefore being about to pay higher wages and make higher profits, the cost was paid by the unemployed who had to live on low incomes from state support. The national economy continued to grow at lower rates than its competitors. The economy even shrunk by 2.3% in the recession between 1990 and 1992.

However, since then the picture has been brighter, with 4 years of steady growth, at rates higher than that in the rest of the European Union. Inflation has been controlled, with the unemployment rate falling, among the lowest in the European Union. Encouraged by low interest rates, investment has increased. Britain's membership of the EU has made it an attractive location for inward investment by companies from outside the **EU** (especially the US and Japan), of which it has received a larger share than any other EU country. Overall it is second only to the US as a destination for international direct investment. It is also itself a major source of international investment—in fact it is the second biggest international investor in the world (1995). According to the World Bank, the GNI per capita of Britain is US $37,600 in 2006.

3. The Current British Economy

The national economies of Britain can be broken down into three main areas: "primary" industries, such as agriculture, fishing, and mining; "secondary" industries, which manufacture complex goods from those primary products; and "tertiary" industries, often referred to as services, such as banking, insurance, tourism, and the selling of goods.

1) Primary Industries

The British agriculture is highly efficient by the standard of France and

Germany. It produces 1.4% of the national wealth, with only 2% of the labor force that grow 58% of the food needed by the nation. The high rate of production is due to the extensive use of modern technical improvements.

Only parts of the country have good soil, and farmland is scare. Three quarters of Britain's land is used for agriculture, with about a quarter of that under crops—wheat and barley are the two commonest. The farmland in the eastern half of the country is used for raising crops. Its chief agricultural products are wheat, barley, oats, potatoes and sugar beets. The rest is grazing for animals, including cattle (both dairy and beef), though sheep are the most numerous livestock. Dairy farming is distributed all over the country but is characteristic of the West of England. Britain is the world's leading exporter of pedigree livestock: cattle, sheep, pigs and horses. Cattle are bred for meat as well as for dairy farming. Sheep are found in hilly counties particularly and are bred chiefly for their meat. Britain's beef, especially the best Scottish meat, is well known for its excellence, and Welsh mutton is the favorite meat in the country. The beef industry has been hit badly by **BSE disease** in cattle leading to a 1996 ban on beef exports. The best agricultural land is in the southeast of England.

Britain has a large ocean fishing fleet and fish is a basic item in the national diet. The fishing industry provides 55% of the UK demand for fish. The leading fish caught are cod, haddock, herring, plaice, turbot and sole. The major fishing areas are the North Sea, the English Channel, the sea area around Ireland and the sea area between England and **Iceland**. Scottish ports land the majority of the fish caught.

Energy production is an important part of the British economy, accounting for 5% of the national wealth. Since the 1970s, when oil and gas were discovered under the North Sea, Britain has become a major oil and gas producer, in addition to its older coal mining industry, which now only accounts for only about a quarter of energy supplies, the rest being divided between oil, gas, and nuclear energy. This abundance of energy resources means that the UK has become an overall exporter of energy. The technology required to extract oil from the difficult offshore conditions has given British companies a strong position in the offshore oil industry around the world. Three of the biggest ten companies in Britain are to be found in the energy sector: **Shell** (half Dutch), **British Pe-**

troleum (**BP**), and **British Gas**. The world's largest mining company, **RTZ**, is a UK company, which operates mines all over the world.

2) **Secondary Industries**

In the secondary sector of the economy, manufacturing industry remains important, producing 22% of national wealth. British companies are active in all major fields of manufacturing industry, but are particularly strong in pharmaceuticals (The British company **Glaxo-Wellcome** is the biggest drug company in the world). Chemicals (including plastics, petrochemicals and pharmaceutical industry. **ICI** is the second largest paint manufacturer in the world), aerospace (overall the UK industry is third in size in the world, with such products as VC 10, the **Trident**, the BAC One-Eleven, and a range of military aircraft including the **Jaguar**, and the **Harrier**, a vertical take-off and landing strike aircraft, and the **Concorde**, the Anglo-French supersonic airliner) and food and drink (Scotch whisky being a major export). Britain has a big electronics industry (the fourth largest in the world, which produces such products as radar, computers, radio and television transmitting equipment, industrial control equipment and consumer goods) but like the car industry (which includes **Ford**, **GM**, **Peugeot**, **Nissan**, **Toyota**) this is in many cases foreign-owned. Britain's last major independent car company, **Rover**, was recently bought by the German company **BMW**. A high-technology engineering industry has developed around the motor-racing business, with many of the world's racing cars, both for **Formula One**, and the American **Indycar** series, being designed and built in Britain. McClaren and Williams are two of the most successful of these companies. The recently privatized British Steel is the world's fourth largest steel company. Other manufacturing industries include mechanical engineering that produces all forms of machinery and industrial plant; instrument engineering, with a product range extending from scientific instruments to photographic equipment and time-pieces; electrical engineering, engaged in the manufacture and installation of generation, transmitting and distribution equipment, telecommunications and broadcasting apparatus, specialized laboratory equipment and domestic electrical appliances. The other leading traditional industries include shipbuilding, textiles, locomotives, food products and consumer goods.

3) Tertiary Industries

Like most developed economies Britain has seen a relative shrinking of the importance of secondary industry and a spectacular growth in tertiary or service industries, which now produce 65% of national wealth. A lot of this is domestic activity such as retailing, tourism, insurance and so on, but Britain is also a major international provider of services, accounting for about 10% of the world's exports of such services. 70% of the UK's work force is employed in the service sector.

Trade is Britain's lifeline. Britain's geographical position makes it a natural transfer point. It imports many goods that are immediately re-exported to other countries in smaller lots, sometimes after some minor processing. Britain remains one of the world's most important trading nations. It exports about one-sixth of the total world exports of manufactured goods. It buys about one-fifth of the raw materials exported in the world.

Britain's traditional customers in trade were the Commonwealth countries and its former colonies. Its trade with highly industrialized nations has gone up since it joined the **European Economic Community (the Common Market)** in 1973. Apart from the Common Market, the United States and Canada are also its important customers in trade now.

The invisible trade makes a great contribution to Britain's balance of payment problems. Earnings from tourism, with the associated shipping, international insurance, banking fees and air services and from private investment overseas constitute one of the largest single sources of foreign currency. A government-sponsored body, the **British Trade Authority (BTA)** is responsible for the overseas promotion of tourism in Britain.

The financial sector is an important part of this service industry, as London is one of the top three financial centers in the world. It has the greatest concentration of foreign banks in the world, accounts for 20% of all international bank-loans, and is the world's largest foreign exchange market. As well as banking, dealing in commodities and insurance are important processes in **"The City"**—the name given to the historic area at the center of London where all this business is concentrated, at the heart of which is the London Stock Exchange, one of the busiest share-dealing centers in the world. Advertising is another major business service in which UK companies are highly successful.

Britain's unit of currency is the pound sterling (£). It did not adopt the new decimal currency system until February 15th, 1971. Before the introduction of the new system, one pound was worth 20 shillings, and one shilling 12 pence. Following the introduction of the decimal currency system, the pound is divided into 100 pence (p) Cupro-nickel coins are issued with denominations of 50p, 10p, and 5p, and bronze coins with denominations of 2p, 1p, and 1/2p. The Bank of England notes are issued for sums of £1, £5, £10, and £20.

The **Bank of England** is Britain's central bank, which was established in 1694, and was brought into public ownership in 1946. It has a wide range of financial and economic responsibilities both as an agent of government policy and in its own right. It acts as banker to the government and to the deposit banks. It advises government on the formulation of monetary policy and plays an important part in making agreed policy effective. In addition, the Bank is the note-issuing authority, the registrar for government stocks and banker to many overseas central banks.

Besides the Bank of England, which acts as a **clearing house**, there are several large joint-stock banks in Britain. The main ones, called the **"Big Four,"** are **Lloyds**, **Barclays**, **Midland** and **the National Westminster Bank Group.** These banks exert great influence on the formulation of the financial and monetary policies in Britain.

Notes

1. the Group of Seven large industrial economies　世界上的七个经济大国:美国、英国、法国、德国、日本、意大利和加拿大。
2. the British Empire　大英帝国
3. NATO　北大西洋公约组织,North Atlantic Treaty Organization 的缩写。
4. stagflation　滞胀是 stagnation (停滞)和 inflation(通货膨胀)的混成词。20 世纪 70 年代首先发生在英国的一种经济现象,俗称“英国病”。
5. Margaret Thatcher　玛格丽特·撒切尔,1979 年,保守党大选获胜,撒切尔夫人成为英国第一位女首相,执政后采用货币主义政策,压缩政府开支、降低贷款利率、鼓励私人投资、大力推行私有化、限制工人罢工,搞所谓人民资本主义,使英国经济在 80 年代得到复苏。
6. EU　the European Union 的缩写,欧洲联盟,简称“欧盟”。
7. BSE disease　俗称“疯牛病”,始发于牛的一种传染性大脑疾病
8. Iceland　冰岛

9. Shell 壳牌石油公司(英国与荷兰的合资公司)
10. British Petroleum (BP)英国石油公司
11. British Gas 英国天然气公司
12. RTZ 英国矿产公司
13. Glaxo-Wellcome 格拉克色·威尔卡姆公司,全球最大的药品公司。
14. ICI 帝国化学公司(Imperial Chemical Industry)的缩写。
15. Trident 三叉戟飞机
16. Jaguar 美洲虎
17. Harrier 猎兔,英国制造的一种垂直起落的小型飞机。
18. Concorde 协和,英法合造的大型客机
19. Ford 福特汽车公司(美国)
20. GM 通用汽车公司(美国), General Motors 的缩写。
21. Peugeot 标致(法国)
22. Nissan 尼桑(日本)
23. Toyota 丰田(日本)
24. Rover 罗孚(英国)
25. BMW 宝马(德国)
26. Formula One 一级方程式赛车世界锦标赛,1950 年设立的职业性比赛。
27. Indycar 全称为 Indianapolis 500, 印第安纳波利斯 500 英里汽车大赛。
28. tertiary industries 第三产业
29. European Economic Community (the Common Market) 欧洲经济共同体,亦称共同市场。
30. BTA (British Trade Authority) 英国贸易管理局
31. The City 伦敦城,伦敦市中心的一部分,是全国的金融中心,在 1.6 平方公里的地方集中了许多家大银行和金融机构。
32. Bank of England 英格兰银行,英国的中心银行。
33. clearing house 票据交换所
34. "Big Four" "四巨头",指英国四大银行:劳埃德(Lloyds)、巴克莱(Barclays)、密德兰(Midland)和国民威斯敏斯特银行(the National Westminster Bank Group)。

Questions for Discussion

1. What are the major causes of the decline of the British economy?

2. Why is it said that the British economic decline is a relative one?
3. Describe the economic situation of Britain in 1970s.
4. Tell what you know about Mrs. Thatcher's economic reform program and its result in the 1980s.
5. Why is it said that British agriculture is highly efficient?
6. Give a brief account of the use of land in Britain.
7. How industries in Britain are classified? Explain each sector.
8. In what fields of manufacturing are British companies particularly strong?
9. Describe the importance of tertiary industries in Britain.
10. Which is the central bank of Britain? What a part does it play in British economy?

Exercises

Ⅰ. Choose the correct answer and circle the letter before it.

1. By the 1880's the British economy produced ________ of the world's manufactured goods.

   A. one fourth B. one third C. half D. over half

2. By the 1890s, Britain had been overtaken by ________ in economy.

   A. The US and Germany B. Japan

   C. France D. Italy

3. The British Empire collapsed immediately after the end of ________.

   A. the 19th century B. the First World War

   C. the Second World War D. the 1960s

4. Which of the following statements about the UK economy is NOT true?

   A. Britain has experienced a relative economic decline since 1945.

   B. Britain remains one of the Group of Seven large industrial economies.

   C. There has been a period of steady decreasing of living standards.

   D. Britain ranks the second in industrial investment abroad.

5. ________ were characteristic of the British economy in relation to other

developed economies.

A. Low rates of military expenditure

B. Low rates of educational investment

C. Low rates of industrial investment

D. Low rates of scientific experiment

6. British economy in the 1970s was characterized by ______.

A. stagnation B. inflation

C. recovery D. stagflation

7. Under Mrs. Thatcher, British economy in the 1980s gradually ________.

A. declined B. recessed

C. recovered D. went down

8. Britain is the ________ largest country invested and the investor abroad.

A. second B. third

C. fourth D. fifth

9. The British beef industry has been hit badly by ________ disease in cattle.

A. SARS B. BSE

C. AIDS D. Non of the above three

10. Which of the following companies is the world's largest mining company?

A. Shell. B. BP.

C. British Gas. D. RTZ.

11. The two companies, McClaren and Williams design and build ________.

A. large ocean ships B. locomotives

C. racing cars D. aircraft

12. Tertiary industries do not include ________.

A. retailing B. insurance

C. electronics D. banking

13. "The City" in this lesson refers to ________.

A. Greater London B. Inner London

C. Outer London D. the City of London

14. Britain did not adopt the new decimal currency system until 15th February, ________.

    A. 1970　　B. 1971　　C. 1973　　D. 1975

15. The central bank in Britain is ________.

    A. Lloyd　　B. Barclay

    C. Midland　　D. the Bank of England

Ⅱ. Fill in the following blanks with proper words or expressions.

1. During World War Ⅱ, Britain was forced to borrow large amounts of money from the ________ and ________.
2. India became independent in the year of ________.
3. Britain had to spend a higher proportion of its national wealth on the ________ than most of its competitors.
4. The failure to ________ sufficiently in industry also reflects a long-standing and continuing problem in the British economy.
5. It should be noted that the decline of British economy was not an ________ decline.
6. Under Margaret Thatcher, public expenditure was ________, foreign exchange controls ________, rules governing banks ________ and worker strikes ________.
7. The Conservative Party carried out an extensive programme of ________ throughout the 1980s.
8. The negative aspect of Thatcher's reform was a rapid increase in ________.
9. Britain's membership of the EU has made it an attractive location for ________ investment by companies from outside the EU.
10. The fishing industry provides ________% of the UK demand for fish.
11. The major fishing areas in Britain are the ________ Sea, the ________ Channel, the sea area around ________ and the sea area between England and ________.
12. The technology required to extract oil from the difficult offshore conditions has given British companies a strong ________ in the offshore oil industry around the world.
13. The British company Glaxo-Wellcome is the biggest ________ company in the world.

14. The German company named ________ recently bought Britain's last major independent car company, Rover.
15. Like most developed economies, Britain has seen a relative ________ of the importance of secondary industry and a spectacular ________ in tertiary industries.
16. Britain's traditional customers in trade were the ________ countries and its former ________. Now Britain trades mainly with the ________ Market, the US and ________.
17. The ________ trade makes a great contribution to Britain's balance of payment problems.
18. The Bank of England advises government on the formulation of ________ policy and plays an important part in making agreed policy ________ and acts as a ________ house.

Ⅲ. Explain the following in English.

1. the Group of Seven large industrial economies
2. NATO
3. stagflation
4. Margaret Thatcher
5. EU
6. primary industries
7. secondary industries
8. tertiary industries
9. Common Market
10. "The City"
11. Bank of England
12. "Big Four"

Lesson 4 Political System: Parliament and Government

Major Points

Britain still keeps an old-fashioned government established on the basis of constitutional monarchy.

Britain has no written constitution.

Theoretically, the Queen has all the power, but in reality, she has no real power at all. Nevertheless, she plays a very important part in the whole system.

British Parliament, the supreme legislative authority in the realm, consists of the Sovereign, the House of Lords and the House of Commons.

The House of Lords comprises hereditary and life peers and peeresses, with the Lord Chancellor as the President of the House.

The House of Commons consists of 650 members elected from the country's 630 constituencies, with Mr. Speaker as the chairman in debates.

Parliament's main functions are: debating, making laws and supervising the government and finance.

The British government is composed of the Prime Minister and other ministers, who are responsible to Parliament.

The most senior ministers compose the Cabinet.

There are over a dozen departments under the leadership of the Prime Minister, some heads of which are entitled "minister" or "secretary" and some have special titles.

Each department has a large staff of professional civil servants.

The Cabinet, the core of the administration, is composed of the heads of the most important department.

The Privy Council has the formal power to make certain executive orders and proclamations.

The Prime Minister is a really powerful leader in Britain, who controls not

only the Cabinet but also the Parliament.

Each of the local administrated areas (counties, regions or districts) has elected council of its own as local authority.

Main Contents

1. A Brief Introduction

The United Kingdom still keeps an old-fashioned government established on the basis of **constitutional monarchy**: the head of the state is a king or queen. In practice, the Sovereign reigns, but does not rule; the country is governed, in the name of the Sovereign, but by His or Her Majesty's Government—a body of ministers who are the leading members of whichever political party the electorate has voted into office, and who are responsible to **Parliament**.

2. The Monarchy

The present Sovereign is Queen **Elizabeth** Ⅱ, daughter of George Ⅵ, who ascended the throne in 1952 and was crowned in 1953. Her eldest son—**Prince Charles**—is the heir to the throne.

The power of the Queen is nowhere exactly defined as Britain has no **written constitution** and many of the rules that govern the system are customs or conventions established through the fact of being observed and ordinary laws passed at various times in response to particular situations. However, as the head of the state, she is will-informed and consulted on every aspect of national life.

Theoretically the Queen has all the power: she is the head of the executive branch of government and gives effect to all laws; she may pardon criminal offenses and cancel punishments; she is the commander-in-chief of the armed forces and the temporal head of the Church of England; she also confers all titles of rank and appoints judges, officers of the armed forces, governors, bishops and diplomats. It is the monarch who has the power to conclude treaties, to declare war upon and make peace with other nations.

In reality, however, almost all these acts are performed only on the advice of the ministers. She does not personally take part in the process in which decisions are made. Though she has **the power of veto in legislation** that power has never been used since the modern political system come into being over two centuries ago. As for her power of appointing a new **prime minister**, she is bound in practice to appoint the very person Prime Minister—the leader of **the majority party in the House of Commons.** So the appointment is only a legal formality.

The importance of the monarchy is found in its effect on public attitude; it is used to represent the continuity and adaptability of the whole political system; it is used as a symbol of the unity of the whole country, an acceptable bound among the peoples who retain many regional and cultural differences. People are convinced that the Queen has no bias towards any nation and exists to help preserve the people's rights, the right to personal property and the right not to be imprisoned without a trial.

Royal duties include visiting many parts of Britain each year to inaugurate scientific, industrial, artistic and charitable works of national importance; paying state visits to foreign countries; and undertaking tours of other countries in the **Commonwealth**, of which the Queen is the head.

3. Parliament

The UK is a unitary, not a federal state. All the four nations of the kingdom are represented in the Parliament at Westminster (London), which is the supreme legislative authority in the realm.

Parliament consists of the Sovereign, the House of Lords and the House of Commons. The Sovereign formally summons a **House of Lords**, dissolves Parliament and generally opens each new annual session with a speech from the throne.

In the past decade, Britain seemed to be moving toward federalism. In 1999, both Scotland and Wales had their own parliament or assembly. Northern Ireland Parliament was open in 2007. We will have to wait to see how much autonomy each regional parliament will have in the future. Moreover, in recent years, membership of the European Union and human rights legislation has suborned its power inasmuch as it must comply with EU treaties and directives and with the principles of the European Convention on Human Rights.

The House of Lords is made up of hereditary and life peers and peeresses. **The Lord Chancellor** is the President of the House of Lords. At present, there are over 1,000 peers who have the right to attend the debates, vote and propose bills and ask questions of government ministers, but not many of them actually use their power. Since they have no urgent government business to deal with, the timetable of the House of Lords is less crowded than that of the House of Commons.

The House of Commons consists of 651 members who are elected from and represent the country's 651 constituencies. It is in the House of Commons that the ultimate authority for making laws resides. The members meet in a Chamber, sometimes called **St. Stephen's Chapel.** They sit on two sides of the Chamber, one side for the Government and the other for **the Opposition**, the party that has won the second largest number of seats in the **House of Commons** in the general election. Between them sits **"Mr. Speaker,"** who acts as Chairman in debates.

The Speaker is elected by a vote of the House at the beginning of each new Parliament to preside over the House and enforce the rule of order. In carrying out his duties he is required to be impartial: he cannot debate or, as a general rule, vote on a measure, and he sees that all points of view have a fair hearing. He has more powers than the Lord Chancellor and rank only next to the Prime Minister.

Parliament's main functions are: debating, making laws and supervising the government and finance. Most of this work is carried on through a system of debates, which is much the same in both houses.

Either House may introduce a bill (draft Act of Parliament) unless it deals with finance or representation, which is always introduced in the House of Commons. Those that pass through all the necessary stages (first and second readings, committee and report stages, and third reading) in both Houses receive Royal assent and become law as Acts of Parliament. The House of Lords may not alter a financial measure, nor can it delay for longer than one year any bill passed by the House of Commons in two successive sessions.

Parliament has the power to supervise the government. The main opportunities offered in the House of Commons for detailed examination of government policy are provided through Parliamentary questions and answers during debates. During **Question Time** (which lasts for just under one hour on four days in the week) questions involving issues of national importance or concerned with purely local or individual matters may be put to the responsible minister by any member of Parliament, provided due notice has been given.

Parliament has the power to supervise finance. The government cannot legally spend any money without the permission of the House of Commons. On **Supply Day** (traditionally set aside for authorizing proposed public expenditure), custom has given the Opposition the right to decide which of the Estimates it wishes to discuss, and thus to criticize government policy and administration on grounds of its own choice. The House of Commons still keeps a rather closer contact with taxation. Each year the taxes are authorized by a finance act, which is based on the budget presented by the **Chancellor of the Exchequer** (head of the Treasury).

4. Government

The British government is composed of the Prime Minister and other ministers, who are formally appointed by the Queen on the advice of the Prime Minister. All the ministers must be members of either the House of Commons or the House of Lords. The most senior ministers constitute the **Cabinet**, which meets regularly under the chairmanship of the Prime Minister to decide government policy on major issues. Ministers are responsible collectively to Parliament for all Cabinet decisions; individual ministers are responsible to Parliament for the work of their own departments.

1) Departments

The principal government departments include: the Treasury, **Ministry of Agriculture, Fisheries and Foods**, Ministry of Defence, Ministry of Post and Telecommunications, **Department of Education and Science**, Department of Health and Social Security, Department of Trade and Industry, **Foreign and Commonwealth Office, Home Office, Scottish Office, Welsh Office** and Northern Ireland Office, Department of Energy, and the **Civil Service Department.**

Most of the offices were founded before the 20th century, while ministries and departments were established during the 20th century. Some heads of ministries are entitled "minister" or "secretary" and some have special titles, such as the Chancellor of the Exchequer, the Lord Chancellor. Even some old offices survive, such as **Lord President of the Privy Council**, **Lord Privy Seal**, **Chancellor of the Duchy of Lancaster**, **Paymaster-General**, and **Minister without Portfolio.** Their duties are nominal, but the Prime Minister uses these posts to give positions in the government to people who he wants to perform special tasks.

2) Civil Service

Besides the ministers, who are politicians, each department has a large staff of professional civil servants who do most of the work of running the department on the minister's behalf. The civil service is non-political. Those of its members who are in any way concerned with administration are forbidden to be candidates for Parliament or to give public support to any political party, though they may vote at elections. Changes of government do not involve changes in departmental staff. They continue to carry out their duties whichever party is in office. Civil servants are recruited mainly by open competition.

"Whitehall" is often used as a synonym for the central core of the Civil Service (the British Government). This is because most Government Departments have headquarters in and around the former Royal Palace of Whitehall.

3) The Cabinet

The Cabinet is composed of the heads of the most important departments with a few ministers without departments. It is the Prime Minister who decides which minister will be included.

The Cabinet meets regularly, usually once a week, in one of the rooms in the Prime Minister's official residence, No. 10 Downing Street. Though there is no law that recognizes the Cabinet as such, it has the real power to take the effective decisions about what is to be done in Britain.

The Cabinet and all its committees work in great secrecy, and this rule is generally well observed. It is connected with the principle of collective responsibility. Whatever decision is made, every office-holder must be prepared to share the responsibility for it and to defend it outside. If he is not prepared to do it, he must resign.

Technically the Cabinet is an informal committee of the Privy Council. Whenever a person is made a minister of Cabinet rank, he is made a member of the Privy Council and remains a member for the rest of his life.

4) The Privy Council

The Privy Council includes all ministers and ex-ministers, the holders of certain offices outside the political executive and some other people to whom membership has been given as an honor. Members of the Privy Council are entitled to the prefix, "the Right Honorable," before their names.

The Privy Council has the formal power to make certain executive orders and proclamations. When the government wishes to have an Order in Council made, it arranges for a meeting of the Council to be held for that purpose. This is usually not very difficult, because any three Councilors constitute a quorum; the meeting, being formal, in fact consists of people who are merely registering decisions that have been made elsewhere. Thus in relation to the study of the real exercise of political power the Privy Council is without importance.

5) The Prime Minister

As the head of government, the Prime Minister controls not only the Cabinet but also the Parliament, as he or she is the leader of the majority party in the House of Commons. Since The Queen has only formal power, with no real power, the Prime Minister is a really powerful leader in Britain. The present prime minister is Gordon Brown, who became prime minister on 27 June 2007 after serving as Chancellor of the Exchequer in three consecutive Labour governments under Tony Blair. He was the only candidate for the premiership when Mr. Blair stood down two years into his third term in office.

5. Local Government

England is divided into 45 counties. Each county is subdivided into about 6 districts. Wales is divided into 8 counties and 37 districts, Scotland 12 regions and Northern Ireland, 26 districts.

Each of these administrated areas has its own elected council as local authority which is responsible for many of the public services, including local health and social services, education, town and country planning, the provision and upkeep of certain roads, traffic management, etc.

The arrangements for the election of the councilors are rather complicated, and are not the same for all types of councils. Members of county councils are elected for three years at general elections taking place every three years. With district council there may be an election every year, but only one-third of the seats in each council are filled at each annual election.

Every **local council** has its presiding officer, and this post is filled by the vote of the whole council, for only one year at a time. The presiding officer of a county or district council is called the Chairman or a more neutral term,

Chairperson is used instead, but in a district that is a borough or city he or she is called Mayor or **Lord Mayor.**

All local councils work through committees. Each council has a committee for each of the main sections of its work. For every important matters the committee can only recommend to the council what is to be done, and the decision is made by the council in general session. Meetings are normally open to the public.

Note

1. constitutional monarchy 君主立宪制
2. Parliament 议会
3. Elizabeth Ⅱ 伊丽莎白二世
4. Prince Charles 查尔斯王子
5. written constitution 成文宪法
6. the power of veto in legislation 立法否决权
7. prime minister 首相
8. the majority party in the House of Commons 下院中占多数席位的政党
9. Commonwealth (of Nations) 英联邦国家
10. House of Lords (议会)上院
11. the Lord Chancellor 大法官,上院议长
12. St. Stephen's Chapel 圣·斯迪文教堂
13. the Opposition (Party) 反对党,即下院中占有次多数席位的党。全称为"英王陛下忠诚的反对党",通常组成"影子内阁"(Shadow Cabinet)。
14. House of Commons (议会)下院
15. Mr. Speaker 下院议长
16. Question Time (议会的)质讯时间,反对党议员向政府大臣进行质询的时间。
17. Supply Day (英下院中)请求批准预算日
18. Chancellor of the Exchequer 财政大臣
19. Cabinet 内阁
20. Ministry of Agriculture, Fisheries and Foods 农业、渔业和粮食部
21. Department of Education and Science 教育和科学部
22. Foreign and Commonwealth Office 外交和联邦事务部
23. Home Office 内政部

24. Scottish Office　苏格兰事务部
25. Welsh Office　威尔士事务部
26. Civil Service Department　文官部
27. Lord President of the Privy Council　枢密院长
28. Lord Privy Seal　掌玺大臣
29. Chancellor of the Duchy of Lancaster　兰开斯特公爵郡大臣
30. Paymaster-General　主计大臣
31. Minister without Portfolio　不管(部)大臣
32. the Privy Council　枢密院
33. local council　地方议会
34. Lord Mayor　大市长

Questions for Discussion

1. What power does the Queen have theoretically? Why is it said she has no real power at all in reality?
2. What a part does the monarch play in the political system of Britain? What are the royal duties?
3. What is the supreme legislative authority in Britain? What does it consist of?
4. What is the duty of "Mr. Speaker"?
5. Point out the main functions of Parliament.
6. Describe the law-making procedures in British Parliament.
7. How does Parliament exercise its power to supervise the government and finance?
8. Describe the organization of British government and its Cabinet.
9. Why is it said that in relation to the study of the real exercise of political power the Privy Council is without importance?
10. Why is it said that the Prime Minister is the really powerful leader in Britain?

Exercises

Ⅰ. Choose the correct answer and circle the letter before it.

1. Which of the following statement is NOT true of British political system?
   A. Britain has no written constitution.
   B. Britain is a federal state.
   C. Britain still keeps an old-fashioned government.
   D. British government is established on the basis of constitutional monarchy.
2. ________ is the second most powerful person in Britain.
   A. The Prime minister　　B. Mr. Speaker
   C. The Lord chancellor　　D. The Queen
3. A bill that deals with finance is always introduced ______.
   A. by the Chancellor of the Exchequer
   B. in the House of Lords
   C. in the House of Commons
   D. in the Privy Council
4. In Britain, government cannot spend any money without the permission of ________.
   A. the Queen
   B. the Prime Minister
   C. the House of Commons
   D. the House of Lords
5. The British government ministers are responsible to ____ for the work of their department.
   A. the House of Lords　　B. Parliament
   C. the Cabinet　　D. the Privy Council
6. All the government ministers of Britain must be members of ________.
   A. the House of Lords　　B. the House of Commons
   C. the Privy Council　　D. Parliament
7. Most of the offices were founded ________.

A. before the 19th century
B. after the 19th century
C. before the 20th century
D. during the 20th century

8. Civil servants who are concerned with administration are forbidden ________.
A. to be voters at elections
B. to be candidates for parliament
C. to continue their work when government changes
D. to compete with others for a higher rank

9. The Cabinet meets ________ in one of the rooms in the Prime Minister's official residence, No. 10 Downing Street.
A. regularly　　B. irregularly
C. twice a week　　D. once a month

10. Whenever a person is made a minister of Cabinet rank, he or she is made a member of ________.
A. Parliament　　B. the House of Lords
C. the House of Commons　　D. the Privy Council

Ⅱ. Fill in the following blanks with appropriate words or expressions.

1. The British government is established on the basis of constitutional ________.
2. The present sovereign of Britain is Queen ________, and Prince ________ is the heir to the throne.
3. Britain has no written constitution and many of the rules that govern the system are ________ or ________ and ________ laws.
4. Theoretically, the Queen has all the power, but in reality, she must act on the advice of the ________.
5. Parliament is the supreme ________ authority in Britain.
6. Parliament consists of the ________, the House of ________ and the House of ________.
7. The President of the House of Lords is the ________, and the presiding officer of the House of Commons is "________."
8. Parliament's main functions are ________, making ________ and supervising the ________ and ________.

9. The British government is composed of the ____________ Minister and other ____________, who are responsible to ____________.
10. The Cabinet is composed of the most ________ ministers who meet regularly under the ____________ of the Prime Minister to decide government ____________ on major issues.
11. The Prime Minister controls not only the ____________ but also the ____________.
12. The Privy Council has the formal power to make certain executive ____________ and ____________.
13. Each of Britain's local administrated areas has its own elected ____________ as the local authority.
14. The presiding officer of a county or district council is called ____________, but in a district that is a borough or city he is called ____________ or ____________.

Ⅲ. Translate the following into Chinese.

1. the House of Lords
2. the House of Commons
3. the Lord Chancellor
4. the Ministry of Agriculture, Fisheries and Foods
5. the Foreign and Commonwealth Office
6. the Home Office
7. the Chancellor of the Exchequer
8. the Lord President of the Privy Council
9. the Lord Privy Seal
10. the Minister without Portfolio

Ⅳ. Explain the following in English.

1. St Stephen's Chapel
2. Mr. Speaker
3. Question Time
4. Supply Day
5. the Cabinet
6. the Privy Council

Lesson 5 Political System: Party Politics and Judiciary

Major Points

Two main political parties dominate the political scene of Britain: the Conservative Party and the Labour Party.

The Conservative Party developed out of the Tory Party. It supports private enterprise and is opposed to nationalization and extending social services.

The Labour Party was founded in 1900 by a union between the Trade Unions, the Independent Labour Party and the Fabian Society. It practices social democracy or bourgeois reformism.

The general election in Britain is held every five years and is controlled by the two principal parties. In the election, each of the 651 constituencies elects one member of the House of Commons. The party that has the majority of seats in the House of Commons will organize Government.

England and Wales have a single system of law and courts, and Scotland has a system of its own.

There is no Minister of Justice in Britain.

There is neither civil code nor criminal code in Britain. The law consists partly of statutes, or Acts of Parliament, and partly of common law. The central courts include the House of Lords and the Privy Council, the High Court of Justice, and the Court of Appeal.

The High Court of Justice has several divisions: the Chancery Division, the Family Division and the Queen's Bench Division. The Crown Court sits at nearly 90 centers.

The local courts in England are the magistrates' courts and county courts.

The local courts in Scotland are High Court of Justice of Scotland, sheriff courts and sheriff-substitute courts.

The death penalty for murder was abolished in 1969,

Outside London the police are all local forces.

The Metropolitan Police in London is under the direct responsibility of the Home Secretary.

Main Contents

1. Political Parties

There are three major national parties in Britain: **The Conservative Party** and **the Labour Party** and **the Liberal Democrats.** Two main political parties dominate the political scene: the Conservative party and the Labour party, which have been in office by turns ever since the end of World War Ⅱ. The two parties are both bourgeois in nature, representing the interests of the big bourgeois and the big land-owning classes. The Conservative party openly helps the monopolists to get super-profits, while the Labor Party practices social democracy or bourgeois reformism. The Liberal Democrats, the third biggest party, occupies the ideological ground between the two main parties.

1) The Conservative Party

The Conservative Party developed out of the **Tory Party**, which was founded in 1679 when Parliament was divided into two political groups over the dispute whether James Ⅱ should be the heir to King Charles. The supporters of James Ⅱ formed the group known as "Tory," while the opponents formed the "Whig." The Tory Party changed its name into the Conservative Party and **Whig** into Liberal Party in 1833.

The Conservative Party was the "Empire Party" during the 19th century. Before World War Ⅰ, the Conservative and the Liberal were two principal parties, taking turns in office. After 1922 the Labour Party (formed in 1900) took the place of the Liberal Party as one of the two main parties.

Now the Conservative Party has about 2 million members. It supports private enterprise and is generally opposed to nationalization and extending social services.

2) The Labour Party

The Labour Party was founded in 1900 by a union between the Trade Unions, **the Independent Labour Party** and **the Fabian Society**. It became the main opposition party after the First World War, and won a majority in the House of Commons in 1945 under **Attlee.** The Labour government put through a large program of social reform, nationalizing about 1/3 of the British economy and introducing the National Health Service. It gave independence to India in 1947. The Labour Party was again in office from 1964 to 1970, and from 1974 to 1978, and from 1997 to the present. That the Labour won the election with a greatly reduced majority in 2005 was widely seen as an expression of dissatisfaction with Mr. Blaire's decision to become involved in the war in Iraq, and much attention will be focused on Mr. Brown's handling of this issue.

3) The Liberal Democrats

The liberal Democrats constitute the third biggest party and may be seen as a party of the "middle," occupying the ground between the two main parties ideologically. In the general election, the Liberal Democrats receive votes both from those who usually vote Labour and from those who usually vote Conservative. They emphasize the need for change in Britain's constitutional arrangements to make government more democratic and accountable, and they are seen by many as comparatively flexible and pragmatic in their balance of the individual and the social.

2. General Elections

The general election in Britain is held every five years and is controlled by the two principal parties, the Conservative Party and the Labour Party.

For the purpose of election, the whole country is divided into 651 electoral areas or constituencies, each of which has more or less 60,000 voters and elects one member of the House of Commons. In each constituency there may be any number of candidates, but the one who wins most votes in the constituency is elected. In order to win the election, each party has a local organization in each constituency. Its main task is to choose the candidate and help him to win.

Any British aged over 18 may vote in the general election, with the exception of lunatics, peers who already have seats in the House of Lords, certain categories of convicted criminals, churchmen and resident foreign citizens. **The UK resident citizens of the Irish Republic** may vote.

Anyone who is eligible to vote can stand as an **MP.** It is necessary to make a deposit of 500 pounds which is lost if the candidate does not receive at least 5% of the vote. This is supposed to stop people running just for a joke: however, no British election would be complete without its eccentric no-hopers running for parties such as the **"Monster Raving Loony Party."** An independent

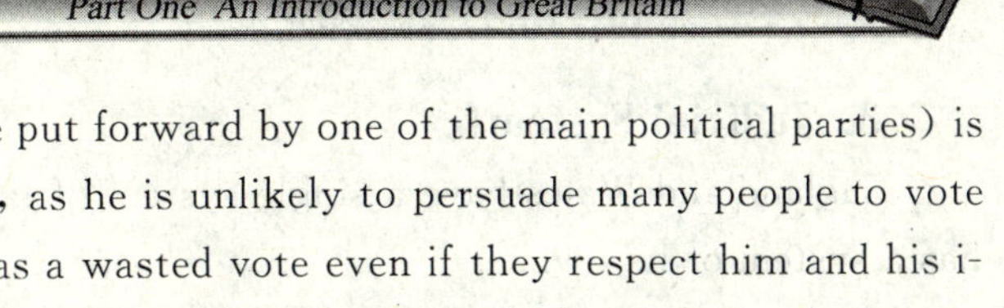

candidate (not the candidate put forward by one of the main political parties) is unlikely to win the election, as he is unlikely to persuade many people to vote for him. Voters will see it as a wasted vote even if they respect him and his ideas, because even if he were to win the seat, he would be powerless in parliament against the big parties' representatives. A vote for an independent candidate effectively prevents the voter from contributing to the competition between the big parties as to which of them will form a government.

In each constituency a suitable person is appointed as **Returning Officer**. A register of voters is compiled each year and he must do some preparation. During the election, each voter must go to his voting station to cast his vote. When he comes in, an official gives him his ballot paper, and his name is recorded as having voted. On the ballot paper the names of all the candidates are printed. The voter must take his paper to a screened cabin, where he puts a cross against the name of the candidate for whom he wishes to vote. He then folds the paper, so that nobody can see how he has marked it, and puts it into a large box. The candidate who receives the largest number of votes is elected. This is so even if there are three or more candidates; in such a case the winner may have much less than half of the votes, but he is elected nevertheless. Many people complain that the simple majority system is unfair, particularly to small parties. There are small parties supporting the independence of each of the three smaller countries in the Union, however, at present they all receive a small share of the vote at election time.

As soon as the results of a general election are known, it is usually clear which party will form the government. If the party that had a majority of seats in the House of Commons has a majority again in the new Parliament, then the government does not change. If the majority changes from one party to the other, as it did in 1945, 1951, 1964, 1970, 1978 and 1995 the defeated Prime Minister usually resigns at once, and the Queen appoints the leader of the new majority party in his or her place. The new House of Commons then meet, with the new Government already in office.

The general election in Britain is a comic scene. Only rich people of great influence can stand as candidates in the election and enter Parliament. The workers cannot afford to take part in the electoral campaigns and the parliament door is closed before them.

3. Judicial System

England and Wales have a single system of law and courts, and Scotland has a system of its own.

There is no **Ministry of Justice** in Britain. Central responsibility for the administration of the judicial system lies partly with **the Lord Chancellor** and partly with **the Home Secretary**, the Secretary of State for Scotland, and **Secretary of State for Northern Ireland.** Judges are appointed by the Crown, on the advice of the Prime Minister, Lord Chancellor or **Secretary of State for Scotland.** A judge holds office for life, and his judicial independence is to some extent guaranteed. The Lord Chancellor or the Secretary of State for Scotland appoints **magistrates** on behalf of the Crown.

1) Law

There is neither civil code nor criminal code in Britain. The law as a whole consists partly of statutes, or **Acts of Parliament**, and partly of **common law,** which may be said to consist of past decisions of judges, with regard to matters not regulated by statutes, in accordance with custom and reason and the previous decisions of courts. A large part of the civil law is not contained in statutes at all but is made up of a mass of precedents, previous court decisions, interpreted in authoritative legal textbooks. The criminal law is contained in statutes. By now, almost all actions for which a person may be punished are those that are specifically forbidden by some statute or other, with the statute usually including a provision for a maximum penalty. It is almost as though there were a sort of criminal code scattered through a large number of laws.

2) Courts

In terms of level all courts in Britain can be divided into the central courts and local courts.

The central courts include the House of Lords, the Privy Council, and **the High Court of Justice** and **the Court of Appeal.** The High Court of Justice has several divisions: **the Chancery Division**, which consists of the Lord Chancellor and ten judges, dealing with questions of company law, bankruptcy, trusts and administration of the estates of people who have died; **the Family Division**, which deals with divorce and questions arising out of wills; and the **Queen's Bench Division**, which consists of the Lord Chief Justice and 39 other judges, dealing with questions arising in trade and maritime affairs, etc. these high court judges divide their time between civil work and the Central Criminal Court in London and visit to the provincial **Crown Courts.** The Crown Court sits at nearly 90 centers, selected as far as possible to be within daily traveling distance from all parts of the country.

The local courts in England are **the magistrates' courts** and county courts and others. Magistrates' courts try the less serious offences. The court generally consists of from 2 to 7 unpaid "lay" magistrates known as **Justices of the Peace**, but in some large cities professional magistrates, known as "stipendiary," may sit alone.

When a criminal case is not finally dealt with in the magistrates' court, it has to go for trial as soon as possible before a judge and jury in a higher court. A jury consists of twelve citizens chosen out of local residents. If the jury finds the accused guilty, then it is for the judge to "pronounce sentence." A person may appeal to **the Court of Criminal Appeal** against conviction or sentence, and the appeal court may quash the conviction or it may reduce or increase the sentence. The highest civil court of appeal is the House of Lords.

The local courts in Scotland are sheriff courts, sheriff-substitute courts and **High Court of Justice.** The High Court of Justice divides into **the Criminal Session** and **the Court of Session** that has an Outer House and the Inner House. In Scotland civil cases of first instance are heard at the sheriff courts and in the Outer House of the Court of Session, which is the supreme civil court in Scotland. The Inner House of the Court of Session hears appeals.

3) Crime and Punishment

If a person is found guilty of a fairly small offence, he may be placed on probation for a period-left at liberty, but under the supervision of a probation officer, who is a trained, professional social worker. Punishments are in the form of fines or imprisonment, and some offenders are given suspended prison sentences. The **death penalty** for murder was first abolished for a five-year period in 1965; it was then completely abolished in 1969. Consequently, some types of crime, including crimes of violence and theft, have increased and young people commit many crimes, and prisons are overcrowded.

Young offenders (between 16 and 21 years old) may be sent to **Borstal institutions** for unspecified periods; these are special establishments, sometimes in ordinary prison buildings, where courses of training are given. There are special juvenile courts; younger offenders my be sent to "**approved schools**" which are run on the line of ordinary schools, with necessary adaptations.

4) The Police

Outside London the police are all local forces, employed and paid by county councils. The central government gives the local authorities grants towards the cost of policing, and inspectors from the Home Office visit the local forces, and the Home Secretary can approve or disapprove of appointments and removals of chief constables, but the actions of a local police force are normally not the responsibility of any minister.

In London the regime is different. **The Metropolitan Police**, whose zone of operation covers Greater London, is under the direct responsibility of the Home Secretary, as good order in the capital concerns the central government. The Metropolitan Police provides certain national police services, including the maintenance of a national registry of all criminals and crimes, to which local police forces may refer. The famous **"Scotland Yard"** is the Criminal Investigation Department (**CID**), which gets its popular name from **New Scotland Yard**, where its offices are situated, close to Whitehall and the House of Parliament.

During the 20th century the English police forces have become well known throughout the world from the great mass of fiction about crime and detection poured out by English authors, and often translated into many other languages.

Notes

1. the Conservative Party 保守党
2. the Labour Party 工党
3. the Liberal Democrats 自由民主党
4. Tory Party 托利党
5. Whig 辉格党
6. the Independent Labour Party 独立工党
7. the Fabian Society 费边社(小资产阶级改良主义团体)
8. Attlee 克莱门特·理查德·艾德礼,1945～1951年任英国工党首相。
9. the UK resident citizens of the Irish Republic 侨居英国的爱尔兰共和国公民。英国与爱尔兰共和国在历史上有着千丝万缕的联系。爱尔兰原为英国殖民地,经过几个世纪的抗争,南部26个自由郡于1922年获得独立,成为后来的爱尔兰共和国,北部的6个郡仍属于英国。

10. MP　Members of Parliament 的缩写，议员。
11. Monster Raving Loony Party　怪物疯话疯子党，20 世纪 60 年代由一个摇滚歌手建立的，没有什么跟随者，但每次选举都参加。
12. Returning Officer　负责选举的官员
13. Ministry of Justice　司法部，英国没有司法部。
14. the Lord Chancellor　大法官，议会上院的议长
15. the Home Secretary　内政大臣，主管社会治安
16. Secretary of State for Northern Ireland　北爱尔兰国务大臣，主管北爱尔兰事务部。
17. Secretary of State for Scotland　苏格兰国务大臣，主管苏格兰事务部。
18. magistrates　（英格兰和威尔士的）地方法官，治安法庭法官
19. Acts of Parliament　议会通过的法案
20. common law　习惯法，主要指法院以往的重大判决。
21. the High Court of Justice　（英格兰）高等法院
22. the Court of Appeal　上诉法院
23. the Chancery Division　大法官庭
24. the Family Division　家事庭
25. the Queen's Bench Division　王座庭
26. Crown Courts　巡回法院
27. the magistrates' court　治安法庭
28. Justices of the Peace　亦称 magistrates，即地方法官。
29. the Court of Criminal Appeal　刑事上诉法院
30. High Court of Justice　苏格兰高等法院
31. the Criminal Session　（苏格兰高等法院的）刑事庭
32. the Court of Session　（苏格兰高等法院的）民事庭
33. death penalty　死刑
34. Borstal institutions　青少年犯管制教养院
35. "approved schools"　青少年犯教养感化院
36. the Metropolitan Police　都市警察，指大伦敦地区警察。
37. Scotland Yard　苏格兰场，因 CID(Criminal Investigation Department 英国刑事侦缉厅)位于新苏格兰场而得名。

Questions for Discussion

1. Give a brief account of the history and the basic policies of the two principal parties in Britain.
2. How do the British choose their Prime Minister in the general election?
3. What officials are responsible for the administration of the judicial system in Britain?
4. What does the British law as a whole consist of?
5. Describe the court system in England and Wales.
6. Describe the court system in Scotland.
7. Make a comment on the abolition of the death penalty in Britain.
8. Tell what you know about the police regime in Britain.

Exercises

Ⅰ. Choose the correct answer and circle the letter before it.

1. The Conservative and the Labour parties have been in power by turns ever since ________.

   A. the end of the 19th century

   B. the end of the First World War

   C. the end of the Second World War

   D. the end of the 1960s

2. ________ is seen as the party of the "middle," occupying the ideological ground between the two main parties.

   A. The Conservative

   B. The Labour

   C. The Liberal Democratic

   D. The Tory

3. The general election in Britain is held every ________ years.

   A. 3 B. 4 C. 5 D. 6

4. Which group of people cannot be voters in the general election?

A. the UK citizens above the age of 18.

B. the UK resident citizens of the Irish Republic.

C. lords in the House of Lords.

D. members in the House of Commons.

5. The deposit a candidate has to pay is supposed to ________.

A. raise money for the election

B. prevent people from running just for a joke

C. prevent the poor from entering Parliament

D. encourage the rich to run

6. Which of the following is the duty of a Returning Officer in a constituency?

A. Compiling a register of voters.

B. Nominating candidates.

C. Deciding the party platform.

D. Winning the election for his own party.

7. The party that has the majority of seats in ________ will form the government.

A. the House of Commons

B. the House of Lords

C. the Privy Council

D. the Cabinet

8. Common law in Britain may be said to consist of ________.

A. acts passed by Parliament

B. ordinary laws

C. previous court decisions

D. cabinet decisions

9. Serious cases arising in trade and maritime affairs in Britain are dealt with by ________.

A. the family Division of the High Court of Justice

B. the Queen's Bench Division of the High Court of Justice

C. the Chancery Division of the High Court of Justice

D. the House of Lords

10. The supreme civil trial court in Scotland is ________.

A. the sheriff court

B. the Inner House of the Court of Session

C. the Outer House of the Court of Session

D. the Criminal Session

11. Which of the punishment forms for criminals in Britain was abolished in 1969?

A. Life imprisonment.

B. Big fines.

C. Probation.

D. Death penalty for murder.

12. Which is true of Borstal institutions for young offenders in Britain?

A. They are just like ordinary prisons.

B. They are just like ordinary schools.

C. They provide courses of training.

D. They are called "approved schools."

13. All police forces in Britain outside London are supported and paid by ________.

A. the central government

B. county councils

C. district councils

D. the Metropolitan Police

14. The famous "Scotland Yard" refers to ________.

A. CIA   B. CID

C. New Scotland Yard   D. House of Parliament

15. The operation zone of the Metropolitan Police covers ________.

A. the City of London   B. Inner London

C. Outer London   D. Greater London

Ⅱ. Fill in the following blanks with appropriate words or expressions.

1. The two main political parties in Britain are both ________ in nature. The Conservative Party openly helps the ________ to get super-profits, while the Labour Party practices social ________ or bourgeois reformism.

2. The Conservative Party developed out of the ________ party, while the Liberal Party developed out of the ________ Party.

3. The Labour Party was founded in 1900 by a union between the ________

_____ Union, the __________ Labour Party and the __________ Society.

4. For the election purpose, Britain is divided into ________ constituencies, each of which elects __________ member of the House of Commons.
5. In each constituency there may be any number of candidates, but the one who wins __________ votes is elected.
6. The party that wins the __________ seats in the House of Commons will be in office.
7. Central responsibility for the administration of the judicial system lies partly with the Lord __________ and partly with the __________ Secretary, the Secretary of State for __________ and the Secretary of State for __________.
8. In Britain the law as a whole consists partly of ________ or conventions and partly of __________ laws.
9. The criminal law is contained in __________ while a large part of the civil law is made up of a mass of __________ court decisions, interpreted in authoritative legal textbooks.
10. The central courts in Britain include the __________ and the Court of __________, the House of __________ and the __________ Council.
11. The three divisions of the High Court of Justice are the __________ Division, the __________ Division and the __________ Division.
12. The local courts in England are the __________ courts and county courts and others.
13. In Britain the highest civil court of appeal is the __________.
14. The Scottish High Court of Justice divides into the __________ Session and the __________ of Session that has an __________ House and the __________ House.
15. Punishment in Britain is in the form of __________ or __________. The death penalty for murder was completely abolished in the year of __________.
16. The police outside London are all __________ forces, employed and paid by local __________.

Ⅲ. Translate the following into Chinese.

1. Fabian Society
2. High Court of Justice
3. Returning Officer
4. Crown Court
5. Monster Raving Loony Party
6. the Lord Chancellor
7. Home Secretary
8. Secretary of State for Scotland
9. magistrate courts
10. common law
11. the Chancery Division
12. the Family Division
13. the Queen's Bench division
14. Lord Chief Justice
15. the Court of Session
16. Justices of the Peace
17. CID

Ⅳ. Explain the following in English.

1. the Conservative Party
2. the Labour Party
3. the Liberal Democrats
4. Returning Officer
5. the Chancery Division
6. the Family division
7. the Queen's Bench Division
8. Borstal institutions
9. Metropolitan Police
10. Scotland Yard

Lesson 6 History: Early Man and the Feudal Society

Major Events

3000 B. C.	Iberians began to migrate to the British Isles.
700 B. C.	Celts began to migrate to the British Isles.
55 & 54 B. C.	Romans under Caesar twice invaded Britain.
A. D. 43	Romans under Claudius conquered Britain.
A. D. 410	the end of Roman Britain
A. D. 449	The migration and settlement of Anglo-Saxons started.
A. D. 597	the arrival of the Christian mission under Augustine
A. D. 787	the beginning of the Danish Invasion of Britain
A. D. 878	Alfred forced the Danes to sign a peace treaty, which defined the Danelaw.
1017—1042	Danish kings ruled England.
1066	Norman Conquest
1086	William I made the Doomsday Book.
1087	William I died.
1100	William II was killed.
1106	Henry seized Normandy.
1135—1154	War between Matilda and Stephen
1154	the establishment of the House of Plantagenet
1215	King John was forced to sign the Great Charter.
1265	All Estates Parliament was summoned.
1295	“Model Parliament” was summoned.

Main Contents

1. Earliest Settlers

1) The Iberians

The earliest settlers on the British Isles were the Iberians, who came from the Iberian Peninsula between 3,000 and 2,000 B. C. They were dark-haired people and nomadic Stone Age hunters, who raised themselves from savagery onto the first steps of the civilized life. They were users of flint. They learnt to tame the dog, the sheep, the goat, the ox and the pig, and adopted the use of bronze and began farming. Their social system was a tribal society. They left no written records and the only relics which gave evidence of their existence were stone monuments, the biggest of which was the Stonehenge, built by the Iberians on the Salisbury Plain about 3,500 years ago.

2) The Celts

From 700 B. C. Celts came in several successive waves from the **Upper Rhineland** and began to inhabit British Isles. The fair-haired Celts imposed themselves as an aristocracy on the conquered tribes of Iberians throughout Britain and Ireland. So these people found refuge in the mountains to the north and west.

At least two big waves of Celtic invasion can be distinguished: first the **Gaels or Goidels**, still found in Ireland and Scotland, came over as early as 600 B. C. ; secondly the Cymric and **Brythons**, still found in Wales, come over before 300 B. C. From the Brythons came the English name for Britain. In the end all the races mixed in blood by intermarriage.

The Celts, like the Iberians before them, remained tribesmen or clansmen. They knew hunting, herding, weaving, bee keeping and the cultivation of wheat, oats and barley. There was no union among the tribes, and wars were frequent.

2. Roman Britain

In 55 and 54 B. C. Britain was twice invaded by Roman troops under **Julius Caesar**, but it was conquered by the Romans under Claudius in A. D. 43 Britain then became a Roman province and so it remained until the beginning of the 5th

century.

Caesar had two reasons to conquer the tribes across the Channel: (1) He needed showy exploits, tributes and slaves to enrich his fighters, and fill his war-chest; (2) the tribes of North **Gaul** and South Britain were so closely allied that Gaul would be more submissive if the neighboring tribes were constrained to pay tribute and to fear the mighty name of Rome.

In 55 B. C. Caesar took a small army and moved ten miles inland from the Dover Straits. As a military action his first expeditions was a failure. The next year, on a larger scale, he won several battles and penetrated into the inland. The Britons put up a stout fight against Caesar, but being undisciplined they lost the war. The expedition had no permanent results, except as a memory on both sides of the Channel. The tribute soon ceased to be paid.

The actual conquest of the island took place in A. D. 43. by the Romans under **Claudius**, the Roman Emperor, who sent Roman Legions to Britain that year. In the following two years the Romans reduced the whole south and east England, and soon the midland. But it was hard for them to conquer Wales and Northern England. Several times the Romans tried to conquer Scotland, but they failed hopelessly and repeatedly.

The Romans were empire builders. For military purposes they built roads, walls and garrisons and villas. They built Roman temples, baths, and occasional theatres. Attempts were made to Romanize Britain.

In A. D. 410, when the Roman Empire was declining, all the Roman troops went back to the continent to join the civil war there and never returned. In the end the Romans left behind themselves only three things of value: Welsh Christianity, the roman roads and cities, especially London.

3. Anglo-Saxon Britain

1) Anglo-Saxon Settlement

From the middle of the fifth century (traditionally A. D. 449) three Teutonic groups began to migrate from the region of **Denmark** and the Low Countries (Holland, Belgium and Luxemburg) and settle in Britain. As they were barbarians, they destroyed much the Romans had built. The Celts were driven westward to Wales and Cornwall.

The three **Teutonic groups** were **Angles**, **Saxons and** Jutes. From the Anglo-Saxon conquerors came the name "England" and "English;" England (An-

gla-land in OE) means the land of the Anglo-Saxons, collectively known as Angles.

The Anglo-Saxons were tribesmen who had developed from pasture farming to settled agriculture. They were mostly freemen, though they had the conquered Celts as slaves. Their social union was not kinsfolk, but the village. Private ownership had come into existence, but everyone was subject to a great deal of control by the village as a whole.

The early Anglo-Saxons were worshipers of natural forces, e.g., thunder, winds and storms. Their outlook upon life and their habit of mind were entirely different from Christian teachings. However, the Pope sent a Christian mission under **Augustine** from Rome in A.D. 597. The missionaries were extremely aggressive personalities, who succeeded in converting one tribal leader after another either by diplomacy or by persuasion. By the end of the 7th century all England had been Christianized. By 737 the Church of England had been well organized.

2) Anglo-Saxon Heptarchy

As time went on, the Anglo-Saxon tribes combined to form small kingdoms. Seven of these are eventually recognized: Northumbria, Mercia, East Anglia, Kent, Essex, Sussex and Wessex, collectively known as the **Anglo-Saxon Heptarchy**. The first three were established by Angles, Kent by Jutes and the last three by Saxons.

In the early part of the 7th century Northumbria gained the political supremacy over a number of other kingdoms. In the 8th century this leadership passed to Mercia and in the 9th century to Wessex under Egbert and later Alfred, the Great. Under Alfred the Great, Wessex attained a high degree of prosperity and considerable enlightenment.

3) Danish Invasion

In the late 8th century (traditionally A.D. 787) the Danes or Scandinavians began to attack the English coast. They made extensive settlements in the eastern half of the island in the late 9th century and turned their attention to Wessex. For 7 years the West Saxons, under the leadership of King Alfred the Great, offered resistance and their courage and persistence triumphed. In 878, a peace treaty was signed between the Danes and Alfred: the eastern half of the island was to be subjected to the Danish law and come to be known as the

Danelaw.

In 1014 Sweyn and Canute of the Danes scored a series of victories in different parts of England and finally seized the throne. From 1017 to 1042 England was ruled by Danish kings.

4) Feudal Society

In early Saxon England, the main classes of people were: (1) noblemen, with the king at the top, who were supposed to be descendants of Gods; (2) freemen, who were independent peasants holding large pieces of land; and (3) slaves, who had no land but were forced to till the land of the noblemen. Probably they came from the conquered Celts.

Gradually changes took place in social relation. The development of agriculture and trade stimulated production and resulted in the accumulation of wealth in the few hands. By the 10th century, a new aristocracy, **the thegn**, had appeared, who was originally a retainer of the king or some nobleman, and was frequently given a gift of land for his service. In the 11th century, the noble classes, whether by blood or through service, were supposed to be protectors of the ordinary people, and for this reason came to exercise economic control and judicial power over the classes below them. It was laid down as a rule of law and police that "every man must have a lord." The old system of clans and kinship had been completely displaced by the system of lords and tenants. At the head of the state was the king. Next to the king was the earl, who ruled many districts. Next to the earl was the thegn, who had become a territorial noble. Below the thegns stood a small class of freemen, who acknowledged the thegns as lords. Further below were serfs, who were bound to the soil. But the process of feudalism was not completed until after the Norman Conquest of 1066.

4. Feudal Society after Norman Conquest

1) Norman Conquest

When Canute died at forty in 1036, he left two sons and both of them were evil men. So Edward, son of Ethelred, was called back from Normandy to be king. His mother was a Norman lady and he was brought up in an abbey in Normandy. He was more French than English, and more like a monk than a king, so he was called Edward the Confessor. During his reign (1042—1066), a strong French atmosphere pervaded his court. He gave Sussex lands to Norman abbeys and put a Norman in command of the Sussex harbors, and he even appointed a Norman archbishop. All this paved the way for the Norman Conquest of 1066.

In January 1066, Edward, the last Saxon king, died childless. Harold, Edward's brother-in-law, and William of Normandy, Edward's Norman cousin, both claimed the throne. When it was reported that Edward had promised to leave the kingdom to his Norman cousin, Duke of Normandy William, the English lords decided to take action. They forced Edward to dismiss his archbishop and appoint a Saxon instead, but they were too disunited to prevent the spread of Norman influence and power. Later Edward died. On his deathbed he chose Harold of Wessex, his wife's brother, to be king in his place.

After Harold had been crowned, Norway's king landed and seized York. Harold had to rush north and destroy him. Three days later, on September 28th, 1066, William Duke of Normandy crossed the Channel with a formidable army, killed Harold and defeated the English army at the battle of **Hastings** on October 14, 1066. South England then offered little resistance. Londoners after a few weeks' hesitation surrendered and invited William to his coronation at Westminster Abbey on Christmas Day. However, the Conquest of England was not complete until 1071.

2) Development of Feudalism After Norman Conquest

After Norman Conquest, feudalism was established in England. The king was the sole and ultimate owner of all land, which he gave to nobles and the Church in return for military and other services. The vassals could subdivide their fiefs into smaller fiefs and bestow them upon their own followers. The king was the lord to his vassals, who in turn were lords to their tenants. Thus a new and more elaborate hierarchy of nobility came into being.

William Ⅰ adopted several measures to consolidate his rule. He required not only his vassals but also the vassals of his vassals to take an oath that they would be faithful to him against all other men. Thus the feudal system of England acquired a more centralized character than those of other European countries of the time.

In 1086, William Ⅰ had his officials go through England and make a record of each man's property. With this record at his elbow he could tell how much each man should and could pay. The people viewed the record with so

much superstitious fear that they called it **Doomsday Book.**

William Ⅰ died in 1087 and left Normandy to his elder son, Robert, and England to his second son, William Ⅱ. An arrow killed William Ⅱ in 1100 while hunting and his brother Henry took his place. Henry led an English army, defeated Robert and seized Normandy in 1106.

On Henry's death, the lords made his nephew Stephen king of England. This caused the war between Matilda (Henry's daughter) and Stephen for 19 years (1135—1154). Finally Henry Ⅱ, son of Matilda, was crowned and began **the House of Plantagenet.**

Under Henry Ⅱ, for the first time, condition became settled enough for a steady increase in trade and in population. But Henry Ⅱ is best remembered for his reform of the courts and law. He improved the courts of justice, introduced the jury system and made the law common throughout the country. To strengthen the King's power, Henry Ⅱ also weakened the power of the lords and knights. He cancelled the feudal services of forty days instead he asked the feudal lords to pay a special tax. This allowed him to hire professional soldiers. All he did greatly strengthened the feudal system in Britain.

3) King John and the Great Charter

Richard Ⅰ, son of Henry Ⅱ, was killed in France in 1199. His brother John succeeded the crown. He was defeated in a war with France and lost Normandy in 1204. He demanded more feudal taxes and army service than custom allowed so as to revenge himself on France. The lords became angry, marched to London and forced him to sign a long document on June 17th, 1215. The document is known as the Great Charter.

The Great Charter contained three sets of provisions: (1) that the king was not to exact extra payments from the feudal vassals (towns) without their consent; (2) that laws were not to be modified by the arbitrary action of the king; (3) that should the king attempt to free himself from law, the vassals had the right to force him to obey law, by civil war or otherwise.

The Great Charter was made in the interests of the feudal lords, great and small. Nevertheless, it had a progressive significance. It granted to the townspeople freedom of trade and self-government. The merchants and craftsmen in England appeared for the first time as a new political force. With the Pope's help, John soon tore up the Great Charter. Fighting broke out again and final-

ly John lost the war and died in 1216.

4) Birth of Parliament

When King John died, his son Henry Ⅲ was crowned. All was peaceful until he became old enough to rule. Like his father, Henry Ⅲ hoped that he could defeat the lords and their Charter with the help of the Pope. Year after year he poured English gold into the Pope's hands and let the Pope fill his church post with foreigners. He filled his own household with foreign advisers. After 30 years of misrule, his treasury was empty.

The contradiction between the king and the lords became acute. Under the leadership of Simon De Montfort, the king's brother-in-law, the lords forced the king to dismiss his foreign advisers and to accept their own council of advisers instead. De Montfort's new council took control of the treasury and all state officials, and then settled down to work their reforms. Simon called a parliament in 1265 after a battle in which Henry Ⅲ was defeated and taken prisoner. In addition to the older group, there were two knights from each shire and two citizens from each town. It was known as the "**All Estates Parliament.**"

Edward Ⅰ succeeded his father, Henry Ⅲ, in 1272. He was an energetic king, who conquered Wales and was engaged in a long war with Scotland. He was in constant need of money, too. In 1295, he summoned the "All Estates Parliament"—more than 400 members in all. As that Parliament was followed as a model, it became known in history as the "**Model Parliament.**"

Edward Ⅱ succeeded his father in 1307. He was a weak and lazy king. He left the work of government to his household favorites. Soon a party of lords formed against him. Parliament approved of their plans, which demanded the public appointment of all state officials. In 1327, Parliament forced him to hand over the crown to his son, and a few months later he was murdered.

Notes

1. Iberians 伊比利亚人
2. Celts 凯尔特人
3. Upper Rhineland 莱茵河上游
4. Gaels or Goidels 盖尔人
5. Brythons 布立吞人
6. Julius Caesar 朱利耶斯·恺撒，罗马大将军。

7. Gaul 高卢(古罗马帝国的一部分)
8. Claudius 克劳迪,罗马帝国皇帝。
9. Denmark 丹麦
10. Teutonic groups 条顿部族,日耳曼部族
11. Angles, Saxons and Jutes 盎格鲁人、撒克逊人和朱特人
12. Augustine 奥古斯丁
13. Anglo-Saxon Heptarchy 盎格鲁—撒克逊七国,七国时代。
14. Danish Invasion 丹麦人入侵
15. Danelaw 丹麦区,指九世纪英格兰东部受丹麦法所管辖的地区。
16. the thegn 乡绅,乡绅阶层
17. Norman Conquest 诺曼征服
18. Hastings 赫斯丁,亦译“哈斯丁斯”,诺曼征服的主战场,位于英格兰东南部。
19. Doomsday Book 《末日审判书》,实指财产调查登记簿。
20. the House of Plantagenet 金雀花王朝,又译为“安茹王朝”。
21. All Estates Parliament 各级议会
22. Model Parliament 模范议会

Questions for Discussion

1. Who were the earliest settlers on the British Isles? Where were they from and how did they live there?
2. Why did Caesar twice invade Britain?
3. Tell what you know about Roman Britain.
4. Describe the Anglo-Saxon settlement and the Heptarchy.
5. Give a brief account of the Danish invasion and the resistance offered by Wessexons.
6. How was feudalism gradually established in England and how was it developed after Norman Conquest?
7. Give a brief account of the circumstances in which Parliament was born in Britain.
8. Tell what you know about Edward Ⅰ and his son, Edward Ⅱ.

Exercises

Ⅰ. Choose the correct answer and circle the letter before it.

1. The earliest settlers on the British Isles were the ________.
   A. Celts B. Gaels
   C. Iberians D. Brythons
2. From 700 B. C. the Celts came from the ________ and began to inhabit British Isles.
   A. Iberian Peninsula B. Upper Rhineland
   C. Lower Rhineland D. Scandinavian countries
3. In A. D. 43 Romans under ________ conquered Britain.
   A. Julius Caesar B. Claudius
   C. Augustine D. the Pope
4. Roman Britain lasted until the year of ________ when all Roman troops went back to the continent.
   A. A. D. 400 B. A. D. 410
   C. A. D. 445 D. A. D. 449
5. Which of the following was NOT a thing of value left behind by Romans.
   A. Welsh Christianity. B. The Roman Roads.
   C. Cities. D. Roman Settlements.
6. In the middle of the fifth century, Anglo-Saxons came from the region of ________ and the Low Countries and settled in Britain.
   A. Denmark B. Norway
   C. Germany D. Holland
7. By the end of the ________ century all England had been Christianized.
   A. 5th B. 6th
   C. 7th D. 8th
8. Which of the following kingdoms was NOT set up by Angles?
   A. Northumbria. B. Mercia.
   C. East Anglia. D. Kent.
9. Which of the following kingdoms was set up by the Jutes?

A. Kent. B. Sussex.

C. Wessex. D. Essex.

10. In the late ________ century the Danes or Scandinavians began to attack the English coast.

A. 6th B. 7th

C. 8th D. 9th

11. The new aristocracy, the thegn, had appeared by the ________ century in Britain.

A. 9th B. 10th

C. 11th D. 12th

12. Edward had promised his kingdom to ________, but on his deathbed he changed his idea and gave the kingdom to ________. This led to the Norman Conquest of 1066.

A. William, Harold B. Harold, William

C. Matilda, Stephen D. Stephen, Matilda

13. Doomsday Book was in fact a record of each man's ______.

A. experience B. behavior

C. property D. reputation

14. The war between Matilda and Stephen resulted in the establishment of the House of ________.

A. Tudor B. Normandy

C. Plantagenet D. Lancaster

15. The Great Charter was made in the interest of ________.

A. the King B. the feudal lords

C. the townsmen D. the merchants

16. The first British parliament was summoned in the year of ________.

A. 1215 B. 1265

C. 1295 D. 1343

Ⅱ. Fill in the following blanks with appropriate words or expressions.

1. The earliest settlers on the British Islands were ________ and ________.

2. In 55 and ________ B. C. Britain was twice invaded by roman troops under Julius Caesar.

3. The Romans under ______ conquered Britain in A. D. 43.

4. From the middle of the 5th century three ____________ groups began to migrate from the region of ____________ and settle in Britain.
5. The early Anglo-Saxons were worshipers of ________. However, a Christian mission under ________ came from Rome in 597, and by the end of the ________ century all England had been Christianized.
6. In the late 8th century the ________ began to attack the English coasts. Under the leadership of King __________, the West Saxons offered resistance.
7. From 1017—1042 England was ruled by ________ kings.
8. In early Saxon England the main classes of people were ________, freemen and ________. By the 10th century, a new aristocracy, the thegn, had appeared.
9. Feudalism was established in England after ________ Conquest.
10. Henry Ⅱ is best remembered for his reform of ________ and ________.
11. The Great Charter aimed at restricting the power of the ________.
12. Simon called the "____________ Parliament" in 1265.
13. King Edward Ⅰ summoned the "All Estates Parliament" in the year of ________, which is known in history as "________ Parliament."
14. In 1327, Parliament forced ______________ hand over his crown to his son.

Ⅲ. Explain the following terms in English.

1. Anglo-Saxon Heptarchy
2. the Danelaw
3. Norman Conquest
4. Doomsday Book
5. Great Charter
6. All Estates Parliament
7. Model Parliament
8. the House of Plantagenet

Ⅳ. Rearrange the following historical events in the order in which they took place.

1. ____ a. Norman Conquest
2. ____ b. Anglo-Saxon Conquest
3. ____ c. the birth of Parliament
4. ____ d. Roman Conquest
5. ____ e. Danish Invasion

Ⅴ. Translate the following into Chinese.

1. Iberians
2. Celts
3. Gaels
4. Roman Conquest
5. Anglo-Saxon Heptarchy
6. Edward, the Confessor
7. Battle at Hastings
8. Doomsday Book
9. the Great Charter
10. All Estates Parliament
11. Model Parliament

Lesson 7 History: Decline of Feudalism and the Bourgeois Revolution

Major Events

1337—1453	the Hundred Years' War
1348—1350	Black Death
1381	Wat Tyler's uprising
1455—1485	Wars of the Roses
1485—1603	House of Tudor
1533	The Church of England began its own journey.
1553	Mary re-established Catholicism in England.
1558	Elizabeth ascended the throne.
1625	Charles I came to the throne.
1640	"Short Parliament" was summoned.
1640—1653	"Long Parliament"
1642—1646	the First Civil War
1648	the Second Civil War
1660	the Restoration of the Stuart
1688	the "Glorious Revolution"

Main Contents

1. The Decline of Feudalism

Several historical events took place in the 14th and 15th centuries, which shook the very foundation of the feudal society and marked the disintegration and decline of feudalism in Britain. These events are as follows.

1) Hundred Years' War (1337—1453)

In the 13th century, the English possessions on the European Continent were greatly reduced. At the beginning of the 14th century, England developed into a stronger state in Europe as its commerce and manufacture grew rapidly. Consequently the rich desired to control more market and the nobility wanted to regain their lost territories on the Continent.

Edward Ⅲ succeeded his father at the age of 15. He launched a war against French the in 1337 for the French crown on the ground that his mother was the daughter of the late king of France. The war, feudal in nature, lasted intermittently for over one hundred years, hence being known as the Hundred Years' War.

The Hundred Years' War was also a trade war. The economic interests of England and France clashed in **Flanders**, one of the richest provinces of **the Netherlands**. The Flemish cloth manufacturing towns were the importers of English wool. These towns owed political allegiance to the French king and the French objected to the wool-based economic ties between England and Flanders and taxed the wool trade heavily. The English king and his barons and merchants desired to get a foothold in Flanders for the expansion of trade.

In the early phase of the war the English were on the offensive and won great victories. Henry Ⅴ was once recognized as heir to the French throne, and his son was acknowledged king of France and England in 1422. In the last phase, when the French peasants came in under **Saint Joan of Arc**, a famous peasant girl, the French began to act on the offensive. By the time the war was concluded, the English had lost all the territories they had gained during the war-except the French port of **Calais.**

During the Hundred Years' War England underwent important political, economic and social changes. While the king was busy with his war, Parliament was frequently summoned. Apart from the right to approve taxes, it acquired the right to issue laws. From 1343 onward, it was divided into two chambers: the House of Lords, a body of leading clergymen and leading vassals, and the House of Commons, a body of small nobility (knights). The commoners were inferior politically because they were inferior economically to the great feudal landowners. They were not prominent until the 16th century. In economy, the English failure to conquer Flanders led the government to encourage the home woolen industry. England soon became more a manufacturer of cloth and less a mere producer of raw wool after the war. The war accelerated the breakdown of feudal society as the heavy cost of the long war inevitably increased the burden on the feudal lords and merchants. The vast expenditure of treasure for war consequently put the money class, the new bourgeoisie, in a more important position in Britain.

2) Black Death

The Black Death was a deadly bubonic plague that struck Europe in the middle of the 14th century and reached England in the summer of 1348. It was the severest of many plagues in **the Middle Ages**. About 40% of the population (3.5 million) died. Consequently, there was shortage of labor. The agricultural labors in villages and under-masters and journeymen in cities struck for higher wages, while the villains whose labor was not free struggled for full freedom. If the Black Death brought higher wages and greater freedom to the wage laborers it brought equal advantages to the villains. This hastened the breakdown of the manorial system in England.

The government of Edward Ⅲ issued in 1349 an order that required all grown-up men and women below sixty, having no land or other means of living, to work for landlords and proprietors at the rate before the plague. The parliamentary statutes of 1351 and 1361 (**"Statutes of Laborers"**) introduced cruel punishments for those who refused to work. A general hatred was aroused against the ministers, lawyers and landlords.

3) Wat Tyler's Uprising (1381)

During the reign of Richard Ⅱ, a new poll tax was imposed upon the peasants. This made the life of the peasants even worse. In the summer of 1381 the peasants in Essex rebelled. They went first to **Maidstone**, where they released John Ball from the county jail. They drove away or killed the king's tax collectors, attacked the nobles' manor houses and monasteries, and even killed the nobles. They were determined to abolish serfdom. They preached equality between the nobles and peasants. **John Ball**, a radical clergyman, who had traveled through southeast England before joining the peasants, served as their spokesman. He voiced the bitterness of the peasants and their strong hatred of the nobles in his famous rhyming jingle that is still remembered by many people in England.

"When Adams delved and Eve span,
Who was then the gentleman?"

Fighting bravely, the peasants soon came to London in June. Richard Ⅱ, being only fourteen years of age, was frightened and had to hold a peace talk with the rebellious peasants. The peasants told the king that they demanded freedom from villain-age, the reform of the church by a re-organization that would leave only one bishop in England, and the establishments of a society in which there should be no class distinction and all men should be equal except the King. The King promised to grant their demands and issued a pardon to everyone who went home in peace. About half of the peasants went home. During the next talk, the Lord Mayor of London, one of the King's followers, treacherously killed Wat Tyler, the leader of the peasant army. Later Richard put hundreds of rebels to death as he passed triumphantly with an army of 40,000 men through Kent and Essex. The Royal army soon suppressed the uprising.

Though the peasants' uprising met with its failure, it gave a heavy blow to the nobles with the king as their head and shook the very foundation of the feudal society in Britain.

4) Wars of the Roses (1455—1485)

From 1399 to 1461 **the House of Lancaster** reigned. The feudal nobility split into two groups: the Lancastrians and the Yorkists. They were contending for power, wealth and ultimately for the possession of the Crown. England had become a feudal anarchy by the middle of the 15th century.

Barely two years after the Hundred Years' War was concluded, England was thrown into another series of civil wars which were fought intermittently between the Lancastrians who wore a red rose and the Yorkists who wore a white rose, from 1455 to 1485, hence the name of Wars of the Roses.

The war began when Richard, the Duke of York, claimed to displace the Lancaster king, Henry Ⅵ. Supporting the Lancastrians were the wild nobles of the Scottish and Welsh Borders. The Yorkists drew most of their support from the progressive South, from East Anglia and London. So in nature the wars were a struggle between the commercial-minded gentry in the South and the backward feudal landowners in the North and West.

The war went on for 30 years. Open battles were few, but murder revenges were common. Political trials after disturbance put many nobles to death. From 1461 the Yorkists reigned, but the wars were not concluded until 1485. During the wars, the common people were little affected and so was the economic life of the time. However, the old feudal nobility was greatly weakened. "It was lucky for England," said Engels, "that the old feudal barons slaughtered one another in the Wars of the Red and White roses." When Henry Tudor, founder of a new monarchy, came to the throne in 1485, the old feudal nobility had been so weakened that it was no longer an important factor in the state.

In 1485, Henry Tudor killed Richard Ⅲ in **Bosworth Field**, putting an end to the wars, and became the founder of a new House-the House of Tudor.

2. The Bourgeois Revolution

The 17th century British Bourgeois Revolution lasted for nearly half a century from 1640 to 1688. In the whole process many historical events took place, such as the two civil wars, the execution of Charles Ⅰ, the suppression of the Diggers and the Levelers, the establishment of the commonwealth by Cromwell, the restoration of the Stuart and the so-called "Glorious Revolution" of 1688. The following is a brief account of the background, the process and the historic significance of the British Bourgeois Revolution of the 17th century.

1) The Background

The 15th and the 16th centuries were marked by the further decline of feudalism and the rapid growth of capitalism in the British History.

(1) Capital Accumulation

The **Tudor** family ruled England from 1485 to 1603. Under the Tudors, England became a national state with an efficient centralized government, and changed from a medieval to a modern country. The Tudor Monarchy, being in a transitional stage from feudalism to capitalism, witnessed many important political, economic and social changes. It reformed church in England and tolerated enclosures. It was under the Tudors that America was discovered and the renaissance spread into England. The Tudors also stimulated English commercial and maritime enterprises. The discovery of the New World and of the new sea routes and the expansion of trade with the Continent and the East brought enormous wealth to the country, and made men think differently.

(2) Religious Reformation

Henry Ⅶ was a strong and sensible king. He weakened the old nobility by forbidding any lords by law to keep any armed followers. He gave the royal court of **the Star Chamber** power to deal severely with any rich man who wronged his poorer neighbors. He organized an efficient tax system and built up a large fortune, which made him independent of parliament. To encourage the weaving industry at home, Henry Ⅶ increased the customs duty on imported cloth; he reduced the rights of foreign traders in London; and he encouraged shipbuilding industry by forbidding the carriage of the imported in foreign ships. Most of all, he encouraged adventurous merchants to explore new lands; he sent Cabot to explore the coasts of Canada and of Newfoundland.

Under Henry Ⅷ, the Church of England got its independence of Rome. In 1533, Henry Ⅷ repudiated papal supremacy over the English Church and declared himself Supreme head of the Church in England by the **Act of Supremacy** (passed by Parliament in 1534). There were reasons for Henry Ⅷ to do so: (1) the wealth and power the Church in Europe gathered through ages attracted the jealousy of kings. Most of the English kings resisted the Pope's interference in their national affairs; (2) by the 16th century the new national spirit of the English people had become impatient with the Church. The greed and laziness of the Church was hindering the social and political progress of England. And the Pope, under the foreign influence, hindered the English commercial progress abroad; (3) the external pretext for the Religious Reformation was the issue over Henry's divorce of his wife Catherine. Henry Ⅷ married **Catherine**, a Spanish princess, his elder brother's widow in 1509 for maintaining the alliance with Spain, with the special permission given by **the Pope**. The marriage gave them a daughter, Mary, but all their sons died at birth. Henry badly needed a son to succeed him, he began to feel that his marriage to Catherine was displeasing to God and decided to divorce her. He asked the Pope Clement Ⅶ to nullify his marriage, but he was refused because the Pope was then under the control of emperor Charles Ⅴ, Catherine's nephew. Henry became angry and began to take action. In the years that followed the repudiation of the Pope, all the religious institutions in England were seized and the crown confiscated their possessions. The English language, instead of Latin, became the language for churches.

Edward Ⅵ succeeded Henry Ⅷ at the age of nine in 1547 and died six years later at the age of fifteen. Then Mary, Edward Ⅵ's half-sister, became Queen of England, who married the King of Spain and re-established Catholic Church in England. She burned about 300 Protestants in a few years of her reign, hence the name of "**Bloody Mary.**" Mary died in 1558 and was succeeded by her half-sister, Elizabeth. Under Elizabeth the Church was re-established on a moderate **Protestant** basis.

(3) The Renaissance

It was under the Tudors that the renaissance spread into England.

The renaissance was a re-birth, i. e. revival of interest in many things that the early Middle Ages had cared little about. It was a cultural movement by progressive thinkers who represented the interests of the rising bourgeoisie and worked for freedom and enlightenment. They were called "humanists." The greatest of the English humanists was Sir Thomas More (1478—1535). In his classical work *Utopia* (1516), he gave an analysis of the social contradictions in England in the period of primitive accumulation. He argued against the savagery of laws, the greed of Enclosers, selfish wars, unjust taxation, and unequal distribution of property. He dreamed of an ideal commonwealth, which he called "**Utopia,**" meaning "nowhere." In his Utopia, there is no private wealth or money, no unemployment, no wars of aggression. In his Utopia, work is made compulsory, but only for six hours a day.

Under Elizabeth the theatre attained great popularity. No less than 2,000 plays were produced between the middle of the 16th century and the middle of the 17th century. The greatest dramatist of the age was William Shakespeare (1564—1616). In more than 30 comedies, tragedies and histories, Shakespeare gave the fullest expression of England and the English in the transitional period from feudalism to capitalism.

The two centuries just before the outbreak of the Bourgeois Revolution were a period of capital accumulation. The first and most important field in which merchant capitalists made their fortune was the wool trade. In order to raise sheep and get wool, the nobles and the bourgeoisie turned vast arable land into pastures. Fences were put around the pastures. The enclosure of land turned a large number of peasants into landless men, who poured into towns and cities. A new proletariat was born out of these landless men. Another way

of accumulating capital was to plunder colonies. Many companies were formed. These companies were to engage in the cruel exploitation of colonies and slave trade. Thus a new bourgeoisie was born out of the merchant capitalists, who worked hand in hand with the new aristocrats who had turned their land into pastures and were also engaged in other adventurous undertakings of the bourgeoisie.

Under Queen Elizabeth Ⅰ, capitalism grew rapidly. As the bourgeoisie was not yet strong enough to threaten the security of the throne, the Queen more or less supported the rising bourgeoisie and the new aristocrats. As the bourgeoisie became more and more powerful, they soon found that feudalism was preventing them from further development. They wanted free trade, but the monarchy controlled trade and commerce and imposed heavy taxes on merchants. Things grew even worse when Charles Ⅰ came to power. The king ruled without Parliament and sold special privileges to nobles to manufacture or sell such articles as soap, paper, coal and salt.

The persecution of Puritans constituted another cause of the bourgeois revolution. The Puritans were also Christians who wanted to make reforms in the Anglican Church. They were opposed to Charles Ⅰ and his idea that the king should no only be the head of state but also head of the Church as his power was a divine gift. They interpreted the Bible in a new way by advocating that the common men and the king were equal in the presence of god, and that the Bible encouraged free trade and the development of individualism. Obviously, Puritanism represented the interests of the new bourgeoisie. Charles chose as his archbishop William Laud (1573—1645), a red-faced, fiery-tempered little man, who did his best to defeat the Puritans. Many of them immigrated to America during the 17th century to free themselves from political and religious persecution at home.

The new bourgeoisie and the aristocrats, relying on the strength of the masses of peasants, with Puritanism as their ideological weapon, found that time had come for them to wage a decisive fight with the landowners, the old aristocrats and the king.

2) The Process

(1) The Outbreak of the Revolution

Charles Ⅰ ascended the throne in 1625. Like his father, he was constantly at loggerheads with Parliament. The Commoners sympathized with the Puritans and tried to make Charles Ⅰ follow their wishes by keeping him short of money. In 1629 Charles Ⅰ decided to call no more Parliaments. By being very thrifty and keeping out of war, he managed to rule without Parliament for 11 years. In 1640 Charles Ⅰ was forced to call a Parliament to get money to subdue the Scots who rose in rebellion. Parliament refused to help the king until English grievances had been considered, and so Charles dissolved it after a few weeks. Hence its nickname "**Short Parliament.**"

But when the Scots invaded England, Charles was forced to call another Parliament in November 1640. This Parliament lasted until 1653 and came to be called "Long Parliament." It declared that all the methods by which Charles Ⅰ had raised money without parliamentary consent were illegal. It abolished the Star Chamber, a special court that Charles had used to enforce his authority.

By the time the **Long Parliament** was called, London had become the center of stirring activity. Mass movements threatened the court. Backed by the masses, Parliament proceeded to struggle against absolutism. William Laud was arrested, and Thomas Wentworth, the Earl of Strafford, was executed before a crowd of 200,000.

In 1641 the Commoners drew up **the Grand Remonstrance** through which they bitterly accused Charles Ⅰ of his tyrannical rule and demanded that they should be given the rights of free trade and free commerce. The king rejected it and burst into Parliament at the head of his troops to arrest those who drew up the Remonstrance on January 5, 1642, but only found with disappointment that "the birds are flown." The merchants, craftsmen, apprentices and laborers as well as peasants in nearby villages came to support Parliament. The King fled and raised an army. When he raised his standard at Nottingham, war broke out between him and parliament.

(2) The First Civil War (1642—1646)

At the beginning of the Civil War, two camps were formed; the king's men were feudal lords, mainly members of the Church who were called "**Cavaliers**" with Oxford as the base and the supporters of Parliament were the bourgeoisie, the new aristocrats, craftsmen and workers and peasants, mostly members of Free churches, who were called "**Roundheads**" because the com-

mon people of London kept their hair very short. The first battle was fought at Edgehill in 1642. At first Charles had better soldiers and leaders than Parliament, and the war went in his favor. But later after Oliver Cromwell (1599—1658) reorganized the parliamentary forces, the King was badly defeated at **Marston Moor** (1644) and **Naseby** (1645). In the next year the King could struggle on no longer and surrendered to his enemies. The first Civil War ended on Jun 24, 1646.

(3) The Second Civil War (1648)

By then the contradictions among the revolutionaries arose. Parliament failed to pay their army and refused complete religious freedom to their Protestant supporters. Its generals marched to London, seized money to pay their men and took control of parliament. The King and his Royalists made use of the contradictions among the revolutionaries, revolting in Scotland and other places. The King ran away to join the revolt in 1648. The quarrel between Parliament and the army had to be settled. They reached an agreement to wipe out the King and his royalists. The army, under the leadership of **Cromwell**, defeated the revolt in a few months. The King was recaptured and was executed on January 30, 1649. England then called itself a Commonwealth.

(4) The Commonwealth (1649—1660)

In the period of Commonwealth Cromwell cruelly ruled the country. In 1649 **the Diggers** opened the wasteland near London suburbs. This movement soon spread over the country nearby. Meanwhile the Levelers in the army were against Cromwell. Cromwell sent the army to suppress the Diggers and kill the soldiers who were **Levelers** in the army. Then he led an army and conquered Ireland. The Irish people were ruthlessly exploited and oppressed by the English rulers.

(5) The Restoration and the "Glorious Revolution"

Cromwell died in 1658. Seeing that the peasants and the Levelers were organizing new uprisings and threatening their security, the bourgeoisie and the new aristocrats compromised with the rightists (Presbyterians) and invited Charles Ⅱ to come back from Holland to the throne on May 29th, 1660. This incident came to be known as the **Restoration of the Stuart**.

Charles Ⅱ ruled the country until 1685 and succeeded by James Ⅱ. Charles Ⅱ adopted some measures to protect the interests of the bourgeoisie,

but took revenge on the people. **Puritans** were persecuted and many were driven to America. Even the corpse of Cromwell was taken out of the grave and hanged in public. Things got even worse during the reign of James Ⅱ.

The expansion of the king's power soon clashed with the interests of the bourgeoisie and in 1688, the two parties of the bourgeoisie united and staged a bloodless coup d'état and put William of Orange (son-in-law of James Ⅱ) on the throne and formed an alliance with the landowners. This came to be known as "the Glorious Revolution."

3) The Historic Significance

The English Bourgeois Revolution is an epoch-making event. It swept away the obstacles of feudalism and paved the way for the development of capitalism in England in the next two centuries. It exerted great influence on the French and American revolutions in the 18th century. It marked the beginning of a new era, the era of capitalism. Since then Constitutional monarchy has become the system of government in England with the passage of **Bill of Rights** of 1689 and **Act of Succession** of 1701.

However, as the leadership of the revolution was in the hands of the bourgeoisie, the revolution was not made in the interests of the peasants and the rank and file, who were most resolutely opposed to the monarchy and made the biggest sacrifice in the revolution, but they were deprived of the fruits of victory. The revolution was the replacement of one exploiting class by another.

Notes

1. Hundred Years' War　英法百年战争
2. Flanders　弗兰德斯,昔日为欧洲的一个国家,今成为比利时东、西弗兰德斯两省及法国北部的一部分。
3. the Netherlands　尼德兰，荷兰的旧称。
4. Saint Joan of Arc　贞德,世称 The Maid of Orleans，法国民族女英雄，她唤起法国民族精神抵抗英国,后被烧死;1921 年尊为圣女。
5. Calais　加来,法国北部之一海港,距英国最近,隔英吉利海峡与英国 Dover 港相对。
6. Black Death　黑死病，一种严重致命的淋巴鼠疫,因尸体颜色发黑而得名。
7. the Middle Ages　中世纪,一般认为,欧洲的中世纪从 5 世纪开始至 15 世纪结束。

8. Statutes of Laborers 《劳工法令》
9. Wat Tyler 瓦特·泰勒,1831年农民起义的领导人。
10. Maidstone 美斯顿,英格兰东南部之一城市。
11. John Ball 约翰·鲍尔,英国教士。
12. the House of Lancaster 兰开斯特王朝(1399～1461)
13. Bosworth Field 博斯沃斯原野
14. Tudor 都铎
15. the Star Chamber 星室法庭
16. Act of Supremacy 《至尊法案》,英国议会于1534年通过的法案。
17. Catherine 凯瑟琳,亨利八世之妻。
18. the Pope 罗马教皇
19. Bloody Mary 血腥的玛丽
20. Protestant 新教的,新教徒
21. Renaissance 文艺复兴
22. *Utopia* 《乌托邦》
23. Short Parliament 短期议会
24. Long Parliament 长期议会
25. the Grand Remonstrance 大抗议书
26. Cavaliers 骑士党
27. Roundheads 圆颅党
28. Marston Moor 马斯顿荒原
29. Naseby 纳斯比
30. Cromwell 克伦威尔,资产阶级革命的领导人,独立派领袖。
31. the commonwealth 共和国
32. the Diggers 掘地派
33. Levelers 平等派,资产阶级革命中的一个激进的派别。
34. Glorious Revolution 光荣革命
35. Restoration of the Stuart 斯图亚特王朝的复辟
36. Puritan 清教徒
37. Bill of Rights 1689年英国议会通过的"权利法案"
38. Act of Succession 王位继承法案,1701年通过。

Questions for Discussion

1. What were the main causes of the Hundred Years' war? And what were the consequences of the war?
2. Give a brief account of Wat Tyler's Uprising.
3. What was the nature of the Wars of the Roses? What were the consequences of the wars?
4. What did Henry Ⅷ do to encourage the development of trade?
5. How did the religious Reformation take place in England?
6. Tell what you know about the renaissance.
7. What were the major causes of the British Bourgeois Revolution?
8. Describe the two civil wars and their consequences.
9. What did Cromwell do after he became the head of the Commonwealth?
10. Tell what you know about the Restoration of Stuart and the "Glorious Revolution."
11. What was the significance of the Bourgeois Revolution in the 17th century?

Exercises

Ⅰ. Choose the correct answer and circle the letter before it.

1. ________ launched the Hundred Years' War.
   A. Edward Ⅰ B. Edward Ⅱ
   C. Edward Ⅲ D. Henry Ⅲ
2. Which of the following statements was NOT true?
   A. Hundred Years' War was a feudal war.
   B. Hundred Years' War was a trade war.
   C. Hundred Years' War lasted for one hundred years.
   D. Hundred Years War is one of the historical events that marked the decline of feudalism in Britain.
3. From ________ onward, Parliament was divided into two chambers.

A. 1337 B. 1343
C. 1453 D. 1455

4. Black Death to some extent brought ________ to villains.
A. higher wages B. greater freedom
C. bitter life D. both A and B

5. The Statutes of Laborers issued by the government of Edward Ⅲ introduced cruel punishments for those ______.
A. who demanded higher wages
B. who worked
C. who hated the ministers, lawyers and landlords
D. who refused to work

6. In 1381, peasants in ________ first rebelled.
A. Sussex B. Essex
C. Wessex D. Kent

7. Wars of Roses were fought ________ between the Lancastrians and the Yorkists from 1455 to 1465.
A. Constantly B. irregularly
C. Continuously D. intermittently

8. During the Wars of Roses common people were ________ affected.
A. greatly B. much
C. a little D. little

9. The House of Tudor was founded in ________.
A. 1455 B. 1465
C. 1475 D. 1485

10. The British Bourgeois Revolution took place in the ______ century.
A. 15th B. 16th
C. 17th D. 18th

11. Which of the following statement about the Renaissance is NOT true?
A. The renaissance was a revival of interest in many things that the early Middle Ages had cared about.
B. The renaissance was a cultural movement by humanists.
C. The renaissance spread into England under the Tudors.
D. During the renaissance, the theatre attained great popularity under Elizabeth.

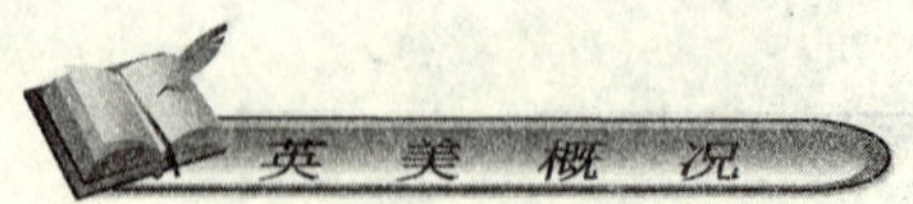

12. The two centuries jus before the outbreak of the Bourgeois Revolution were a period of ________.
    A. capital accumulation
    B. colonization abroad
    C. foreign territorial expansion
    D. Enlightenment
13. Which of the following is NOT true of Puritans?
    A. Puritans were Christians.
    B. Puritans were opposed to Charles Ⅰ and his ideas.
    C. Puritans wished to purify the Church of England.
    D. Puritans chose William Laud as archbishop.
14. Charles Ⅰ ruled without Parliament for ________ years.
    A. 10　　B. 11
    C. 12　　D. 13
15. The Commoners who drew up the Grand Remonstrance ________.
    A. were arrested by Charles Ⅰ
    B. were killed by Charles Ⅰ
    C. had already escaped before Charles Ⅰ burst into parliament
    D. had resigned from Parliament
16. The king's men at the beginning of the First Civil War were called ________.
    A. Cavaliers　　B. Roundheads
    C. Puritans　　D. Presbyterians
17. The First Civil War lasted for ________ years.
    A. 3　　B. 4　　C. 5　　D. 6
18. The Second Civil War was fought in the year of ________.
    A. 1646　　B. 1647　　C. 1648　　D. 1649
19. Which of the following statements is NOT true of the Commonwealth period?
    A. Cromwell suppressed the diggers.
    B. Cromwell killed Levelers in the army.
    C. Cromwell conquered Ireland.
    D. Cromwell restored the House of Stuart.
20. The "Glorious Revolution" of 1688 put ________ on the throne.

A. Charles Ⅰ　　B. Charles Ⅱ

C. James Ⅱ　　D. William of Orange

Ⅱ. Fill in the following blanks with appropriate words or expressions.

1. The Hundred Years' War was a war against ________ for the ________ crown and for the industrial city of ________.
2. In the 14th century, Parliament acquired the right not only to approve taxes but also to issue ________. From 1343 onward, it was divided into two ________.
3. The Black Death caused a ________ of labor. The laborers struck for higher ________, and villains struggled for full ________. But the "________ of Laborers" introduced cruel punishment for those who refused to work.
4. In 1381, the peasants in ________ rebelled. They were determined to abolish ________.
5. Wars of the Roses were wars fought between ________ and ________. The old feudal nobility was greatly ________ as a result of the Wars.
6. The 15th and 16th centuries were marked by the ________ of feudalism and the ________ of capitalism in the English history.
7. The enclosure of land turned a large number of peasants into ________.
8. The two major causes of the British Bourgeois Revolution were the ________ conflict between the bourgeoisie and the Monarchy and the persecution of ________.
9. The Commoners drew up the ____________ in 1641.
10. In the First Civil War, the king's men were called ______ and the supporters of Parliament were called ________.
11. The Second Civil War was fought in the year of ________.
12. England was cruelly ruled by ________ in the period of Commonwealth.
13. The restoration of Charles Ⅱ took place in the year of ________.
14. The "Glorious Revolution" was actually a bloodless ______ by the bourgeoisie in 16 ________.
15. The British bourgeois Revolution exerted great influence on ________ and the ________ revolutions in the 18th century.

Ⅲ. Rearrange the following historical events in the order in which they took place.

1. ____ a. the outbreak of the Wars of the Roses
2. ____ b. the outbreak of the Hundred Years' War
3. ____ c. Wat Tyler's Uprising
4. ____ d. the Black Death
5. ____ e. the "Glorious Revolution"
6. ____ f. the call of the Long Parliament
7. ____ g. the restoration of Charles Ⅱ
8. ____ h. the execution of Charles Ⅰ
9. ____ i. the call of the Short Parliament
10. ____ j. the re-organization of Parliamentary forces by Cromwell

Ⅳ. Explain the following in English.

1. The Enclosure
2. Puritans
3. The Grand Remonstrance
4. The Hundred Years' War
5. Short Parliament
6. Long Parliament
7. Black Death
8. Cavaliers and Roundheads
9. Restoration of the Stuart
10. "Glorious Revolution"

Lesson 8 History: The Industrial Revolution and the Chartist Movement

Major Events

1651	The first Navigation Act was passed.
1652—1674	Three wars were fought between England and Holland.
1756—1763	the Seven Years' War
1765	James Hargreaves invented the "Spinning Jenny."
1769	Richard Arkwright invented a spinning machine run by waterpower.
1785	Edmund Cartwright invented the power loom.
1784	James Watt improved the steam engine.
1814	George Stephenson invented the steam rail locomotive.
1819	Peterloo Massacre
1832	The Reform Bill was passed.
1837	The People's Charter was drawn up.
1846	The Corn Laws were repealed.
1847	The Ten-Hour Act was enacted.

Main Contents

1. The Industrial Revolution

The Industrial Revolution, a revolution in both the method of production and the relations of production, was one of the direct results of the primitive accumulation of capital and the rapid development of capitalism in Britain after the Bourgeois Revolution. It began with the introduction of machinery in the textile industry in the 1760's and lasted until the 1840's when machinery was widely used in practically every field of major industries.

1) Conditions for the Industrial Revolution

(1) After the "Glorious Revolution," enclosures continued on an even larger scale and were sanctioned by Parliament in the 18th century. Consequently there was a large transfer of land from one class to another, and thousands of small peasants were deprived of their land. Large modern capitalist farms took the place of the small pieces of land tilled by peasants. Agricultural production increased and supplied the industrial cities with raw materials and foodstuffs. The peasants who were deprived of land became either farmhand workers working on modern capitalist farms or "a reserve army of wage earners" in towns or cities. They had to make a living by selling their labor and buying foodstuffs and daily necessities, so there was not only an appearance of labor reserve but also an expansion of domestic market. Both were essential conditions for the Industrial Revolution.

(2) In the 17th and 18th centuries, England fought a series of wars against Holland and France, England's strong rivals at sea, and won the supremacy.

After England defeated **the Spanish Armada** in 1588, England entered into rivalry with Holland and France. In order to keep the Dutch vessels from trading between England and other lands, the British Parliament passed the first **Navigation Act** in 1651, which provided that no goods should be imported from abroad except in English ships or those of the country that produced the goods. This Act led to the outbreak of the war between the two countries. In the years from 1652 to 1674, three wars were fought and consequently Holland was completely defeated. In **the Seven Years' War** (1756—1763), Britain won Canada from the French and destroyed French power in India, and became the world's leading colonial power.

(3) The British foreign trade and slave trade constituted a great source of wealth. After the Seven Years' War, England became the strongest sea power and dominated world trade until the end of the 19th century. The wool trade continued to enjoy its prosperity and the slave trade increased after the middle of the 17th century when Negro labor was in great demand in sugar and tobacco plantations in South America.

(4) The colonial exploitation constituted another great source of wealth.

From the colonies in America and India the English bourgeoisie plundered enormous wealth for developing its industries. For example, **the East India Company** had the monopoly of the transport of goods to and from Europe, and its higher employees had the monopoly of the coastal trade as well as the internal trade of India. The officers of the Company were enriched through corruption and illegal trading and returned home with untold wealth.

2) The Process of the Industrial Revolution

The Industrial Revolution first began in the textile industry and was marked by a series of important inventions. James Hargreaves, a carpenter made the first invention. Before his invention the spinning wheel consisted chiefly of one large wheel that turned a spindle on which the thread was spun and wound. In 1765, he made a machine with eight spindles and with bars and clamps to take the place of human fingers in guiding and holding the threads. He gave credit of his invention to Jenny, his daughter, and in compliment to her he called it the **"Spinning Jenny."** In 1769 a barber by the name of Richard Arkwright invented a spinning machine run by waterpower. The great increase in the production of spinning would inevitably promote the demand of a fast weaving speed. In 1785, Edmund Cartwright invented the **power loom**, which greatly increased the speed of weaving. All these inventions gave a great impetus to the development of the textile industry.

The most important was the invention of the steam engine in 1769 and its improvement by James Watt in 1784. The steam engine was soon applied to coal mining, textile, iron and steel and machine industries.

The expansion of the market and the growth of world trade also called forth new means of transportation. In 1814 further improvements were made on the steam locomotive, which was used on the railway. In 1803 a young American of Irish origin successfully built a steamboat after making improvements on those made by his predecessors. In 1819 the first steamboat crossed the Atlantic and in 1825 the first locomotive railway was built between Liverpool and Manchester.

3) The Consequences of the Industrial Revolution

(1) The industrial bourgeoisie gained supremacy in the 1840s not only in the economic but also in the political life of the country.

(2) Productivity was greatly increased. In 1850, the total industrial out-

put value of England was 39% of that of the whole world and its iron output more than half of that of the world. England became the most advanced industrial country in the world and its financial center.

(3) As a result of the growth of industry, population was more and more concentrated in towns and cities. Many new cities sprang up. Manchester, Leeds, Birmingham and Sheffield were notable examples. By 1850 the urban population was half of the whole population of England.

(4) The rapid growth of capitalism, while bringing enormous wealth to the industrial bourgeoisie, caused miseries and disasters among the working people. As a result of the introduction and use of machinery, unskilled workers, mostly women and children, displaced handicraftsmen and skilled workers. Working and living conditions were horrible for the workers. Those who could not earn a living and who were found by the police wandering in the street would be thrown to the "**workhouse**," where they were brutally treated and were forced to do various kinds of hard work. Charles Dickens (1812—1870) gave a vivid picture of the workhouse of his time in his novel ***Oliver Twist***.

As the capitalists intensified their exploitation of the working class, the latter took action against the bourgeois government. In 1818—1819, mass rallies were held in Birmingham, Manchester and Leeds in protest against the government's decision to place a ban on all wheat import when the price fell below 50 shillings per quarter. On August 16th, 1819,80,000 people were gathered at **St. Peter's Fields**, Manchester, demanding Parliamentary Reforms and the repeal of the **Corn Laws**. No sooner had the speaker taken the platform than the soldiers sent by the government fired at the masses. Eleven were killed and about 400, including 100 women, were wounded. This incident was called the "**Peterloo Massacre**" in the English history.

2. The Chartist Movement

Towards the end of the 18th century, the industrialists became much stronger economically in Britain. They demanded a reform in the constituencies of the House of Commons so as to allow the growing town in the Midlands and North of England to be represented equally in Parliament and the abolition of the "**Rotten Boroughs**," a name given to a constituency that was represented in the House of Commons by the nominee of a peer though there was not a single

inhabitant in it. The industrial and commercial classes, with the support of the working class, demanded the reformation of the old voting system. After years of debate, in 1832 **the Reform Bill** was passed, which redistributed MPs so as to correspond to the great centers of population, but limited the franchise to those who possessed a low level of income. The working classes were still excluded from franchise and their living and working conditions were going from bad to worse. They began to realize that only by securing enough representation in Parliament could they force the government to pass laws in favor of the poor. This belief led to the outbreak of the Chartist Movement.

In 1837, workers in London, who were organized in **the London Workingmen's Association**, drew up a petition to Parliament, in which were embodied the Six Points that afterwards became known as the **People's Charter**. The Six Points were equal electoral districts, abolition of the property qualifications for MPs, universal manhood suffrage, **annual Parliament**, **vote by ballot**, and **the payment of MPs**. These demands were accepted with enthusiasm by hundreds of thousands of industrial workers who saw in them the means to remove their intolerable economic grievances. The People's Charter was endorsed at gigantic meetings all over the country. This was called the Chartist Movement.

As the movement spread beyond London, its character changed and sharp division arose among its leaders. The right wing leaders were opposed to the use of force and held the view that by the influence of moral force and through legal channels, Parliament could be persuaded to accept the people's demand. The left wing leaders called for an armed insurrection if Parliament should reject the People's Charter. They demanded the nationalization of all land and mines, the eight-hour working day, the elimination of social inequality, the abolition of child labor, the abolition of **the Poor Law**, and freedom of speech and of press.

The Chartist Movement reached its height in 1839—1842. From 1839 to 1848, three petitions were presented to Parliament, but all were rejected.

The first petition, signed by more than one million persons, was presented in 1839. Riots occurred in London and Birmingham. About 450 persons were arrested. **The "moral force" group** got frightened and left the movement.

The second petition was signed by more than three million persons and presented in 1842. Torch meetings were held by thousands of workers at night. The government made more arrests.

The third petition was presented in 1848. Over 5 million persons signed the petition. The government was alarmed. Troops were brought to London and special constables were enrolled. A procession of 20,000 bearing the petition was stopped just outside London. A rising had been planned, but instead of giving signal for the rising, O'Connor, the leader of the movement, played safe and dispersed the workers.

The Chartist Movement declined after 1848, though the National Charter Association lingered on until 1858.

The failure of Chartism is largely due to divided leadership and lack of a strong basis for class unity. The working class was still immature, not yet organized into a strong political party with socialism as its programme. Utopian and petty bourgeois ideologies enjoyed currency among the proletarians. A number of Chartists believed in peaceful reform and were even ready to come to a compromise with the bourgeoisie. The movement was weakened by internal dissension under a strong bourgeois influence.

However, Chartism was "the first broad, really mass, politically formed, proletarian revolutionary movement." (Lenin) Beginning with Chartism, the English working class entered the period of conducting independent political movements against the bourgeoisie. And it was the Chartists that compelled the ruling class to make substantial concessions. In 1846 were repealed the Corn Laws. In 1847 was enacted **the Ten-Hour Act**, whereby young persons and females were prohibited to work in any factory longer than ten hours a day.

3. The Growth of Economics

The social and economic changes brought about by the Industrial Revolution stimulated the growth of economics, which stems chiefly from Adam Smith, whose ***Wealth of Nations*** (1776) argued for non-interference by government with business, on the ground that each man is the best judge of his own economic affairs, that free competition and the universal desire for enrichment would result in the maximum increase in total wealth, and that the individuals' collective activity would automatically tend to the economic welfare of all though they might be selfish and unconcerned with the common good.

The doctrine of *laissez faire*, which advocated that government should merely be an omnipresent policeman protecting property and compelling the performance of contracts, appealed strongly to the new capitalists of the Industrial Revolution.

The school of "classical economists" headed by **Thomas Malthus** and **David Ricardo** later developed Smith's thinking of economy. Malthus formulated his "principle of population" in 1798, which asserted that any improvement in the economic condition of the poor would be counterbalanced by an increase in population since population tends to increase to the limit of the means of subsistence. Ricardo enunciated the celebrated "iron law of wages," which stated that wages must inevitably tend to an amount just capable of maintaining life, much as the coal fed into a steam engine was just capable of maintaining the fire under the boiler.

Against the terrible pessimism of the individualist economists arose the socialists, who refused to accept as irremediable the bad conditions brought by the Industrial Revolution. The experiment by **Robert Owen** at New Lanark was a cooperative community scheme for improving the condition of the workers. The success of the experiment at New Lanark raised hopes for a rapid improvement of social conditions, but later experiments of the same sort by Owen and others were disappointing. However, they created a public opinion against the system of *laissez faire*, which demanded better working conditions, a higher standard of living, an increased leisure, and a greater freedom for women and children.

Notes

1. the Spanish Armada　西班牙无敌舰队
2. Navigation Act　航海条例
3. the Seven Years' War　七年战争(1756～1763)，英法争夺世界霸权的一次大决战。
4. the East India Company　东印度公司，成立于1600年。
5. Spinning Jenny　珍妮纺纱机
6. power loom　自动织布机
7. workhouse　劳动院
8. *Oliver Twist*　《雾都孤儿》
9. St. Peter's Fields　圣彼得广场

10. Corn Laws 谷物法
11. Peterloo Massacre 彼得卢大屠杀
12. Rotten Boroughs 有名无实的选区
13. the Reform Bill 选举法改革法议案
14. the London Workingmen's Association 伦敦工人联合会
15. the People's Charter 人民宪章
16. annual Parliament 议会每年改选一次
17. vote by ballot 采用无记名投票方式
18. the payment of MPs 下院议员实行支薪制
19. the Poor Law 济贫法
20. the "moral force" group "道义"派
21. the Ten-Hour Act 十小时工作制法
22. *Wealth of Nations* 《国富论》
23. doctrine of *laissez faire* 放任主义,指经济按其自身的规律发展,故政府不宜干预经济的观点。
24. Thomas Malthus and David Ricardo 托马斯·马尔萨斯和大卫·李嘉图
25. Robert Owen 罗伯特·欧文

Questions for Discussion

1. Give a brief account of the nature and process of the British Industrial Revolution.
2. What were the consequences of the British Industrial Revolution?
3. What did Lenin say about the Chartist Movement?
4. What were the Six Points contained in the People's Charter?
5. Comment on the ideas of the British classical economists.
6. Tell what you know about the experiment by Robert Owen and its significance.

Exercises

Ⅰ. Choose the best answer and circle the letter before it.

1. The British Industrial Revolution first began in the ______ industry.
   A. iron and steel　　B. textile
   C. coal mining　　D. ship-building
2. ________ invented the "spinning Jenny."
   A. James Hargreaves　　B. Richard Arkwright
   C. Edmund Cartwright　　D. James Watt
3. As a result of the Industrial Revolution, which of the following statement is NOT true?
   A. Productivity was greatly increased.
   B. Unskilled workers were employed.
   C. Many new cities sprang up.
   D. Workers' living and working conditions were improved.
4. One of the Corn Laws placed a ban on ________ import when the price fell below 50 shillings per quarter.
   A. corn　　B. wheat
   C. barley　　D. any food
5. The term "Rotten Boroughs" means ________.
   A. boroughs that had gone rotten
   B. dirty boroughs
   C. boroughs in which there were no inhabitants
   D. constituencies that were represented in the House of Commons though there was not an inhabitant in it
6. The People's Charter was not ________.
   A. a long document drawn up by workers organized in the London Workingman's Association in 1837
   B. accepted by Parliament
   C. endorsed at gigantic meetings
   D. presented to parliament
7. The failure of the Chartist Movement was caused by the following rea-

sons except ________.

A. divided leadership

B. a strong party with socialism as its program

C. influence of Utopian and petty-bourgeois ideologies

D. immaturity of the working class

8. The Ten-Hour Act prohibited ________ to work in any factory longer than ten hours a day.

A. skilled workers

B. unskilled workers

C. young persons and females

D. all workers

9. The author of *Wealth of Nations* is ________.

A. Adam Smith B. David Ricardo

C. Thomas Malthus D. Robert Owen

10. The principle of population was formulated by ________.

A. Adam Smith B. David Ricardo

C. Thomas Malthus D. Robert Owen

Ⅱ. Fill in the following blanks with appropriate words or expressions.

1. The Industrial Revolution was a revolution in both the ________ of production and the ________ of production. It began in the ________ industry in the 1760s and lasted until ________.

2. The enclosures in the 18th century resulted in the appearance of ________ farms, ________ reserve and an expansion of ________ market.

3. In the 17th and 18th centuries, England fought a series of wars with ________ and ________ and won supremacy.

4. After the ________ War England became the strongest sea power and dominated world trade.

5. As a result of the Industrial Revolution, the ________ bourgeoisie gained supremacy in both economic and political life of the country. Productivity was greatly ________. Many ________ sprang up.

6. The rapid growth of capitalism caused ________ and ______ among the working people.

7. *Oliver Twist* was written by ________.

8. The People's Charter was a petition to Parliament drawn up by workers

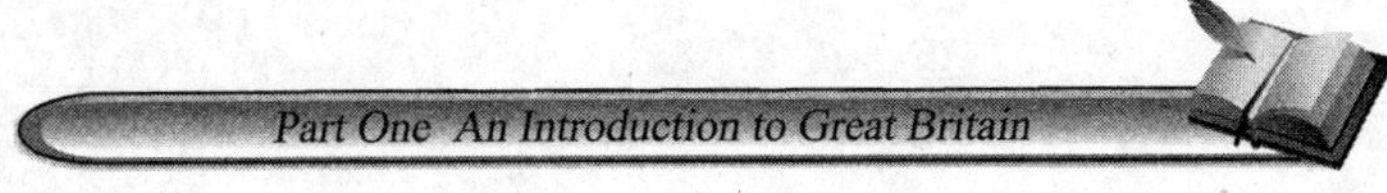

organized in ____________ in 1837.

9. The Chartist Movement reached its height in 18 ____—18 ____.

10. The failure of Chartism is largely due to the divided ______ and lack of a strong basis for class ______.

Ⅲ. Explain the following in English.

1. the Navigation Act of 1651
2. the Seven Years' War
3. Peterloo Massacre
4. the People's Charter (including the Six Points)
5. the doctrine of *laissez faire*

Ⅳ. Match the inventions in Column B with the inventors in Column A.

	Column A	Column B
1. ____	James Hargreaves	a. spinning machine run by water power
2. ____	Richard Arkwright	b. the steam engine
3. ____	Edmund Cartwright	c. the "Spinning Jenny"
4. ____	James Watt	d. the power loom

Lesson 9 History: The British Empire and Britain in Two World Wars and Post-War Periods

Major Events

1583	the founding of Newfoundland
1775—1783	the War of American Independence
1857	the Indian Mutiny
1840	the Opium War
1899	the Anglo-Boer War
1914—1918	the First World War
1929—1933	the world economic crisis
1931	Italy invaded Abyssinia.
1936	the Spanish Civil War
1937	the Japanese invasion of Central China
1938	the Munich Agreement
1941	Germany attacked the Soviet Union.
1945	the end of World War Ⅱ
1979	Mrs. Thatcher was elected Prime Minister.
1990	John Major was elected Prime Minister.

Main Contents

1. The Formation of the British Empire

The British Empire began with the founding of **Newfoundland** in 1583, the first British colony overseas. At the beginning of the 17th century, some large companies, such as the East India Company, London Company, and Plymouth Company were chartered. These companies were the earliest colonists. During the 17th and the 18th centuries other colonies were set up in North America, and trading posts were established in India by the East India Company, and in Africa and the **West Indies.**

In the 350 years from the first British colonists setting foot on the soil of America and India to the collapse of the British Empire at the end of World War Ⅱ, the British colonists subjected other peoples to their cruel rule. In the hundred years after the Industrial Revolution, the Empire kept expanding. In 1876 the total area of the British colonies was 22,500,000 square kilometers. By 1914 it had increased to 33,500,000 square kilometers, that is, 130 times that of Britain, with a colonial population 9 times that of Britain. The Empire embraced about one-fourth of the world population, and its combined territory covered nearly one fifth of the world land area. It was an Empire boasted as one "on which the sun never sets."

The British colonists perpetrated atrocities in the colonies. In America, they slaughtered millions of native **Indians** and deprived many Africans of their lives through slave trade. The strict and unimaginative colonial policies of the British government cause the American colonies to rebel, fight the **War of American Independence**, and form the United States (1775—1783). In India, the East India Company was given the right to enlist army, enforce law, declare war and make peace. The Company reaped fabulous super profits by buying low-priced cotton cloth, silk and jute in India and selling them at high prices in England and other parts of Europe. In the 17th century the East India Company seized three important cities: **Bombay, Madras and Calcutta**, and then gradually took control of almost the whole country. Under the British rule, the Indian people were in dire distress. When famine broke out in 1700, ten million people died in Bengal. There was a continuous wave of rebellion of the Indian people against the British rule. In 1857 the Indians rose in revolt in Delhi and other places. The rebels killed British officers, burned down garrisons and set free political prisoners. This incident is known as **the Indian Mutiny.**

India served as a gangplank for the British colonists to expand their colonies and **spheres of influence** in Asia. It was from India that the colonists shipped opium to China in exchange for China's tea and silk and extended their rule to **Burma, Malaysia, Singapore, Ceylon (Sri Lanka)**, etc.

In 1840 the British colonists launched an aggressive war against China and forced the corrupt Qing government to conclude the *Treaty of Nanking* in

1842, whereby Hong Kong was ceded to Britain as colony and five ports (Shanghai, Fuchow, Amoy, Ningpou and Canton) were opened as trade ports, and the colonists were granted special privileges for travel and missionary activities in China.

From 1856 to 1860 Britain and France jointly waged a war of aggression against China and occupied such major cities as **Canton, Tientsin and Peking.** They plundered and burned down the Yuanmingyuan and forced the Qing government to conclude the *Treaty of Tientsin* and the *Treaty of Peking*. In 1900, Britain allied with seven imperialist powers, invaded China in an attempt to further dominate over China.

In Africa, Britain occupied **Azania** in 1902, **Botswana** in 1885, Egypt in 1882, Gambia in 1889, Ghana in 1879, Kenya in 1895, Malawi in 1891, Nigeria in 1851, Somalia in 1887, Sudan in 1898, Uganda in 1896, Zambia in 1889, Zimbabwe in 1895, Tanzania in 1890, and other small countries. In fact, Britain occupied one-third of the whole Africa. In 1899 the sharply divided interests of Boer farmers (the Dutch settlers) and British miners led to a war known as the **Anglo-Boer War**. After two years of struggle Britain defeated Boers in South Africa, and annexed South Africa as colony.

The British Empire reached the peak of its colonial expansion after the Boer War. Britain not only had colonies all over the world, but also owned a large and powerful fleet and possessed the strategic spots along the route from Europe to Asia: **Gibraltar**, **Malta**, **Cyprus**, **Suez**, **Aden**, etc.

By 1900 Britain had been transformed from capitalism into imperialism. Besides the foreign territorial expansion, another important feature of imperialism was the export of capital, which was linked with territorial expansion both as cause and effect. By 1900 the total amount of British investments abroad was about 2,000 million pounds, from which a yearly income of 100 million pounds was drawn, which, in turn, brought about great changes in the nature of the exploiting class at home. The Typical capitalist was now no longer a factory owner running his own business and making efforts to develop industry, but a shareholder—drawing dividend from the investment of a vast capital.

Another key feature of imperialism was monopoly. In Britain monopoly developed strongly from the closing years of the 19th century. This was especially the case in the iron and steel and some new industries like the manufacture of chemicals, soap and margarine, in shipping and shipbuilding, and in railways and bank.

2. Britain in World War Ⅰ and Post-War Period

By the beginning of the 20th century, the world had entered the period of imperialism. Owing to the law of the uneven growth of capitalism, Germany and the U.S. became strong imperialist powers in the late 19th century and they, together with Japan, Italy, France and Russia competed with Britain for world domination. When the imperialist powers attempted to re-divide the world, an imperialist war was inevitable.

On the eve of World War Ⅰ, two imperialist blocs had formed. Germany, Austria-Hungary and Italy formed the **Triple Alliance** and Britain, France and Russia were held together by a firm alliance known as the **Triple Entente.**

On June 28th, 1914 the Austrian Archduke Francis Ferdinand and his wife were shot and killed by a young Yugoslav in Sarajevo. This incident was used as a pretext by Austria-Hungary to declare war against Serbia. On the side of Austria-Hungary were Germany, Bulgaria and Turkey. Italy, though a member of the Triple Alliance, joined the **Allies** against **the Central Powers.** Four years of the imperialist war ended with the Allies victorious.

The War came to the end in 1918. During the war, nearly three million British soldiers were killed, wounded, or disabled. Seventy percent of her merchant ships were sunk or damaged. Britain had lost her sea supremacy by the end of the War. The situation at home was worse than it was during the pre-war days. Though victorious, Britain came out of the War with a huge national debt, ten times as large as that before the War. Business was slack, many factories were closed down and taxes were unbelievably heavy.

In 1920 and 1921, an economic crisis broke out for the first time since the end of the War. Industrial production dropped by 46% during the crisis.

The world economic crisis lasted from 1929 to 1933. It was the most serious economic crisis that Britain had ever experienced. In the depression years, factories and mills closed down, banks failed and foreign trade shriveled. The number of unemployed people in 1932 reached three million. The total value of her export decreased to half the amount of the pre-war level, whereas her import doubled. Britain's position in the capitalist world was further weakened.

After World War Ⅰ the political consciousness of the British working

class was heightened. They fought one battle after another against the capitalist class. Their post-war struggle reached its climax in the General Strike of 1926 when six million men went on strike on May 4.

3. Britain in World War Ⅱ

Britain's foreign policy in the years between the two world wars was characterized by its hostility toward the young Soviet and the policy of non-intervention and appeasement towards Fascist aggression. In 1919, British imperialists mobilized 14 states for an armed intervention in Soviet Russia. On the other hand, Britain connived at Fascists' aggression on weak nations and instigated them to direct their spearhead towards the Soviet Union. When the Japanese Fascist forces invaded China and occupied Manchuria in 1931 and the Italian Fascist troops invaded Abyssinia in 1935, **the League of Nations**, controlled by the British and French governments, took no action to check the Fascist aggression. In the Spanish Civil War, the Fascist powers were again given a free rein to pursue their policy of aggression. In 1937, the Japanese militarists seized Peking and invaded Central China. The German fascists annexed Austria and proceeded to invade Czechoslovakia in 1939. By then the Second World War had actually begun. The League of Nations met again and again. Much was talked, but little was done to check the aggressors. The British Prime Minister **Neville Chamberlain** still thought he could keep the peace by making concessions to Hitler. At the Munich Conference in 1938, Hitler was allowed to take over the Sudetenland section of Czechoslovakia. The Munich Agreement was in essence a non-aggression pact between Britain and France on the one hand and Nazi Germany on the other. However, Hitler was not satisfied with this for long. He soon attacked Poland, which Britain and France were bound by treaty to defend. So Britain was forced to declare war on Germany on September 23, 1939, and France followed the next day. The next year Chamberlain resigned and **Winston Churchill** became Prime Minister.

Germany invaded France successfully and forced it to surrender in June 1940. England was in a very dangerous position, as German planes were able to bomb English cities and towns from French bases. Italy also entered the war on the side of Germany. Then in 1941 the pressure was somewhat relieved for England when Germany attacked the Soviet Union, and Japan attacked the United States at **Pearl Harbor** on December 7, 1941. World War Ⅱ marked the

first since the Norman Conquest of 1066 that England being an island did not save it from direct attack. Although England was not invaded, enemy planes did great damage in London and other cities. Fighting with Germany stopped in May 1945, and Japan surrendered in August of the same year.

4. The Fall of the British Empire

World War Ⅱ sealed the fate of the British Empire, though the collapse of the Empire had begun years earlier. In 1931 Australia, Canada and New Zealand became independent countries. After World War Ⅱ, a wave of national liberation and a movement of national independence swept over Asia, Africa and Latin America. India and Pakistan became independent in 1947, followed by Ceylon and Burma in 1948. The countries that became independent in the 1950s and 1960s were: Sudan, Ghana, the Federation of Malaya, **Somaliland**, Cyprus, Kuwait, Tanganyika, **Trinidad and Tobago**, Uganda, Western Samoa, Kenya, Malawi, Malta, Zambia, Gambia, **Maldives Is.**, Guyana, Botswana, People's Republic of Yemen, Nauru, Mauritius and Swaziland, followed by **Tonga and Fiji** in 1970. In July 1966 Egypt seized the Suez Canal. The British Empire had completely disintegrated. But the British government still tries to maintain the British Commonwealth of Nations, which is, in fact, a phony organization, as there is no ideology, legal bonds or military commitments to unite its members.

5. Britain in the Post-War Period

The Second World War, like the first, caused a tremendous loss to Britain. Domestic capital was seriously depleted, and over 1,000 million pounds of overseas investments were sold and new external debts incurred. While the Labour Party was in office from 1945 to 1951, some very important industries, like coal mining and railroads, were nationalized.

Britain lost the greater part of her export owing to the collapse of the Empire. Her export trade has been falling as compared with other capitalist countries. For most of the years since World War Ⅱ, Britain has had a deficit in the balance of international payments.

Britain's serious economic troubles produced the following effects: 1) devaluation of pound sterling, and 2) inflation and debts. The pound was worth US $4.03 before it was devalued in 1949, but it was worth only US $1.60 in 1976. Prices of consumer goods have kept going up since the end of the War.

When Wilson became Prime Minister in 1974, he had to face the problem of a brisk inflation and sluggish economy. In order to increase its trade, England joined the **European Economic Community (Common Market)** in 1973. The oil and natural gas deposits discovered off the Scottish coast, beneath the waters of the North Sea helped Britain tide over her economic problems.

In 1979, Mrs. Margaret Thatcher was elected Prime Minister and the Conservative Party was back in office. The political and economic policies pursued by Mrs. Thatcher in the 1980s are known as **Thatcherism**, the underlying aim of which is denationalization, i. e., to shift the economic emphasis back to private enterprise, directly contrary to nationalization carried out by the Labour government. This involves cutting public expenditure, returning state-owned enterprise to private ownership wherever possible, curbing the power of the trade unions, restraining the workers from striking, associating wages of workers with the profit of their enterprises and reducing inflation by **"monetarist financial policies."**

In the early 1980s, this "hard-line" right-wing doctrine was moderated slightly, partly because of the opposition from within the Conservative Party, and partly because most of the Conservative voters seemed to prefer less extreme policies. However, if modern British governments are judged merely on their economic records, by any standard Mrs. Thatcher's economic record since 1983 was extremely good. It was on this record that she won the general election in 1987. She served as Prime Minister until 1990 when she lost the support of the voters mainly because of a high rate of unemployment and was succeeded by **John Major**. In 1996 general election, the Conservative was defeated by the Labour and Blair became the prime minister, who remained in office till 2007 when he resigned and was succeeded by Gordon Brown.

Tony Blair is the first Labour leader to serve three terms. He once declared that his actions were guided by a strong "moral compass," and has pledged to make education and health the key issues of his premiership. In the foreign policy arena, Mr. Brown, the present prime minister, is regarded as more of an Atlanticist than a Europhile. He has also been long committed to increasing aid to Africa. He faces the challenge of restoring the British people's confidence in a Labour government before the next general election, due in a few years' time.

In May 1997, Labour under Blair won landslide election victory. In April 2001, Blair postponed country-wide municipal elections due in May as an outbreak of foot-and-mouth disease amongst cattle, sheep and pigs continues to spread. In June 2001, the Labour Party won a second successive general election victory. Following September 11, 2001 attacks on targets in the US, the prime minister Tony Blair offered strong support for US-led campaign against international terrorism. British forces took part in air strikes on targets in Afghanistan. In March 2003, UK joined US-led military campaign against Iraq after UN-based diplomatic efforts to ensure Baghdad has on weapons of mass destruction are perceived to have failed. That the Labour won the election with a greatly reduced majority in 2005 was widely seen as an expression of dissatisfaction with Mr. Blair's decision to become involved in the war in Iraq, and much attention will be focused on Mr. Brown's handling of this issue.

6. Sino-British Relations

Although the two countries are far apart geographically and have different social systems and cultural traditions, there is no conflict of fundamental interests between China and Britain. There is a long history of contacts and a traditional friendship between the Chinese people and the British people. Britain recognized the People's Republic of China in 1950. The two countries established diplomatic relations at the rank of the Chargé d'affaires in 1954, and at the ambassadorial rank in 1972. Since then, the friendly relations between the two countries have ceaselessly been consolidated. The Hong Kong issue, a legacy of the past, has already been settled satisfactorily through friendly talks between the two governments. Hong Kong was returned to China on July 1, 1997. The Chinese government began to exercise the sovereignty over Hong Kong on that day, and Hong Kong has become a special administrative region of China since then. The smooth settlement of the Hong Kong issue has pushed forward the political and economic relations between China and Britain.

Notes

1. the British Empire　大英帝国
2. Newfoundland　纽芬兰
3. West Indies　西印度群岛
4. Indian　印第安人
5. War of American Independence　美国独立战争

6. Bombay, Madras and Calcutta　孟买、马德拉斯和加尔各答，印度城市。
7. the Indian Mutiny　印度兵变
8. spheres of influence　势力范围
9. Burma, Malaysia, Singapore, Ceylon (Sri Lanka)　缅甸、马来西亚、新加坡、锡兰(斯里兰卡的旧称)
10. Canton, Tientsin and Peking　广州、天津和北京。
11. Azania　阿扎尼亚(非洲)
12. Botswana　博茨瓦纳
13. Anglo-Boer War　英布战争
14. Gibraltar, Malta, Cyprus, Suez, Aden　直布罗陀、马耳他、塞浦路斯、苏伊士、亚丁
15. Triple Alliance　三国同盟
16. Triple Entente　三国协约
17. Allies　协约国
18. the Central Powers　同盟国
19. the League of Nations　国际联盟
20. Neville Chamberlain　尼维尔·张伯伦
21. Winston Churchill　温斯顿·丘吉尔
22. Pearl Harbor　珍珠港
23. Somaliland　索马里兰
24. Trinidad and Tobago　特立尼达和多巴哥
25. Maldives Is.　马尔代夫群岛(亚洲)
26. Tonga and Fiji　汤加和斐济
27. European Economic Community (Common Market)　欧洲经济共同体(共同市场)
28. Thatcherism　撒切尔主义
29. monetarist financial policies　货币主义的金融政策
30. John Major　约翰·梅杰

Questions for Discussion

1. What do you know about the British Empire?
2. What atrocities did the British colonists in the colonies in America and India perpetrate?
3. What wars of aggression were waged by Britain against China in the 19th century?
4. What countries in Africa were once British colonies? Name some of them.
5. Point out the causes and consequences of the Anglo-Boer War.
6. What are the key features that marked the formation of British imperialism at the end of the 19th century?
7. What were the major causes of the First World War? What a great loss was brought to Britain by the War?
8. Describe the economic and political situation in Britain in the period between the two World Wars.
9. Make a comment on Britain's foreign policy in the years between the two World Wars. Give examples.
10. Give a brief account of the fall of the British Empire.
11. Describe the economic situation of Britain in the 1970s.
12. Tell what you know about Thatcherism.
13. Give a brief account of the Sino-British relations.

Exercises

Ⅰ. Choose the correct answer and circle the letter before it.

1. The first British colony was ________.

   A. New England　　B. Newfoundland

   C. West Indies　　D. India

2. Which of following is NOT true of the Indian Mutiny?

   A. The rebels burnt opium.

B. The rebels killed British officers.

C. The rebels set free political prisoners.

D. The rebels burned down garrisons.

3. The British colonists forced the Qing government to conclude the *Treaty of* ________ in 1842.

A. *Peking* B. *Nanking* C. *Tientsin* C. *Canton*

4. The British Empire reached the peak of its colonial expansion after the ________.

A. Anglo-Boer War B. the First Opium War

C. World War Ⅰ D. World War Ⅱ

5. Which of the following is NOT the feature of imperialism?

A. Foreign territorial expansion.

B. Export of capital.

C. Free competition.

D. Monopoly.

6. Which is NOT the member country of the Triple Alliance?

A. Germany. B. France.

C. Austria-Hungary. D. Italy.

7. Which is NOT the member country of the Triple Entente?

A. Britain. B. France.

C. Russia. D. Italy.

8. Which of the following is NOT true of the depression in the 1930's?

A. Factories closed.

B. Banks failed.

C. Foreign trade shriveled.

D. Unemployment rate was low.

9. In the 1930s, the League of Nations was controlled by ____.

A. Russia and the US B. Britain and The US

C. Britain and France D. Germany and Britain

10. The Munich Agreement was a non-aggression pact between ________ on the one hand and Nazi Germany on the other.

A. Czechoslovakia B. The US

C. Britain and France D. Britain and Russia

11. In which year did Japan attack Pearl Harbor?

A. 1939. B. 1940. C. 1941. D. 1942.

12. The British Commonwealth of Nations is a ________ organization.

A. military B. cultural C. economic D. phony

13. Which of the following terms best describe the economic situation of Britain in the 1970s?

A. Devaluation. B. Inflation.

C. Stagflation. D. Debts.

14. The underlying aim of Thatcherism is ________.

A. nationalization

B. denationalization

C. cutting wages

D. increasing public expenditure

15. Mrs. Thatcher failed to win the general election in 1990 mainly because of ________.

A. the slow development of the British economy

B. the high inflation

C. the high rate of unemployment

D. the high rate of taxes

16. China and Britain established the diplomatic relations at the ambassadorial rank in the year of ________.

A. 1950 B. 1954 C. 1972 D. 1997

Ⅱ. Fill in the following blanks with appropriate words or expressions.

1. The British Empire began with the founding of ________ in 1583, and fell after the ________ of the Second World War.

2. The East India Company was given right to ________, ________, ________ and ________ in India.

3. India served as a ________ for the British colonists to expand their colonies and spheres of influence in Asia.

4. The British Empire reached the pinnacle of its colonial expansion after the ________ World War.

5. The three features of imperialism were foreign territorial ________, the export of ________ and ________.

6. The two imperialist blocks that had been formed just before the outbreak of World War Ⅰ were ________ and ________.

7. Nearly ________ million British soldiers were killed and wounded and ____% of her merchant ships were sunk or damaged in World War Ⅰ. Consequently Britain lost her sea ________ after the end of the War. And she came out of the War with a huge ________.
8. In 19 ____ and 19 ____ an economic crisis broke out for the first time since the end of the First World War. The most serious economic crisis that Britain had ever experienced before World War Ⅱ lasted from 19 ____ to 19 ____.
9. The working class struggle reached its climax in the ________ of 1926.
10. Britain's foreign policy in the years between the two World Wars was characterized by its ________ toward the young Soviet and the policy of ________ and ________ toward Fascist aggression.
11. The World War sealed the fate of the British Empire.
12. Britain's serious economic troubles after the Second World War produced such effects as ________ of pound Sterling, ________ and ________.
13. In 19 ____ Britain recognized the People's Republic of China. And in 19 ____ China and Britain established diplomatic relations at the ambassadorial rank.

Ⅲ. Re-arrange the historical events in the order they took place by putting the symbolic letter in the corresponding blank.

1. ____ a. Anglo-Boer War
2. ____ b. the Munich Agreement
3. ____ c. the Indian Mutiny
4. ____ d. the First Opium War
5. ____ e. the Spanish Civil War

Ⅳ. Explain the following in English.

1. the Indian Mutiny
2. the Treaty of Nanking
3. the Munich Agreement
4. the British Commonwealth of Nations

Lesson 10 Education in Britain

Major Points

Education in Britain is carried out in three stages: primary, secondary and higher education. Education is compulsory for children between the ages of 5 and 16.

Independent schools are fee-paying institutions, providing pupils with two stages of education: in prep schools and public schools.

Public schools are the most expensive and the best known of independent schools for their house system and prefect system.

Examinations for secondary schooling are represented by the three main certificates: the certificate of Secondary Education (CSE), the Ordinary Level of the General Certificate of Education ("O" Level of GCE) and the Advanced Level of the General Certificate of Education ("A" Level of GCE).

All universities are private institutions, each having its own governing council and deriving nearly all of its funds from state grants.

Universities in Britain can be roughly divided into three groups: Oxbridge, redbrick and new universities.

"Oxbridge" refers to the two most famous higher education institutions in England: Oxford and Cambridge. Included in this group are four other universities founded in Scotland in the 15th and 16th centuries.

"Redbrick" is a name for a group of universities founded between 1850 and 1930, aimed at providing higher education for local inhabitants who could not afford the cost of going away from home for their studies.

The New universities were all founded after World War Ⅱ. Despite the newness of these institutions, they quickly became popular because of their modern approach to university courses.

What deserve special attention of the three categories of universities are the college system and the tutorial system of Oxford and Cambridge.

The Open University is an innovation in the late 1960's, which provides chances for people of all ages and to which entry is much less restricted.

Schoolteachers must have a certain qualification for teaching and are paid according to a set standard, with supplements.

The central Department of Education and Science and the Local Education Authorities (LEAs) jointly administered education in Britain, with the main responsibility left to the LEAs.

The LEAs control all state schools, and each school has a governing board. An independent school has a separately constituted board of governors, which controls the finances and appoints the headmaster. The majority of children attend state schools.

State education is in two stages: primary education and secondary education. Primary education takes place in three categories of schools: nursery schools, infant schools and junior schools, and secondary education in a variety of schools: grammar schools, secondary modern schools, technical schools and comprehensive schools.

Main Contents

1. Educational System

Education in Britain is carried out in three main stages: primary education, secondary education and higher education. All children must, by law, receive full-time education between the ages of five and sixteen. Primary and secondary education takes place in schools, which may be divided into two categories: the **independent schools** and the **state schools.**

Independent schools, also known as private schools, are fee-paying educational institutions. Many private schools are long established and have gained a reputation for their high academic standards. However, only about 6% of all children attend these schools. Apart from the independent schools, there is a complete system of state primary and secondary education. Any child may attend, without paying fees, a school provided by the public authorities, and the great majority of children attend such schools. Numerically small as they are, the independent schools have made the most peculiar and characteristic contribution to education in Britain and they have an immense influence on the whole of English educational practice.

Examinations are very important in British education. Though not its main purpose, they are required for qualification for a higher level of education. Under the old selective system, pupils take an examination called the **"eleven plus"** in their last year at primary school when they are 11 years old. The results of this examination determine whether they will go to a grammar school, a technical school or a secondary modern school. For secondary schooling students, at least one of the three main certificates is required to demonstrate their educational attainment. Moderately assiduous children take the Certificates of Secondary Education (**CSE**), which indicates satisfactory completion of schooling to the age of 16. More ambitious children take the examinations for the General Certificate of Education at Ordinary Level (**"O" Level of GCE**), which is the required starting-point for many types of professional training. Most young pupils who stay at schools after passing their Ordinary Level examinations prepare themselves for the Advanced Level of GCE (**"A" Level of GCE**), which is the standard for entrance to universities and other higher education and to many forms of professional training.

The examinations for the GCE are not conducted by the state or by any public authority, but by eight independent **examining boards**, most of them being connected with universities. Each of the examining boards arranges its syllabus, prepares questions, grades the candidates and awards certificates. Thus, the examinations set by the different boards are similar in difficulty, but differ in contents and arrangement. Each school has its choice from these boards for preparing its pupils for examinations.

Universities in Britain are formerly restricted to the rich. They are now open to all intelligent young people, both male and female. Thanks to the availability of the many scholarships awarded both by the state and by local authorities, students who receive further fulltime education after the age of eighteen and whose parents cannot afford to pay for their children's education at university can receive a grant to cover most of their fees and living expenses, with the rest being paid by their parents. Rich parents have to pay for all the fees and living expenses for their children's education. Still, the number of secondary school students who can enter universities is limited due to the fact that the capacity of universities is not enough to take for admission all those who are able to get the necessary "A" Level of GCE at school. In practice, therefore, entry to universities is competitive. To remedy this insufficiency of capacity, polytechnics were established, where degree courses are also available. The **Open University**, a phenomenon in education first appeared in 1969, provides chances for people of all ages. Entry to the Open University is much less restricted.

In the teaching profession there is no clear distinction between elementary and advanced level teachers. All men and women who have not been to universities but wish to teach in state schools must spend three years in a college of education to get their teaching certificates. Students of a university, however, need only one year in the department of education of a university. All teacher-training courses include teaching practice in the classroom. The standard salary scale for teachers in schools is called the **Burnham Scale**, first established in 1924 by a committee chaired by Lord Burnham. Supplements are paid to teachers who have first or second class honors degrees from their universities and to those who have posts of special responsibility. Schools outside the state system make their own arrangements for paying their teachers, but often follow the Burnham Scale.

The academic year for schools begins after the summer holidays and is divided into 3 terms, namely, the Autumn term (also called the Christmas Term) from early September to mid-December, the Spring Term (also known as Easter Term) from early January to the end of March or the beginning of April, and the Summer Term from the end of April to early or mid-July. The intervals between terms are formed by the Christmas, Easter and summer holidays. The exact dates of the holidays vary from area to area, the general pattern being about 2 weeks at Christmas and Easter and 8 weeks in the summer. School hours are usually from 9:00 a. m. until 3:30 or 4:00 p. m. University terms are shorter and often have religious names: **Michaelmas** for October-December term, **Lent or Hilary** for the January-March term, and **Trinity** for the April-June term.

2. Administration of Education

Education in Britain is not as centralized as it is in many other countries. The central Department of Education and Science in London guides, advises,

and inspects, but the planning and organization of education in England and Wales are left to the Local Education Authorities, the local government bodies that are responsible for the state schools in a district and that engage teachers, maintain school buildings and supply school equipment and materials.

The **LEAs** are controlled by the Education Committees of the county and metropolitan councils. Most of the money needed comes from the general grant provided by the Treasury, but the LEAs have a great deal of freedom in their administration. In the same way, the LEAs interfere as little as possible with schools. The headmaster or headmistress of a school thus has a great deal of autonomy in deciding what is to be taught and how the teaching is to be carried on. Teachers in schools choose their own books and are free to experiment in many different ways.

Education is compulsory for all from the ages of five to sixteen. Children receive their education in two systems of schools: the state schools and the independent schools. All state schools are under the control of the LEAs. Each school has a board of unpaid governors or managers, a group of local citizens who give help and advice to the schools. Nearly 94% of British schools are state schools. They are non-fee-paying, as distinct from independent schools, which are fee-paying schools operating outside the state system. Each independent school has a board of governors separately constituted. They control the finances and appoint the headmaster, who in turn appoints the other teachers. Now about 96% of all children go to state schools, only 4% of them attending independent schools. All schools, including independent schools, are subjected to inspection by officials sent out by the Department of Education and Science.

State education is in two main stages: primary education up to the age of eleven, and secondary education from eleven to sixteen or eighteen; all children, therefore, have a minimum of eleven or thirteen years of compulsory full-time education.

Higher education in Britain takes place in universities. All British universities are private institutions. Each has its own governing council, including some local businessmen and local politicians as well as a few academics. The state began to give grants to them in the 1920s, and by 1970 each university derived nearly all of its funds from state grants. The government gives money to the universities to cover the cost of buildings and to cover almost all their current expenditure, but it does no control them. The Department of Education and Science has an important influence on new developments in higher education through its power to allocate funds.

3. State Schools

State education in Britain is in two main stages: primary education up to the age of eleven, and secondary education from eleven to eighteen. Primary education is divided into three categories: nursery schools, from the age of 2 to 5; infant schools, from 5 to 7; and junior schools, from 7 to 11. Most children start at the age of 5 in an infant school, where boys and girls are kept together. Some children go before the age of 5 to kindergartens, officially called nursery schools. After two years of study in an infant school, children enter a junior school, where boys and girls are often—but not always—kept together. The work for children in these schools is a little more advanced.

For all children in state schools, primary education is followed by a secondary school from the age of eleven to sixteen. Primary school pupils are formerly selected on the basis of the "eleven-plus" for an appropriate secondary education. Those with the highest marks go to the **grammar schools**. Others go to technical schools. The rest—by far the majority—are admitted by **secondary modern schools**. Though the "eleven plus" examination is widely distrusted, it is still loosely used to apply to a similar selection procedure operated in Britain by some LEAs. At present, however, most school pupils can go to comprehensive schools without taking any exams.

Grammar schools take pupils aged between eleven and eighteen, preparing pupils for the General Certificate of Education. The name "grammar" comes from the fact that Latin grammar constituted an important part of teaching in the original grammar schools. At grammar schools, the work is oriented towards possible university entrance or some other form of higher education. In grammar schools, mostly maintained by local education authorities, a class is often called a "form," never a "grade," which is an American term. Teaching at Grammar schools is much concerned with the business of preparing pupils for their examinations, and the advanced-level work in the sixth form tends to be rather specialized. Pupils in the fifth form take the GCE "O" Levels at the end of the year. "A" Levels are usually taken at the end of the second year in

the sixth form.

Secondary modern schools offer a more general and technical and less academic education than grammar schools. These schools are designed to give secondary education to children up to the age of fifteen. Inside a secondary modern school the children in each group are often placed in three "streams." Letter "A" denotes the stream which is learning most quickly, and the "C" stream is for the children of the least academic type, concentrating mainly on practical work and other activities which can best develop the capacities of the children who are placed in that stream.

Many secondary modern schools are very anxious to have their "A" stream pupils develop good academic standards, and plan their "A" steam teaching so as to lead to the General Certificate of Education for those of their pupils who are capable of attempting it and prepared to stay at schools for an extra year. To further raise the prestige of the secondary modern schools, the Minister of Education announced in 1961 that there would be a new school-leaving examination at a lower level than GCE—the Certificate of Secondary Education (CSE). This examination should be within the reach of the children learning at the secondary modern school at the age of fifteen. A more recent event is that another new school-leaving examination, the General Certificate of Secondary Education (GCSE), was introduced, which was intended to replace the two examinations taken by secondary school students—the GCE and the CSE.

Within the state school system the most important are the **comprehensive schools**. By 1980 eight out of ten children were going to comprehensive schools, and it was assumed that British state education would become almost totally comprehensive.

Ever since the first comprehensive school was opened under a Labour government in 1945, there have been bitter arguments for and against this "revolution" in education. In 1965, for example, the Labour Party made "comprehensive education for all" its official policy, and requested all the LEAs to produce plans to "go comprehensive." Though the Conservative Party protested with the battle cry "save the grammar schools," very few LEAs refused. In 1976 a Labour government made comprehensive education compulsory despite fierce opposition from the Conservatives. Today there is still much disagreement about the good and the bad in the comprehensive system. But the good comprehensive schools have shown that the academic and non-academic children need not be kept apart. In some comprehensive schools, state examination results are better than in the old days of grammar and secondary modern schools.

"Comprehensive" means "all inclusive." At the age of eleven children educated in state primary schools go to a comprehensive school. The boys and girls are of mixed abilities and come from a variety of backgrounds. At a comprehensive school, pupils study a wide variety of subjects for two or three years, and then they may choose to study only those subjects they like best. Apart from all the ordinary subjects, they may be able to take more unusual subjects such as economics, commerce and typing. There are also many school and out-of-school activities, which they can share: singing, acting, woodwork, cooking and games. At the age of fifteen or sixteen, pupils at these schools will take an examination, either the "O" Level of GCE or the Certificate of Secondary Education. Those who decide to stay at school after this will have another examination, the "A" Level of GCE, at the age of eighteen, and can go on to university if they do well in this examination.

For state education, some LEAs have introduced variations of the comprehensive system by dividing their age groups into smaller units. First schools are a type of primary school for children aged five to eight; Middle Schools, a separately organized stage between primary school and secondary school, are for pupils aged between nine to fourteen; and Secondary or High Schools for students of the age from fifteen to eighteen. Several LEAs have also introduced Sixth Form Colleges, further education colleges for those aged between sixteen to eighteen, even those who are not preparing for university exams.

4. Independent Schools

Operating outside the state school system is a different system of schools-the independent schools. These schools are supported entirely by fees and private funds; thus they are also known as private schools.

The best known of the private schools are the **public schools**. The oldest of public schools were founded to give free education to clever boys whose parents could not afford to educate them privately. They were under "public" management or control. Today, however, these schools are the most expensive of the independent schools in Britain. They are mostly boarding schools, where pu-

pils live as well as study.

Independent schools usually provide pupils with two stages of education. However, the terms "primary" and "secondary" are not usually applied to independent schools at different levels because the age of transfer from a lower to a higher schools is normally thirteen or fourteen instead of eleven. The principal schools for children of over thirteen (13—18) are usually called public schools and those for younger pupils (8—13) are usually called "preparatory" (colloquially "prep") schools.

There is an important difference of construction between the preparatory and the public schools. Some preparatory schools are private in the fullest sense; they are operated as private enterprises as if they were shops or factories. Such a school is often the personal property of its headmaster, who is not controlled by a governing body, but works as an independent businessman. The public schools, on the other hand, are not normally called "private schools;" they are not private in the fullest sense. They are generally under the control of governing bodies. They do not try to make financial profits, but only to balance their budgets. Their income is mainly from fees paid by parents, supplemented by gifts and endowments.

Most public schools, particularly the most eminent ones, are called by the name of the town or village in which they are situated. Some of them are called "college." In public schools boys and girls are usually educated separately. The four most famous of all the boys' public schools are **Eton College, Harrow School, Winchester College and Rugby School**, and the two best known of all the girls' public schools are **Roedean School and Sheltenham Ladies' College**. Such a school is never referred to as "a college." One way to determine that a particular institution is a public school is the tendency that people usually refer to it by the name of the town or village in which it is located, without adding the word "college" or "school" at all.

Public schools are subject to the inspection by inspectors of the Department of Education and Science, but otherwise they are quite independent. Each school has a board of governors separately constituted. They control the finances and appoint the headmaster or headmistress, who in turn appoints the other teachers.

Public schools are well known for their **house system** and their **prefect sys-**

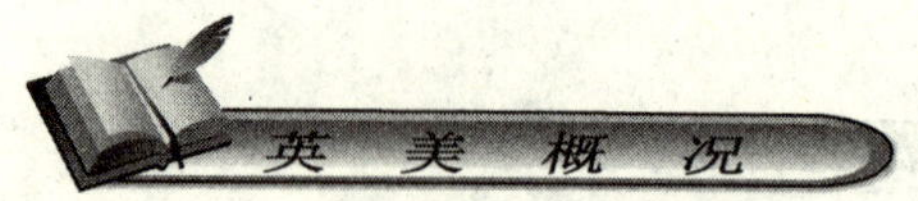

tem. In a boys' public school, for instance, though the teaching is arranged centrally for the school as a whole, the boys live in a separate "houses." A house is a building where a group of pupils lives. Each group of pupils is seen as having a distinctive group identity especially in competitions within the schools. A typical house has about fifty boys, and they are all under the special care of a housemaster and his wife. The housemaster appoints about six of the oldest boys as "prefects," who are given certain powers and duties with regard to keeping order over the other boys. They form a sort of government of the community, with one boy holding the office of "Head of the House," or "House Captain." The housemaster keeps himself a little in the background and leaves as much as possible of the government to the head boy and other prefects.

A typical preparatory school is very small, with between fifty and a hundred children, either all boarders, or all day-pupils, or some of each. Many of these schools are housed in old buildings of the nineteenth century. The pupils are usually taught in five or six forms; the headmaster or headmistress will themselves work as ordinary teachers, and will have four or five assistants working for them. The preparatory schools prepare pupils for the Common Examination for Entrance to Public Schools and for public school life. A typical boarding prep school is run rather like a house in a public school. Prep schools usually have very small classes, and the better prep schools have the benefits of ample space, good playing fields, and pleasant surroundings.

Despite the fact that public schools are long established and have gained reputation for their high standards, there has been disagreement of opinion about the good and the bad of public schools. The greatest argument for public schools is the superiority of public school education, which is proved by the strikingly high proportion of ex-public-schoolboys occupying senior posts in the government, the armed forces, the church, the universities, the professions, and even in businesses. Accidentally, it is this point that constitutes the greatest argument against public school education; it simply proves the social exclusiveness or favoritism of public schools. Nowadays, however, public schools are no longer as superior and as exclusive as they once were. Their prefect system and their house system have been widely adopted in state secondary schools, and many grammar schools have academic records which many

a public school might envy. Moreover, many so-called public schools are dependent on an annual grant from the central government, and admit pupils at eleven, just like grammar schools. And more public schools are liable to be inspected by the state

5. Higher Education

British higher education mainly takes place in universities. In 1960 there were only twenty-three universities in Britain. Today, there are well over forty universities, about twice as many as in 1960. They can be roughly divided into three groups: **Oxbridge**, **Redbrick**, and **New**.

"Oxbridge" is a term used to refer to the two most famous higher education institutions in Britain: Oxford University and Cambridge University. They were the only universities in England until the 19th century. However, four universities had been founded in Scotland before it was united with England to become part of the United Kingdom. They are St. Andrews (1411), Glasgow (1450), Aberdeen (1494) and Edinburgh (1583).

"Redbrick" is the name for a group of universities founded between 1850 and 1930, including London University. They were so called because red brick was the favorite building material of the time. As the term "redbrick" already fell into disfavor, they are sometimes called middle-aged universities. Most of these higher education institutions were founded in the biggest industrial towns and in a few other centers. For a long time they could not give degrees themselves, but prepared students for the London University examinations. Students who successfully passed these examinations were awarded degrees by London University. They were then called "university college," because they were not universities in their own right. Their first purpose was to provide higher education for local inhabitants who could not afford the cost of going away from home for their studies. As these universities grew bigger and more solidly established, all of them have achieved independent status. There are now established universities in London, Durham, Manchester, Liverpool, Birmingham, Leeds, Bristol, and so on. In Wales, there were four similar institutions, united rather comfortably as the University of Wales.

The new universities were all founded after the Second World War, with the first created in 1949 in the grounds of an old country mansion at Keele, Staffordshire. Following this, the early 1960s produced a large number of new foundations, each in a campus near a not-too-large, nor-too-industrial town. They included the University of York and Lancaster, of Sussex, Kent, Warwick, Essex, and East Anglia. Then in the middle of the 1960s, a number of local technical colleges were given charters as new universities. Most of these are in the biggest cities where there are already established universities: The University of **Aston** is in Birmingham, **Salford** close to Manchester, **Strathclyde** in Glasgow, **Heriot-Watt** University in Edinburgh, **Brunel** in London, and **City University of London**. Although these universities were new, some of them quickly became popular because of their modern approach to university courses.

Of the three categories of universities, what merits special attention are the college system and the **tutorial system** at Oxford and Cambridge. Indeed, it is impossible to begin to understand the structure of Oxford or Cambridge without first understanding the nature and function of the colleges, which have no resemblance whatever with the institutions which are also called "colleges" in American universities. In fact, the college system at Oxford and Cambridge is unlike that of any other university in Britain. In order to enter the university, a student must first apply to a college and become a member of the university through the college. All colleges are parallel and equal institutions. None of them is connected with a particular study and all are governed by twenty or thirty "Fellows." Fellows of a college are tutors, that is, teachers, often called dons. They teach their own subject to those students in the college who are studying it, and they are responsible for the students' academic progress.

The university is a sort of federation of colleges. It prescribes syllabuses, arranges lectures, conducts examinations, and awards degrees. Most dons give one or two lectures a week, which students from any college may attend. Each student gets personal tuition once a week in his tutor's own room. This, with a weekly program of private study, is considered so important that no lectures are compulsory; tutors usually advise their students which lectures they should go to.

Each college has its own completely separate living quarters, its own dining hall, and its own chapel. Colleges were formerly founded to admit students of one sex, either males or females. Now most of them have become co-educational. Cambridge University, for example, had five women's colle-

ges. It has at present twenty-eight colleges, of which only one is for men and two for women only. The remaining twenty-five take both men and women. And Oxford University has thirty-five colleges, with only three for women and the rest taking both men and women.

British higher education is divided into undergraduate and graduate studies. At most universities an honors degree is taken in one main subject and one subsidiary, or secondary subject. A general (or **"pass") degree** is taken in a variety of subjects, but carries less weight than an **honors degree**. An honors degree is a first degree at a university obtained by a student with distinction: The honors degree is given to the students who are more successful in their examinations. Honors degrees are classified according to the candidates' examination performance as First Class, Second Class, or Third Class, as distinct from a pass degree. Few students get First Class degrees, however, so these are a valuable qualification for a job. Students with any class of degree, either a pass degree or an honors degree, become **Bachelors of Arts or Science**. If they wanted to go a step further and became **Masters of Arts or Science**, they would have to write an original paper, or thesis, on some subject. Oxford and Cambridge are peculiar in that the former usually awards an MA to anyone who has an Oxford BA degree, who has been a member of the university for at least twenty-one terms, and who pays a small sum of money (five pounds in 1986), and the latter awards an MA degree to any one who has had a Cambridge BA degree for at least two years and who requests it, with no fee being paid.

A striking feature for British higher education is that all British universities are private institutions. They are all independent and self-governing. Each has its own governing council, including some local businessmen and local politicians as well as a few academics. The state began to give grant in the 1920s, and by the end of the 1960s each university received nearly all of its funds from state grants, which were aimed to cover the cost of buildings and to cover the whole of its current expenditure. Students have to pay fees and living costs, but every student may get from the LEA of the place where he/she lives a personal grant, which is enough to pay his full costs. The size of the LEA's grant depends on the size of his parents' income; rich parents have to pay both fees and living expenses for their children of university age.

Following the creation of new universities in the 1960s, there was a new

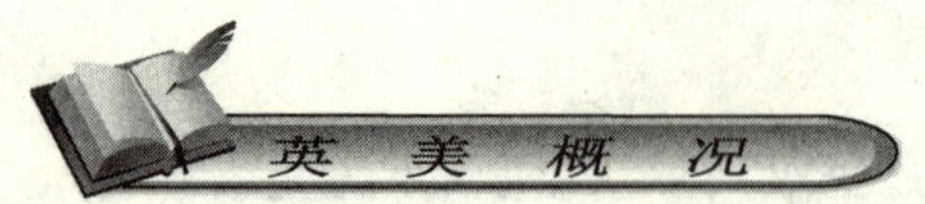

further development in the 1970s. Two other forms of higher education were established. First, a number of technical colleges became "**polytechnics.**" These could be called the "comprehensives of further education," where students can study for diplomas or even degrees, or else just continue their education in the subjects of their choice. The polytechnics offer full-time or part-time courses for students of all ages over eighteen. There are thirty polytechnics in England and Wales, and fourteen similar colleges in Scotland. All of them have gained the status of universities.

The most interesting innovation of all is the Open University, which was founded in 1969 and began its first course in 1971. This educational institution is so named because it is "open" to all to become students with no formal qualifications to study for a degree. Courses are followed in the students' spare time; lectures are broadcast on radio and TV, and students correspond with their tutors by post. For some of the Open University courses students have to attend one-week summer schools, which are held in many of Britain's traditional universities. At the end of the course, successful students are awarded a university degree.

Notes

1. independent school　独立学校(私立学校),指独立于国立学校教育体制以外的学校。
2. state school　国立学校
3. eleven plus　11 岁儿童参加的小学毕业考试
4. CSE　中等教育证书,the Certificate of Secondary Education 的缩写形式。
5. "O" Level of GCE　普通中等教育证书的一般水平测试,是 the Ordinary Level of the General Certificate of Education 的缩写形式。
6. "A" Level of GCE　普通中等教育证书的高级水平测试,是 the Advanced Level of the General Certificate of Education 的缩写形式。
7. examining boards　考试委员会
8. Open University　开放大学,创建于 1969 年,1971 年开课,对各个年龄段的学生开放,故称"开放大学"。通过电台、电视授课,学生通过书信与导师联系,有的课程于暑期集中面授一周。成绩合格,学生可获得学位。我国现行的自考、电大、函授等教育方式均受到开放大学的启示。
9. Burnham Scale　伯纳姆教师工资标准

10. Michaelmas, Lent (Hilary) and Trinity 英国大学每学年的三个学期带有宗教色彩的名称,分别译为:米迦勒、封齐期(希勒里)和三位一体。
11. LEAs 地方教育局,是 Local Education Authorities 的缩写形式。
12. grammar school 文法中学,因教授拉丁文法而得名。
13. secondary modern school 现代中学
14. comprehensive school 综合中学,有工党政府于 1945 年所创立而又极力推崇的非选拔制中学。
15. public school 公学,早期的公学是为其父母无力供孩子上学而向聪明儿童提供免费教育而办的学校,因此而得名。
16. Eton College, Harrow School, Winchester College and Rugby School 英国四所最有名的男子公学名称,分别称为:伊顿、哈洛、温切斯特和拉格比。
17. Roedean School and Sheltenham Ladies' College 英国两所最有名的女子公学,分别称为:罗迪恩、谢尔顿厄姆。
18. house system 寄宿制
19. prefect system 级长制
20. Oxbridge 是 Oxford and Cambridge 的缩写,指英国古老大学。
21. redbrick universities 指英国工业革命后建立的、以红砖建筑为特点的大学。
22. new universities 新兴大学,指英国 20 世纪 60 年代后建立的大学。
23. Aston 阿斯顿大学
24. Salford 索尔福德大学
25. Strathclyde 斯特拉斯克莱德大学
26. Heriot-Watt 哈利特—瓦特大学
27. Brunel 布鲁内尔大学
28. City University of London 伦敦城市大学
29. tutorial system 导师制
30. "pass" degree "合格"学位,亦称 general degree,普通学位。
31. honors degree 优等学位,大学毕业少数优秀学生可以获得的第一个学位,分为一、二、三等。
32. Bachelor of Arts or Science 文科或理科学士
33. Master of Arts or Science 文科或理科硕士
34. polytechnics 理工学院

Questions for Discussion

1. Give a brief description of the British educational system.
2. What are the main examinations for secondary school pupils?
3. What are the qualifications for a teacher of a state school?
4. How are teachers of a school paid?
5. Describe the different terms of an academic year.
6. How is British education administered at different levels?
7. Describe the operation of a grammar school, a secondary modern school and a comprehensive school.
8. Describe the house and the prefect systems of a public school.
9. How is a typical prep school operated?
10. What is the greatest argument for and against public schools?
11. Describe the college system and tutorial system of Oxbridge.
12. What are the degrees a university can offer? Explain.

Exercises

Ⅰ. Choose the correct answer and circle the letter before it.

1. Which of the following statements is NOT true?
   A. Education in Britain is carried out in three stages.
   B. Education in Britain is compulsory for children between the ages of 5 and 16.
   C. All children go to state schools in Britain.
   D. All state schools in Britain are non-fee paying institutions.
2. Which of the following examinations is NOT for secondary schooling?
   A. CSE.　　B. "O" Level of GCE.
   C. "A" Level of GCE.　　D. eleven plus.
3. Universities that were founded between 1850 and 1930 are called ________ universities.
   A. Oxbridge　　B. Redbrick

C. New D. Old

4. All universities in Britain are ________.

A. state institutions

B. private institutions

C. research-oriented institutions

D. founded before World War Ⅱ

5. The main responsibility for administering education in Britain is left to ________.

A. the Department of Education and Science

B. Local Education Authorities

C. Local Councils

D. Board of governors

6. The examinations for the GCE are conducted by ________.

A. the public authority B. each school

C. examining boards D. universities

7. Entry to universities in Britain is ________.

A. compulsory

B. competitive

C. non-competitive

D. arranged by LEAs

8. All teachers in the state system must ________.

A. be advanced level teachers

B. be university graduates

C. get a MA degree

D. spend some time in the department or school of education of a university

9. Supplements are paid to teachers who ________.

A. work hard

B. have first or second class honors degrees

C. have third class honors degrees

D. have posts of special responsibility outside the school

10. The term from early September to mid-December is known as ________.

A. Christmas Term B. Easter Term

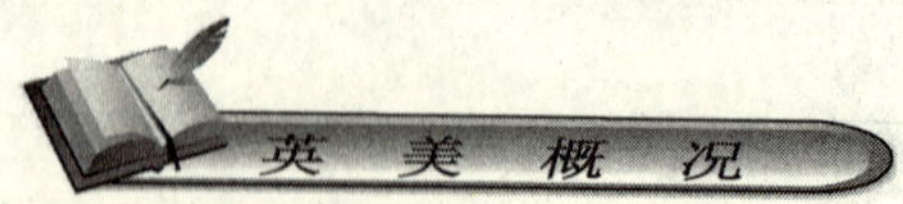

C. Summer Term D. Spring Term

11. University terms are ________.

A. longer B. shorter

C. larger in number D. smaller in number

12. The general grant needed by state schools in Britain is provided by ________.

A. the Treasury

B. the Local Education Authorities

C. LEAs

D. The Education Committees of the local councils

13. In Britain, most children start their schooling at the age of 5 in a (an) ________ school.

A. nursery B. junior

C. infant D. kindergarten

14. Pupils with the highest marks in the "eleven plus" examination go to ________ schools.

A. grammar B. secondary modern

C. comprehensive D. public

15. "Co-educational" means ________.

A. with boys and girls mixed together

B. with boys only

C. with girls only

D. with cooperation between boys and girls

16. Those who do well in the examination of ________ can go on to university for study.

A. "O" Level of GCE B. "A" Level of GCE

C. CSE D. eleven plus

17. Independent schools are schools that ________.

A. operate outside the state school system

B. have independent public funds

C. are free from the inspections of the Ministry of Education and Science

D. are independent in deciding their own teaching curriculum

Ⅱ. Fill in the following blanks with appropriate words or expressions.

1. Independent schools in Britain are ________ educational institutions.
2. Any child may attend, without ____________, a state school in Britain.
3. British education is conducted in ________ main stages.
4. Under the old ________ system, pupils sit for an examination called the ____________ in their last year at primary school.
5. Secondary school students are required to take at least one of the three certificates to demonstrate their ____________.
6. The Open University is so called because it is ________ to people of ________ ages.
7. The academic year for schools begins after the ________ holidays and is divided into ________ terms.
8. The general pattern for school holidays is about ________ weeks at Christmas and Easter and ________ weeks in the summer.
9. Each state school has a ________ board of governors or managers.
10. Education in Britain is ________ for all pupils from the ages of 5 to 16.
11. Primary school pupils are formerly selected for an appropriate ________ education on the basis of the ______ examination.
12. Grammar schools are so called because ________ grammar constituted an important part of the teaching in the original grammar schools.
13. In a secondary modern school, the children in each group are often placed in 3 ________.
14. State primary education falls into 3 categories: ________ schools, ________ schools and ________ schools.
15. The work at grammar schools is oriented towards possible university ________ or some other form of ________ education.
16. The first comprehensive school in Britain was opened in ________ under a ________ government.
17. Prep schools are ________ in the fullest sense because they are operated as private ________ as if they were ________ or ________.
18. A ________ in a public school is a building where a group of pupils live and study.

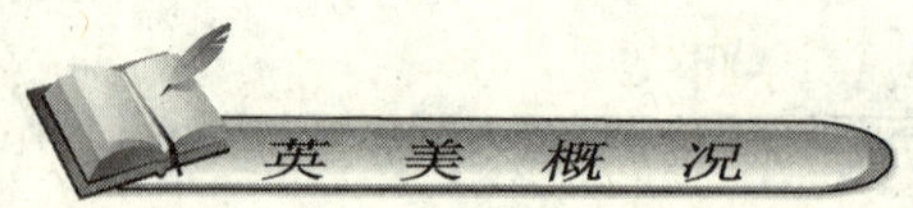

19. The prep schools prepare children for the common ______ for the entrance to ______ schools and for ______ school life.
20. Oxford and Cambridge were the only universities in ______ until the 19th century.
21. ______ universities were founded between 1850 and 1930, and sometimes called middle-aged universities.
22. Middle-aged universities were called "______ college" because they were then not ______ in their own right.
23. All new universities were founded after the ______ World War, with the first created in the year of ______.
24. ______ degree is classified according to the candidate's examination performance as First Class, Second Class or Third Class.
25. In the Open University, courses are followed in the students' ______ time, lectures are delivered on ______ and TV, and students correspond with their ______ by letters.

Ⅲ. Match each of the school examinations with the age at which it is usually taken.

1. ____ "O" Level of GCE — a. 17/18
2. ____ CSE — b. 15/16
3. ____ "A" Level of GCE — c. 11
4. ____ eleven plus — d. 15

Ⅳ. Match each academic term with one of the dates.

1. ____ Autumn term — a. end of April to early/mid-July
2. ____ Spring term — b. early Sept. to mid-December
3. ____ Summer term — c. early January to the end of March/beginning of April

Ⅴ. Translate the following into Chinese.

1. eleven plus
2. independent school
3. state school
4. General Certificate
5. Certificate of Secondary Education
6. Open University

7. Local Education Authorities
8. grammar school
9. secondary modern school
10. comprehensive school
11. the house system
12. the prefect system
13. Common Examination for Entrance to Public Schools
14. college system
15. tutorial system
16. honours degree
17. polytechnics
18. public school

Ⅵ. Explain the following in English.

1. the selective system of education
2. General Certificate of Education
3. the Burnham Scale
4. Local Education Authorities
5. public school
6. preparatory school
7. Oxbridge
8. Open University

Key to Exercises

Lesson 1 Geography: The land

Ⅰ. **Choose the correct answer and circle the letter before it.**

1. B 2. B 3. A 4. D 5. A
6. D 7. A 8. C

Ⅱ. **Fill in the following blanks with appropriate words or expressions.**

1. the North Sea, Strait of Dover, the English Channel
2. 244,019
3. Pennines, Cumbrian
4. Ben Nevis, Grampian
5. Clyde, Forth, Tay
6. Snowdon, Cambrian
7. Clyde, Forth
8. temperate
9. coal, petroleum
10. North Sea

Ⅲ. **Match the names of the rivers in Column A with the names of their ports in column B. Put the letter before the name of a city in the corresponding blank.**

1. c 2. d 3. a 4. b 5. f 6. e

Ⅳ. **Translate the following into Chinese.**

1. 大不列颠及北爱尔兰联合王国 2. 多佛尔海峡
3. 英吉利海峡 4. 格林尼治
5. 海峡群岛 6. 澳柯尼群岛
7. 设特兰群岛 8. 不列颠群岛
9. 奔宁山脉 10. 康布里安山脉
11. 坎布里安山脉 12. 格兰扁山脉
13. 泰晤士河 14. 塞文河

15. 讷湖
16. 湖区
17. 马恩岛
18. 爱丁堡
19. 格拉斯哥
20. 加的夫

Ⅴ. Explain the following in English.

1. Lake District is a region in Northwest of England, which is very famous for its many beautiful lakes and the Lake Poets who were once born and lived there.
2. Edinburgh was once the capital city of Scotland. It is located in the eastern part of the Central Lowlands of Scotland, a very beautiful city, built partly on the plain and partly on rolling hills.
3. Cardiff is the capital city of Wales, located in the southern part of Wales. Coal is mined in the area between this city and Swansea.
4. Glasgow is the largest city in Scotland, located on the bank of River Clyde. It leads the nation in ship-building, serving as the industrial and commercial centre of Scotland. It is the third largest city throughout Britain.
5. Lough Neagh or Lake Neigh is the largest lake in Britain, which is located in the centre of Northern Island. It covers an area of about 396 square kilometers.

Lesson 2 Geography: The People

Ⅰ. Choose the correct answer and circle the letter before it.

1. B 2. C 3. C 4. D 5. B
6. A 7. A 8. D 9. A 10. B

Ⅱ. Fill in the following blanks with appropriate words or expressions.

1. 58.4, 239
2. Anglo-Saxons, Celts
3. English, Gaelic, Welsh
4. established
5. Free, Baptists, the United Reformed Church, Methodists, Quakers
6. Reformation
7. Jews, Moslems, Buddhists
8. Christian

9. Sabbath
10. metric, monetary

Ⅲ. Explain the following in English.

1. Old English (449—1150) is the language of Anglo-Saxons who invaded the British Isles in the Middle of the 5th century. It is one of the three stages that the English language has experienced in its evolution. Old English is quite different from Modern English in phonology, orthography, morphology and syntax.
2. Middle English (1150—1500) took shape in 1150 after the Norman Conquest of 1066 when English became a language of a subjugated people and underwent tremendous changes through contact with the Danes and Norman French, such as the loss of inflections and borrowing and assimilating thousands of French words. English entered the second stage, a transitional period, in its evolution from Old English to Modern English. It was in the late of this period that the Great Vowel Shift took place and English triumphed in England and displaced both French and Latin as the written literary language of the people.
3. Modern English (1500—present) is the third stage that English has experienced in its evolution. It developed out of Middle English as London dialect was disseminated throughout England and established as the literary standard for the country. Now it has become the language widely used for international communication.
4. The Church of England is the established church of the English nation, with the king or queen as the head of the Church and being crowned by the Archbishop of Canterbury in Westminster Abbey.
5. Free Churches are Protestant churches outside the Church of England, including Baptists, the United Reformed Church, Quakers and Methodists. They suffered religious and political persecution in the 17th century, and were excluded from many offices and places, until the early 19th century. They were once called "dissenters" and "non-conformists," now they are called members of Free Churches.
6. Christmas Day is Christians' annual festival, kept on December 25th in memory of the birth of Jesus Christ. People exchange gifts with friends and relatives. Children believe that Santa Claus comes to leave them

presents.

7. Easter is a Christian festival, kept on the first Sunday after the first full moon after the vernal equinox, commemorating Christ's resurrection. Parents usually color hard-boiled eggs before Easter. Late Saturday night or early Sunday morning the eggs are hidden, and the children have an Easter egg hunt Sunday. Little children believe the Easter rabbit comes and leaves the eggs for them.
8. Westminster Abbey is an ancient church where kings and queens are crowned and where, particularly in Poets' Corner, many famous men and women are buried.
9. The English Reformation began as a political movement as much as a religious one: when the Pope would not let Henry Ⅷ divorce his first wife, Catherine of Aragon. Henry declared himself head of the English Church (1534) and dissolved the monasteries. Protestantism, of a Calvinist type was introduced under Edward Ⅵ, Mary Ⅰ brought a Catholic reaction, but with Elizabeth Ⅰ the Church of England was established on a moderate Protestant basis.
10. Protestants were Christians who seceded from the Roman Catholic during the religious Reformation in the early 16th century. From then on, they form a Christian denomination and distinguish themselves from the Roman Catholics. In Britain, such religious sects as Baptists, Methodists, the United Reformed Churches and Quakers, all are Protestants.
11. The City of London is a borough of Greater London, located at its center and covering an area of 1.6 square kilometers. The City of London is managed by the Lord Mayer and serves as the financial center of Great Britain, where there is a concentration of banks, including the Bank of England, insurance companies and stock exchanges.
12. Outer London refers to the 20 boroughs surrounding Inner London.
13. Poets' Corner is a corner of Westminster Abbey where many famous men and women are buried.
14. Birmingham is the second largest city in Britain, with a population of over one million. It is a metropolitan district of West Midlands and one of the nation's leading industrial centers.

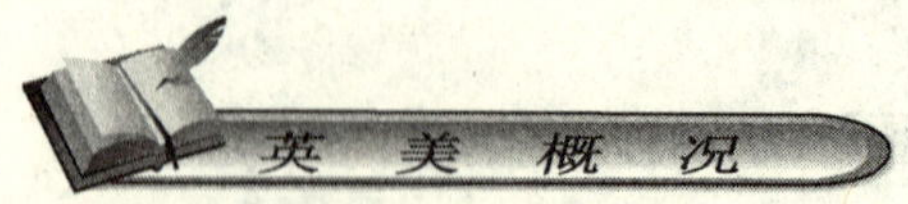

15. Glasgow is the largest city in Scotland. It is a shipping, industrial and commercial center of Scotland. It leads the whole country in shipbuilding.

Ⅳ. **Match the names of the cities in Column A with the descriptions in Column B. Put each of the letters before the descriptions in the corresponding blank in Column A.**

1. f　2. c　3. a　4. b　5. g
6. d　7. e　8. i　9. j　10. h

Lesson 3 British Economy

Ⅰ. **Choose the correct answer and circle the letter before it.**

1. B　2. A　3. C　4. C　5. C
6. D　7. C　8. A　9. B　10. D
11. C　12. C　13. D　14. B　15. D

Ⅱ. **Fill in the following blanks with proper words or expressions.**

1. the United States, Canada
2. 1947
3. international obligations
4. invest
5. absolute
6. reduced, lifted, loosened, restricted
7. privatization
8. taxation
9. inward
10. 55
11. North, English, Ireland, Iceland
12. position
13. drug
14. BMW
15. decline, growth
16. Commonwealth, colonies, Common, Canada
17. invisible
18. monetary, effective, clearing

Ⅲ. Explain the following in English.

1. The Group of Seven large industrial economies include the United States, Britain, Germany, France, Japan, Italy and Canada.
2. NATO is the abbreviation of the North Atlantic Treaty Organization, a military block in Europe.
3. The word "stagflation" is a blending, formed by combining elements of the words stagnation and inflation, meaning "stagnation and inflation at the same time. "This is an economic phenomenon that first appeared in the 1970s of Britain.
4. Margaret Thatcher is the Prime Minister of Great Britain in the period between 1979—1990, the leader of the Conservative Party and the first woman Prime Minister of Britain.
5. "EU" is the abbreviation of the European Union, formally (1993) European Community. It was instituted by the Maastricht Treaty (Nov. 1993). The EU is a legal, political and economic entity. It is supported by three pillars: the European Community, common foreign and security policy, internal affairs and justice.
6. Primary industries refer to those providing primary products, such as agriculture and fishing.
7. Secondary industries are those manufacture complex goods from those primary products.
8. Tertiary industries are often referred to as services, such as banking, insurance, tourism, and the selling of goods.
9. Common Market is another name for the European Economic Community. After 1993, it came to be called EU. The single European currency was adopted from 1 January 1999, by most of its member countries.
10. "The City" in this lesson refers to the City of London, the center of Greater London, which is the financial center of the whole country, where all business is concentrated. The London Stock Exchange, one of the busiest share-dealing centers in the world and Bank of England, the central bank of Britain, are both located in the City of London.
11. Bank of England is Britain's central bank, which was established in 1694 and nationalized in 1946. It has a wide range of financial and eco-

nomic responsibilities both as an agent of government policy and in its own right. It acts as banker to the government and to the deposit banks. It advises government on the formulation of monetary policy and plays an important part in making agreed policy effective. It is the note-issuing bank and the registrar for government stocks and banker to many overseas central banks.

12. "Big Four" is used to refer to the four big banks in Britain: Lloyds, Barclays, Midland and the National Westminster Bank group. The Big Four exert great influence on the formulation of the financial and monetary policies in Britain.

Lesson 4 Political System: Parliament and Government

Ⅰ. Choose the correct answer and circle the letter before it.

1. B 2. B 3. C 4. C 5. B
6. D 7. C 8. B 9. A 10. D

Ⅱ. Fill in the following blanks with appropriate words or expressions.

1. monarchy
2. Elisabeth II, Charles
3. customs, conventions, ordinary
4. ministers
5. legislative
6. monarch/sovereign, Commons, Lords
7. Lord Chancellor, Mr. Speaker
8. debate, laws, government, financing
9. Prime Minister, ministers, Parliament
10. senior, chairmanship, policies
11. Cabinet, Parliament
12. orders, proclamations
13. council
14. Chairman, Mayor, Lord Mayor

Ⅲ. Translate the following into Chinese.

1. 上院 2. 下院 3. 大法官 4. 农业、渔业和粮食部
5. 外交和联邦事务部 6. 内政部 7. 财政大臣

8. 枢密院长 9. 掌玺大臣 10. 不管大臣

Ⅳ. **Explain the following in English.**

1. St Stephen's Chapel: a chamber in which members of Parliament meet; on one side of the chamber sit the Opposition and the other the Government.
2. Mr. Speaker is the Chairman of the House of Commons, who is elected by a vote of the House at the beginning of each new Parliament to preside over the House and enforce the rule of order. Mr. Speaker must be impartial in carrying out his duties. He or she cannot debate or, as general rule, vote on a measure, and he or she sees that all points of view have a fair hearing.
3. Question Time lasts just under one hour on four days in the week, during which questions involving issues of national importance or concerned with purely local or individual matters may be put to the responsible minister by any member of parliament, provided due notice has been given.
4. Supply Day is a day traditionally set aside for authorizing proposed public expenditure in the House of Commons.
5. The Cabinet in Britain comprises the most senior government ministers designated by the Prime Minister. The Cabinet meets regularly under the chairmanship of the Prime Minister to decide government policy on major issues. It has the real power to take the effective decisions about what is to be done in Britain.
6. The Privy Council includes all ministers and ex-ministers, the holders of certain offices outside the political executive and some other people to whom membership has been given as an honor. It has the formal power to make certain executive orders and proclamations, actually decisions are made elsewhere.

Lesson 5 Political System: Party Politics and Judiciary

Ⅰ. **Choose the correct answer and circle the letter before it.**

1. C 2. C 3. C 4. C 5. B
6. A 7. A 8. C 9. B 10. C

11. D 12. C 13. B 14. B 15. D

Ⅱ. Fill in the following blanks with appropriate words or expression.

1. bourgeois, monopolists, democracy
2. Tory, Whig
3. Trade, Independent, Fabian
4. 651, one
5. majority
6. majority
7. Chancellor, Home, Scotland, Northern Ireland
8. customs, common
9. statutes, previous
10. High Court of Justice, Appeal, Lords, Privy
11. Chancery, Family, Queen's Bench
12. magistrate
13. House of Lords
14. Criminal, Court, Inner, Outer
15. fine, imprisonment, 1969
16. local, councils

Ⅲ. Translate the following into Chinese.

1. 费边社 2. 高等法院 3. 负责选举的官员
4. 巡回法院 5. 妖怪疯话疯子党 6. 大法官/上院议长
7. 内政大臣 8. 苏格兰国务大臣 9. 地方治安法院
10. 巡回法庭 11. 大法官庭 12. 家事庭
13. 王座庭 14. 高等法院院长 15. 民事庭
16. 治安推事 17. 刑事侦缉厅

Ⅳ. Explain the following in English.

1. The Conservative Party is one of the two principal parties in Britain. It developed out of the Tory Party. The Conservative Party is in favor of privatization and openly helps the monopolists to make profits.
2. The Labour Party is one of the two principal political parties in Britain. It was formed in 1900 by a union between the trade union, the Independent Labour Party and the Fabian Society. It took the place of the Liberal Party after the First World War and came into office immediately after the Second World War and since then it has taken turns in

office with the Conservative Party. The Labour Party practices bourgeois democracy or social reformation and nationalization of public enterprises.

3. The Liberal Democrats constitute the third largest political party in Britain. It may be seen as a party of the "middle," occupying the ground between the two main parties ideologically. The Liberal Democrats emphasize the need for change in Britain's constitutional arrangements to make government more democratic and accountable.
4. The Returning Officer is a person appointed in each constituency to compile a register of voters and make some preparation for the general election.
5. The Chancery Division is one of the three divisions of the High Court of Justice. It consists of the Lord Chancellor and ten judges, dealing with questions of company law, bankruptcy, trusts and administration of the estates of people who have died.
6. The Family Division, one of the three divisions of the High Court of Justice, deals with divorce and questions arising out of wills.
7. The Queen's Bench Division consists of the Lord Chief Justice and 39 other judges, dealing with questions arising in trade and maritime affairs, etc.
8. Borstal institutions are special establishments for young offenders (between 16 and 21 years old), where courses of training are provided.
9. Metropolitan Police refers to the police forces in Greater London, whose zone of operation covers Greater London. The Metropolitan Police, under the direct responsibility of the Home Secretary, provides certain national police services such as maintaining a national registry of all criminals and crimes, to which local police forces may refer.
10. Scotland Yard is the popular name of the Criminal Investigation Department, which gets the name from New Scotland Yard, where its offices are situated.

Lesson 6 History: Early man and the Feudal Society

Ⅰ. Choose the correct answer and circle the letter before it.

1. C 2. B 3. B 4. B 5. D

6. A　7. C　8. D　9. A　10. C
11. B　12. A　13. C　14. C　15. B　16. B

Ⅱ. Fill in the following blanks with appropriate words or expressions.

1. Iberians, Celts　2. 54
3. Claudius　4. Teutonic, Denmark
5. natural forces, St. Augustine, 7th
6. Danes, Alfred　7. Danish
8. nobles, slaves　9. Norman
10. laws, courts　11. king
12. All Estates　13. 1295, the Model
14. Edward Ⅱ

Ⅲ. Explain the following terms in English.

1. Anglo-Saxon Heptarchy is the collective name for the seven small kingdoms established by the Angles, Saxons and Jutes after they settled in the British Isles in the middle of the fifth century. They were Northumbria, Mercia, East Anglia, Essex, Sussex, Wessex and Kent. The small kingdoms existed until the late of the 8th century when the Danes began to invade Britain. There were no union among them, and wars were frequent.
2. The Danelaw is a term used in the English history to refer to the northern and eastern part of England subjected to the Danish law. It was the treaty signed between Alfred, the Great and the Danes in 878 that defined the boundary of the Danelaw.
3. Norman Conquest is an important historical event that took place in 1066. In that year, after Henry died childless, Harold and William, Duke of Normandy, both claimed the throne. On September 28, William crossed the Channel with a formidable army, killed Harold and defeated the English army at the battle of Hastings on October 14 and finally conquered England. This event was referred to as Norman Conquest.
4. Doomsday Book was really a record of each man's property made by William the First's officials in 1086. With this record at his elbow, he could know how much each man should and could pay. People viewed it with so much superstitious fear that they called it "Doomsday

Book."

5. Great Charter was long document that King John was forced to sing in 1215 because he levied more taxes and army service than customs allowed to revenge himself upon France and seize back Normandy. It contained three sets of provisions: 1) that the king was not to exact extra payments from the feudal vassals or towns without their consent; 2) that laws were not to be modified by the arbitrary action of the king; 3) that should the king attempt to free himself from law, the vassals had the right to force him to obey law, by civil war or otherwise. It was made in the interest of the feudal lards. However, it granted to the towns-people freedom of trade and self-government in England.
6. All Estates Parliament was the first parliament summoned by Simon De Monfort in 1265. In addition to the older group, there were two knights from each shire and two citizens from each town. It was known as the "All Estates Parliament."
7. Model Parliament was the All Estates Parliament summoned by Edward Ⅰ to collect money to suppress the Scots in 1295, with more than 400 members attending it. As that Parliament was followed as a model, it has become known as the Model Parliament.
8. The House of Plantagenet was established as a result of the war between Matilda and Stephen from 1135 to 1154, in which Stephen was defeated and Henry Ⅱ, son of Matilda, was crowned king of England. The House of Plantagenet was replaced by the House of Lancaster in 1399.

Ⅳ. Rearrange the following historical events in the order in which they took place.

1. d　　2. b　　3. e　　4. a　　5. c

Ⅴ. Translate the following into Chinese.

1. 伊比利亚人　　2. 凯尔特人　　3. 盖尔人
4. 罗马征服　　5. 盎格鲁—撒克逊七国
6. 爱德华(信教者)　7. 哈斯丁斯战役　　8. 末日审判书
9. 大宪章　　10. 各级议会　　11. 模范议会

Lesson 7 History: Decline of Feudalism and the Bourgeois Revolution

Ⅰ. Choose the correct answer and circle the letter before it.

1. C　2. C　3. B　4. D　5. D
6. B　7. D　8. D　9. D　10. C
11. A　12. A　13. D　14. B　15. C
16. A　17. B　18. C　19. D　20. D

Ⅱ. Fill in the following blanks with appropriate words or expressions.

1. France, French, Flanders
2. laws, chambers
3. shortage, wages, freedom, Statutes
4. Essex, serfdom
5. Lancastrians, Yorkists, weakened
6. decline, rise
7. landless men
8. economic, Puritans
9. Grand Remonstrance
10. Cavaliers, Roundheads
11. 1648
12. Cromwell
13. 1660
14. coup d'état, 88
15. French, American

Ⅲ. Rearrange the following historical events in the order in which they took place.

1. b　2. d　3. c　4. a　5. i
6. f　7. j　8. h　9. g　10. e

Ⅳ. Explain the following in English.

1. The Enclosure refers to a movement that started in England in the 14th and 15th centuries and continued till the 18th century, in which the feudal aristocracy enclosed large pieces of land with fences and turned arable land into pastures for raising sheep, which was much profitable. As a result of the Enclosure, thousands of peasants lost their land and became landless men. In order to make a living, they had to poured into cities and became the "reserved army of wage earners," who constituted a major source of free labor for the later Industrial Revolution.

2. Puritans were Christians who wanted to make reforms in the Anglican Church, or to "purify" the Church of England. They were opposed to Charles I and his idea that the king should not only be the head of state but also the head of the Church. They interpreted the Bible in a new way by advocating that the common men and the king were equal in the presence of God, and that the Bible encouraged free trade and the development of individualism. They represented the interests of the new bourgeoisie.
3. The Grand Remonstrance is a document drawn up by a group of Commoners in 1641, whereby they bitterly accused Charles I of his tyrannical rule and demanded that they should be given the rights of free trade and free commerce.
4. The Hundred Years' War was a war launched by Edward III in his effort to claim the French throne and fought against France contending for the important industrial city Flanders. The War was a feudal war and a trade war in nature. It started in 1337 and lasted intermittently for more than one hundred years until 1453, hence the name Hundred Years' War. In the first phase of the War, the English won a series of victories, but by the War was concluded, the English has lost all the territories they had gained during the war, except the French port Calais. The Hundred Years' War accelerated the breakdown of feudal society as the heavy cost of the long war inevitably increased the burden on the feudal lords and merchants. The vast expenditure of treasure for war consequently put the money class, the new bourgeoisie, in a more important position in Britain.
5. Short Parliament was summoned by Charles I in 1640 to get money to subdue the Scots who rose in rebellion after he managed to rule the country without Parliament for 11 years. However, Parliament refused to help the King until their grievances would have been considered. Charles I dissolved the Parliament in three weeks after it had been called, hence its nickname "Short Parliament."
6. Long Parliament was summoned by Charles I in November 1640 when the Scots invaded England and Charles was forced to collect money. This Parliament declared that all the methods by which Charles I had

raised money without parliamentary consent were illegal. It abolished the Star Chamber, demanded the punishment of Charles the First's favorite officials, William Laud and Thomas Wentworth, the Earl of Strafford and proceeded to struggle against absolutism. By the time when the Long Parliament was summoned, the Civil War actually began. This Parliament lasted until 1653, hence the name "Long Parliament."

7. Black Death was a deadly bubonic plague that struck Europe in the middle of the 14th century and reached England in the summer of 1348. About 40% of the population died of the Black Death. As a result, there was a severe shortage of labor. The agricultural labors in villages and under-masters and journeymen in cities struck for higher wages while the villeins struggled for freedom. However, the government of Edward Ⅲ issued an order that required all grown-up men and women below sixty, having no land or other means of living to work for landlords and proprietors at the rate before the plague in 1349. The Parliamentary statutes of 1351 and 1361 (the Statutes of Laborers) introduced cruel punishments for those who refused to work. The Statutes of laborers aroused a general hatred among the masses against the ministers, lawyers and landlords.
8. Cavaliers and Roundheads were two opposing groups in the First Civil War of the 17th British Bourgeois Revolution. Cavaliers were the Royalists, the supporters of the King Charles Ⅰ, who took Oxford as their base. The "Roundheads" were the supporters of Parliament, who took London as their base. Because the common people of London kept their hair very short, hence the name "Roundheads."
9. After Cromwell died in 1658, seeing that the peasants and the Levelers were organizing new uprisings and threatening their security, the bourgeoisie and the new aristocrats compromised with the rightists (Presbyterians) and invited Charles Ⅱ to come back from Holland to the throne on May 29th, 1660. This incident was referred to as the Restoration of the Stuart.
10. After the Restoration of the Stuart, the King adopted some measures to protect the interests of the bourgeoisie, but took revenge on the

revolutionaries. Under the reign of James Ⅱ, the expansion of the king's power soon clashed with the interests of the bourgeoisie and in 1688, the two bourgeois political parties, the Tories and the Whigs, united together and staged a bloodless coup d'état and put William of Orange on the throne. They formed an alliance with the landowners. This was spoken of by Englishmen as the "Glorious Revolution."

Lesson 8 History: The Industrial Revolution and the Chartist Movement

Ⅰ. Choose the best answer and circle the letter before it.

1. B 2. A 3. D 4. B 5. D
6. B 7. B 8. C 9. A 10. C

Ⅱ. Fill in the following blanks with appropriate words or expressions.

1. method, relations, textile, 1840s
2. Capitalist, labor, national
3. Holland, France
4. Seven Years'
5. Industrial increased, cities
6. miseries, disasters
7. Charles Dickens
8. London Workingmen's Association
9. 39,42
10. leadership, unity

Ⅲ. Explain the following in English.

1. The Navigation Act of 1651 was the first Navigation Act passed by the British Parliament, which provided that no goods should be imported from abroad except in English ships or those of the country that produced the goods. This act led to the outbreak of the war between England and Holland.
2. The seven Years' War was a decisive fight between England and France in the period from 1756—1763 for the world power. They fought in Europe, at sea, in India and in North America. The war lasted for seven years, hence the name. As the result of the War, France was com-

pletely defeated and the French colonies in Canada were ceded to Britain and Britain also destroyed the French power in India and became the world's leading colonial power after the war.

3. On August 16th, 1819, 80,000 people were gathered at St. Peter's Fields, Manchester, demanding Parliamentary Reforms and the appeal of the Corn Laws. No sooner had the speaker taken the platform than the soldiers sent by the government fired at the masses. Eleven were killed and about 400, including 100 women, were wounded. This incident was called the "Peterloo Massacre" in the English history.
4. In 1837, workers in London, who were organized in the London Workingmen's Association, drew up a petition to Parliament, in which were embodied the Six Points that afterwards became known as the People's Charter. The Six Points were equal electoral districts, abolition of the property qualifications for MPs, universal manhood suffrage, annual Parliament, vote by ballot, and the payment of MPs.
5. The doctrine of *laissez faire* advocated that government should merely be an omnipresent policeman protecting property and compelling the performance of contracts. The doctrine appealed strongly to the new capitalists of the Industrial Revolution.

Ⅳ. Match the inventions in Column B with the inventors in Column A.

1. c 2. a 3. d 4. b

Lesson 9 History: The British Empire and Britain in Two World Wars and Post-War Periods

Ⅰ. Choose the correct answer and circle the letter before it.

1. B 2. A 3. B 4. A 5. C
6. B 7. D 8. D 9. C 10. C
11. C 12. D 13. C 14. B 15. C 16. C

Ⅱ. Fill in the following blanks with appropriate words or expressions.

1. Newfoundland, end
2. enlist army, enforce law, declare war and make peace
3. gangplank
4. First

5. expansion, capital, monopoly
6. Triple Alliance, Triple Entente
7. three, 70, supremacy, debt
8. 20, 21, 29, 33
9. General Strike
10. hostility, non-intervention, appeasement
11. Second
12. devaluation, inflation, debts
13. 50, 72

Ⅲ. Re-arrange the historical events in the order they took place by putting the symbolic letter in the corresponding blank.

1. d 2. c 3. a 4. e 5. b

Ⅳ. Explain the following in English.

1. The Indian Mutiny was an event that took place in 1857 in Indian under the colonial rule of Britain. The rebels killed British officers, burned down garrisons and set free political prisoners. This incident is known as the Indian Mutiny.
2. The Treaty of Nanking was an unequal treaty that the British forced the Qing government to conclude in 1842 after the First Opium War in 1840, according to which and the treaties signed later Hong Kong was ceded to Britain as colony and five ports were opened as trade ports, and the colonists were granted special privileges for travel and missionary activities in China.
3. The Munich Agreement was made at the Munich Conference in 1938. It was in essence a non-aggression pact between Britain and France on the one hand and Nazi Germany on the other, which allowed Hitler to take over the Sudetenland section of Czechoslovakia.
4. The British Commonwealth of Nations is a free association of sovereign nations. It consists of over thirty independent member countries, all of them former dependencies of the British Empire. It is, in fact, a phony organization as its members are not united by ideology, legal bonds or military commitments.

Lesson 10　Education in Britain

Ⅰ. Choose the correct answer and circle the letter before it.

1. C　2. D　3. B　4. B　5. B
6. C　7. B　8. D　9. B　10. A　11. A
12. A　13. C　14. A　15. A　16. B　17. A

Ⅱ. Fill in the following blanks with appropriate words or expressions.

1. private　2. paying fees
3. three　4. selective, eleven-plus
5. educational attainment　6. open, all
7. summer, three　8. 2, 8
9. separately established　10. compulsory
11. secondary, eleven-plus　12. Latin
13. streams　14. nursery, infant, junior
15. entrance, higher　16. 1945, Labor
17. private　18. house
19. examination, public, public　20. England
21. Redbrick/Middle Aged　22. university, universities
23. Second, 1949　24. Honors
25. spare, radio, tutors

Ⅲ. Match each of the school examinations with the age at which it is usually taken.

1. b　2. d　3. a　4. c

Ⅳ. Match each academic term with one of the dates.

1. b　2. c　3. a

Ⅴ. Translate the following into Chinese.

1. 英国儿童11岁参加的小学毕业和升中学的考试
2. 独立学校　3. 国立学校
4. 普通毕业证书　5. 中等教育证书
6. 开放大学　7. 地方教育局
8. 文法中学　9. 现代中学
10. 综合中学　11. 舍长制
12. 级长制　13. 公学入学统考
14. 学院制　15. 导师制

16. 大学优秀毕业文凭　　17. 理工学院
18. 公学

Ⅵ. **Explain the following in English.**

1. The selective system of education is a type of educational system, in which the enrollment of students into schools or universities is determined by the results of examinations. For example, in the past, in Britain children who wanted to go to secondary schools had to take the eleven-plus examination, the result of which will determine what secondary schools they will go to, either the grammar school, secondary modern school, or the comprehensive school.
2. General Certificate of Education is a type of certificate that the British pupils have to obtain after they take the examination at the end of the secondary education to indicate their academic attainment. The examination is within the reach of the children learning at a secondary modern school at the age of fifteen.
3. The Burnham Scale is the standard salary scale for teachers in British schools. It was first established in 1924 by a committee chaired by Lord Burnham. Schools outside the state system make their own arrangements for paying their teachers, but often follow the Burnham Scale.
4. Local Education Authorities are the local government bodies that are responsible for the state schools in a district and that engage teachers, maintain school buildings, and supply schools equipment and materials.
5. Public schools are best-known private schools in Britain. The oldest ones were founded to give free education to clever boys whose parents could not afford to educate them privately. They were under "public" management or control. Today, however, these schools are the most expensive of the independent schools in Britain. They are mostly boarding schools, where pupils live as well as study.
6. Preparatory schools are private schools in Britain. Preparatory schools provide education for children between 8 and 13. Such schools prepare pupils for the entrance of public schools and the public school life. Preparatory schools are private in the fullest sense; they are operated as

private enterprises as if they were shops or factories. Such a school is often the personal property of its headmaster, who is not controlled by a governing body, but works as an independent businessman.

7. Oxbridge is a term used to refer to the two most famous higher education institutions in Britain: Oxford University and Cambridge University.

8. Open University was founded in 1969, the most interesting innovation in the British education. It began its first course in 1971. It is so named because it is "open" to all to become students with no formal qualifications to study for a degree. Courses are followed in the students' spare time; lectures are broadcast on radio and TV and students correspond with their tutors by post. For some of the Open University courses students have to attend one-week summer schools, which are held in many of Britain's traditional universities. At the end of the course, successful students are awarded a university degree.

Part Two
An Introduction to the United States

Lesson 11 Geography: The Land

Major Points

The USA is located in the southern part of N. America and has a total area of 9,327,200 square kilometers.

The USA is divided into three major geographic regions: the highlands in the east, the mountains in the west, and a vast plain in between.

The two youngest of the 50 states of America are Alaska and Hawaii, which are far away from the continental United States.

The longest river in the USA is the Mississippi, which has the Missouri river and the Ohio River as its two main tributaries.

The other important rivers are: the Hudson River, the Columbia River, the Colorado River, the St. Lawrence River and Rio Grande.

The five Great Lakes are: Lake Superior, Lake Michigan, Lake Erie, Lake Huron and Lake Ontario.

The climate in the USA varies from extremely cold in Alaska to semitropical in southern Florida and Hawaii, and the climate is temperate in most of the places of continental United States.

The USA is rich in natural resources, such as fresh water, forests, minerals and metals.

Washington, D.C. is the seat of the federal government of the USA.

New York City is the largest city and port in the USA, and the seat of the United Nations.

Chicago is the third largest city in the USA. The working class there has a glorious revolutionary tradition.

Los Angeles, the largest city on the Pacific coast, ranks the second among the largest cities in the USA.

Philadelphia, one of the largest cities in the USA, was once the seat of the Continental Congress and the birthplace of the American Declaration of Independence and the United States Constitution.

Detroit is known as "the Motor City, USA," and Houston "Space City, USA."

San Francisco, the second largest city on the Pacific coast, is an ideal summer resort, where there is the largest Chinese settlement in the USA.

Boston, one of the oldest cities in the USA, is one of the great seaports of the country. During the American Revolution, several noteworthy events took place in Boston.

Pittsburgh is one of America's top steel making and mining areas. Its iron and steel output is only next to that of Chicago.

Main Contents

1. Location, Size and Administrative Areas

The United States of America is situated in the southern part of North America (except **Alaska** and **Hawaii**). The continental United States stretches 4,500 kilometers from the Atlantic Ocean on the east to the Pacific Ocean on the west. It is bounded by Canada on the north and by Mexico and the **Gulf of Mexico** on the south, with a distance of 2,575 kilometers in between.

The United States is the fourth largest country in the world in terms of area. Its total area is 9,631,420 square kilometers.

The whole country is divided into 50 states and a federal district, the **District of Columbia**, in which the capital city of Washington is located on **the Potomac River**. Alaska is the largest in area of all the 50 states, and **Texas** is

the second. Texas alone is larger than France, and Alaska is twice as big as Texas.

2. Geographic Features

Geographically the country may be separated into three major divisions: the highlands in the east, the mountains in the west, and a vast plain region in between.

The eastern part consists of highlands formed by the **Appalachian Range.** These highlands are comparatively low, having an average elevation of 800 meters above the sea level. The highest peak contained by the Appalachian Mountains is **Mount Mitchell** (6,684 feet). East of the Appalachian Highlands is the narrow Atlantic Coast plain, which merges with the wide Gulf plains in the south.

The western part of the country is composed of high plateaus and mountainous country formed by the great **Cordillera Range**, which consists of **the Coast Range**, **the Sierra Nevada**, **the Cascades** and **the Rocky Mountains.** In general, they are high, rugged and volcanic.

The Rocky Mountains rise over 3,000 meters above the sea level and form the continental divide of the United States. West of the Rockies are the two great plateaus: **the Columbia Plateau** in the north and **the Colorado Plateau** in the south, with **the Great Basin** in between. The best known of the Colorado Plateau is **the Grand Canyon** of the Colorado River, with a maximum depth of 1,800 meters. Few of the rivers in the Great Basin find outlets to the sea, and most of them are shallow and salty. The most famous salt lake is **Great Salt Lake in Utah.**

The Pacific Mountain System consists of three regions: the Cascade Range, the Sierra-Nevada, and the Pacific Coast Range. **Crater Lake**, the deepest of its kind in the US, lies in the region of the Cascades. The Sierras contain **Mount Whitney** (14,495 feet), the highest peak in the US outside Alaska. **Death Valley** in eastern California, 85 meters below sea level, is the lowest point in the whole of North America. The Pacific Coastal Region consists of a chain of low parallel mountains and a series of great valleys. In some places of the region there are plains bordering the Pacific.

The central part of the United States is composed of vast plains between the Appalachian Mountains and the Rocky Mountains. This is a region of

plains drained by **the Mississippi River** and its tributaries and is usually divided into two regions: **the Central Lowland** in the east and **the Great Plains** in the west. The central lowland stretches from the five Great Lakes to central Texas. Much of the land surface of the Great Plains consists of vast treeless plains. The eastern half of the Great Plains consists of the most important agricultural areas in the US, while the western half, getting less and less rainfall as it extends westward to the Rocky Mountains, consists largely of the great prairies.

Alaska, which was bought by the USA from Russia in 1867, occupies the extreme northwestern part of North America, and is only 82 kilometers from Russia. It consists of the Mainland and **the Aleutian Islands**, which form one of the longest volcanic island chains in the world.

Hawaii is situated in the central Pacific Ocean, approximately 3,200 kilometers away from the mainland of the US. It consists of a long chain of islands, including 8 main islands and over a hundred atolls and uninhabited islets. The Hawaiian Islands are volcanic, but only the Island of Hawaii has active volcanoes. **Mauna Loa** is the world's largest active volcano.

3. Rivers and Lakes

The Mississippi River and **the Missouri River** and their branches form a 19,000-kilometer system of waterways that are connected to the Great Lakes in the north by a canal. The Mississippi is one of the world's great rivers; it was the "father of waters" to American Indians. Water from the source of its main branch, the Missouri River, flows about 6,400 kilometers from the northern Rocky Mountains, to the mouth of the Mississippi in the Gulf of Mexico.

Other important rivers are **the Yukon** in Alaska, about 3,000 kilometers long; **the Rio Grande**, which flows for some 3,200 kilometers and forms part of the United States-Mexico border; **the Columbia River**, which rises in western Canada and continues in the U. S. for about 1,900 kilometers west of the Rockies; and **the Colorado River**, which begins in the Rocky Mountains and flows southwest for some 2,300 kilometers. For 342 of these kilometers the Colorado flows through the magnificent Grand Canyon. In the east **the Hudson River** flows through the state of New York. Linked by canals with the five Great Lakes, the Hudson River serves as a main artery for inland waterway traffic. The Potomac River, bordering the national capital at Washington, flows southeast from **the Allegheny Mountains** to **the Chesapeake Bay**. **The Ohio River**, a branch of the Mississippi, flows west from the Appalachian Mountains and joins the Mississippi at **Cairo**, **Illinois**.

The five Great Lakes are **Lake Superior**, **Lake Michigan**, **Lake Erie**, **Lake Huron and Lake Ontario**. They form the most important system of inland waterways in the world. Except Lake Michigan, which is wholly within the United States, part of the national boundary between the United States and Canada runs through this chain of lakes. The **St. Lawrence River** flows from Lake Ontario to the Atlantic Ocean. Connected by rivers and canals, the five Great Lakes are open to navigation by large steamers and are thus linked to many inland industrial areas. The famous **Niagara Falls** are located on the US-Canadian boundary between Lake Erie and Lake Ontario. The American Falls are 1,240 meters wide and 49 meters high.

4. Climate

Affected by such factors as latitude, altitude, distance from oceans and prevailing winds, the climate varies from extremely cold in northern Alaska to semitropical in southern **Florida** and Hawaii. The coasts of **Oregon** and **Washington** are among the rainiest places in the world, while **the Mojave Desert** in **Arizona** and **California** is one of the driest. Between these extremes are many kinds of climate.

New England states have a somewhat cold climate, where winters are long and snowy, and summers are short and warm.

The Middle Atlantic States have a temperate climate, where there are four definite seasons.

The south has a warm climate, which varies with the geographical position of the individual state.

The climate of **the Midwest** is temperate. This region is a great valley between the Allegheny Mountains and the Great Plains. Alternative north and south winds sweeping over this region freely often cause sudden and extreme changes in temperature.

The climate in the Great Plains also varies greatly. The northern part of the Great Plains has a continental climate, where extreme cold and hot weather are often experienced. Affected by the Rocky Mountains, the Great Plains receive little rainfall throughout the year. Farther south the climate grows

progressively milder.

The Rocky Mountains are cooler or colder than other regions in the same latitude because of their high altitude.

Affected by prevailing westerly winds that blow inland off the Pacific, the Pacific coast has a mid and humid climate throughout the year, with remarkably equable temperatures. The climate of the northern part of the Pacific coast is similar to that of England.

5. Natural Resources

1) Water

The United States is blessed with large supplies of fresh water except in the dry desert regions of the West.

Water has played a very important part in America's growth; the early development of a prosperous agricultural system and the later development of an industrial base were made possible largely by rich water resources. Rivers and lakes have provided from the time of the first settlement excellent means of transportation. Today the rivers and streams of America furnish 63% of the fresh water used daily by cities, and by farms for irrigation, and over 90% of the fresh water used for generating electric power.

2) Forests

The United States is rich in lumber resources. About a third of the land area are covered by forests, of which more than 600 million acres are commercial forest land.

Forests are chiefly found in the eastern and western highlands of the country. The greatest wonder of all is found in the forests of sequoia and fir trees on the northwest coast, where the mountains catch the heavy Pacific rains. Some of these great trees are 3,000 years old, and are among the largest and oldest living things known. The state of Washington leads the nation in annual growth of trees of commercial value and its sawmills and factories produce large amounts of lumber, paper, and other wood products.

3) Minerals and Metals

The United States is rich in mineral resources. Its output of iron, coal, petroleum, copper, zinc and lead accounts for a large portion of the total output of the capitalist countries. The important mining areas of the country are: the northern part of the Appalachian Highlands, the Great Lakes area, and the Western mountainous regions.

The coal deposits in the US rank first in the world. The most important coal mining area is the northern part of the Appalachian Highlands. Pennsylvania is the leading state in the whole country in the production of coal, with West Virginia the second. The West and Alaska are also rich in coal deposits.

The US produces over 100 million tons of iron a year for its manufacturing industries. The most important iron ore mining areas are the Lake Superior region of the five Great Lakes, the northern part of the Appalachian Highlands near Pittsburgh, and some places in the West. About three quarters of the iron ore comes from the Lake Superior region.

The US ranks first in the world in natural gas deposits, and second in those of oil. It produces more than 370 million tons of petroleum annually. Texas leads the whole country in the production of oil, with California second. The oil produced in Alaska is brought to the mainland by a 1,289-kilometer pipeline. Natural and manufactured gas supplies more than 33% of the nation's power.

The western mountain ranges are rich in nonferrous metal deposits such as gold, silver, copper, zinc, lead and tin. Gold was discovered in California in 1848. In one of the greatest mass movements of modern history, thousands of people came to California from all over the world to seek their fortunes in the rocks. Partially because of this **"Gold Rush"** the whole continent was settled within the century and many kinds of mineral veins were discovered. The Black Hills of South Dakota was found to be rich in tin ores. Silver, lead and copper were found in **Butte, Montana**. Today the major mining activity here is in copper and to a lesser degree in lead and uranium, with most of the silver deposits now exhausted. Now most of the Rocky Mountain gold is gone. Some other minerals have also vanished much too quickly due to rapacious mining methods.

Arizona leads the whole country in the production of copper, followed closely by Utah, **New Mexico** and Montana. The country's largest open-pit copper mining center is **Bingham, Utah**, where the mining of ore costs only a few cents per ton and the enormous supply will last for many years.

6. Principal Cities

Washington, D. C., the capital of the US, is situated on the Potomac River and covers an area of over 174 square kilometers. It has a population of over 570,898 (2003) and ranks ninth in size. Washington is a beautiful city of wide streets, broad avenues, plazas and public buildings, such as **the United States Capitol**, **the White House**, and **the Pentagon Building**. The city is now the seat of the federal government as well as a leading cultural center and a center of world affairs.

New York City, the largest city and chief port of the United States lying at the mouth of the Hudson River in New York State, has a population of 18.5 million (2003) with about 8 millon in the urban area and over 10 million in the suburbs. The five boroughs (**Manhattan**, **Brooklyn**, **the Bronx**, **Queens and Richmond**) that comprise the city are separated by waterways lined by docks. It leads the whole country in business, manufacturing, communications, transportation and entertainment.

Manhattan Island, the central part of the city today, was "bought" by the Dutch from the Indians in 1626, and was conquered by the English fleet sent by the English Duke of York in 1664 and was renamed New York. The city took a leading part in the War of American Independence, and the opening of **the Erie Canal** in 1825 marked its economic expansion.

The city's development became rapid only in the 19th century. Now it has developed into an international city with the tallest buildings in the world.

New York Harbor, with 840 kilometers of waterfront, is one of the largest harbors in the world. It handles 35% the nation's international shipping. **The Statue of Liberty**, a gift from the French people in 1886, was placed on Liberty Island, directly in the center of New York Harbor.

The United Nations Headquarters stands along the East River at 42nd Street in the city. Here representatives from countries of the world meet to talk over world problems.

Los Angeles, a seaport in southwest California, is the second largest city of the US, with a population of 3.82 million. The city now has developed into the world's largest metropolitan area. With its man-made harbor at San Pedro Bay, Los Angeles serves as an important shipping, industrial, communications and aviation center. It leads the country in the manufacture of aircraft and

parts. The city has also become an important electronic center and the film center of the United States.

Chicago, the third largest city in the US, lies on the southwest shore of Lake Michigan, with a population of nearly 8. 711 million in the metropolitan area and 2. 869 million of city proper (2003). The advantageous location has made it the greatest transportation center in the country ever since the beginning of the settlement. As a chief railway center for the USA with a harbor opening to ocean traffic by the St. Lawrence Seaway, it is now a commercial, financial and industrial center of the Midwest region. Its most important industries are steel and meatpacking.

The working class in Chicago has a glorious revolutionary tradition. Both May Day and International Working Women's Day were decided to support the workers' and women's movements in Chicago in the late 19th century and early 20th century respectively.

Philadelphia, one of the largest cities of the US, has a population of over 1. 479 million. It was founded by William Penn in 1682 as a Quaker settlement and was once the largest of all American cities in the colonial days and the seat of **the Continental Congress** during the War of Independence and served as the national capital for 10 years from 1790 to 1800. It is now an international port, a commercial and industrial center on **the Delaware River**, East **Pennsylvania**.

The major historical shrines in Philadelphia are clustered in **the Independence Hall** or State House. It was in this hall that the **American Declaration of Independence** was signed on July 4, 1776 and **Constitution of the United States of America** was framed.

Phoenix, the capital city of Arizona, has developed into one of the largest cities in the southwest of the United States. Its population increased very rapidly in recent years, and has reached 1. 388 million (2003).

San Diego, with a population of over 1. 226 million (2003), has now become one of the largest port cities on the pacific coast, located south of Los Angeles.

San Antonio is a city located in the central-southern part of Texas. It has a population of 1. 214 million (2003), a little larger than that of Dallas (1. 208 million). It has become one of the largest cities in the south of the US.

Detroit has a population of 911, 402 (2003), of which 40% are black

people. The city, situated on the Detroit River between Lakes Huron and Erie, is the largest center of the automobile industry in the US and is known as "the Motor City." More than 90% of all automobiles made in America are produced in Detroit.

Houston, with a population of over 2 million, is the largest city in the state of Texas and the sixth largest city in the United States, and the center of the petrochemical industry. It not only manufactures oil field equipment but also ranks first in the country as a refinery center. With the manned Spacecraft Center, Houston has won the name "Space City, USA." It is a major port, too, linked with the Gulf of Mexico by the Houston Ship Channel.

San Francisco, has a population of over 700,000 and it is a chief port and financial center on the Pacific coast in North California. It serves as one of the principal gateways to the Orient. San Francisco was founded by the Spanish in 1776 and grew rapidly at the time of the California gold rush. The San Francisco Bay area, with its beautiful hills, parks and fine climate, is an ideal summer resort. The San Francisco Bay, which connects the Pacific through the Golden Gate, ranks among the largest natural harbors of the world. The city and its surrounding counties comprise the San Francisco-Oakland metropolitan area. The **Chinatown** in San Francisco is the largest Chinese settlement in the United States. With over 18 universities and colleges, the city is also one of the foremost cultural and educational centers in the United States.

Boston, the capital of Massachusetts, with a fine natural harbor, is one of America's great seaports and the largest leather, shoe and wool market of the country.

First settled in 1630, Boston was one of the centers of resistance to the British rule during the American Revolution; several noteworthy events took place in Boston, among which were **the Boston Tea Party**, the first shot in the War of Independence fired in Lexington, and the first real battle of the Revolution fought on **Bunker Hill** on June 17th, 1775.

The city is also a major medical center of the US, and there are also many colleges and universities in the Boston area, among which are **Harvard University**, **Massachusetts Institute of Technology** (MIT) and **Boston University**.

Pittsburgh, Pennsylvania, is one of America's top steel making and mining areas. One-fifth of the country's steel-making capacity is concentrated in this

area. There are also nuclear facilities, among which are America's first full-scale nuclear power plant and the first industrial-owned nuclear testing reactor.

Notes

1. Alaska 阿拉斯加,美国的两个海外州之一。阿拉斯加和阿留申群岛是美国政府于1867年从沙皇俄国购买的。
2. Hawaii 夏威夷,美国的两个海外州之一。地处太平洋中心,夏威夷的珍珠港是空中或海上运输的中继站。
3. Gulf of Mexico 墨西哥湾
4. District of Columbia 哥伦比亚特区,美国首都华盛顿所在地,地处马里兰州境内,是联邦政府为了建造首都而专门划出的特区。
5. the Potomac River 波多马克河,流经华盛顿市,注入大西洋。
6. Texas 得克萨斯,美国南方一州,盛产石油。
7. Appalachian Range 阿巴拉契亚山脉,北起圣劳伦斯河,向南延伸至阿拉巴马州的中部,全长两千多公里,其不同的部分尚有其他名称,如北部的格林山(Green Mountains)、怀特山(White Mountains)和中部的蓝岭山脉(the Blue Ridge)、阿勒格尼山脉(the Allegheny Mountain Range)等。
8. Mount Mitchell 米切尔山,阿巴拉契亚山脉的最高峰。
9. Cordillera Range 科迪罗拉山系,美国落基山以西各山脉的总称。
10. the Coast Range 海岸山脉
11. the Sierra Nevada 内华达山脉
12. the Cascades 喀斯喀特山脉
13. the Rocky Mountains 落基山脉,北美大陆的分水岭。
14. the Columbia Plateau 哥伦比亚高原,在落基山与喀斯喀特山之间。
15. the Colorado Plateau 科罗拉多高原,在落基山与内华达山之间。
16. the Great Basin 大盆地,地处哥伦比亚高原和科罗拉多高原之间。
17. the Grand Canyon 大峡谷
18. Great Salt Lake in Utah 大盐湖城,地处犹他州。
19. Crater Lake 火山口湖,美国最深的湖泊。
20. Mount Whitney 惠特尼山峰,美国本土的最高峰。
21. Death Valley 死谷,北美大陆的最低点。
22. the Mississippi River 密西西比河
23. the Central Lowland 中央低地,密西西比河以东,五大湖以南辽阔的

平原。

24. the Great Plains　大平原,密西西比河以西,落基山以东的平原。
25. the Aleutian Islands　阿留申群岛
26. Mauna Loa　冒纳罗亚火山,夏威夷最大的活火山。
27. the Missouri River　密苏里河，密西西比河的主要支流之一。
28. the Yukon　育空河
29. the Rio Grande　格兰德河,沿美国与墨西哥的边界向东注入墨西哥湾。
30. the Columbia River　哥伦比亚河,北起加拿大,流经哥伦比亚高原,向西注入太平洋。
31. the Colorado River　科罗拉多河,起源于落基山,流经科罗拉多高原,进入墨西哥境内,注入太平洋。
32. the Hudson River　哈得孙河,流经纽约州,向南于纽约市入海。
33. the Allegheny Mountains　阿勒格尼山脉，见注释7。
34. the Chesapeake Bay　切萨皮克湾
35. the Ohio River　俄亥俄河,密西西比河的两条主要支流之一。
36. Cairo, Illinois　伊利诺伊州的开罗
37. Lake Superior, Lake Michigan, Lake Erie, Lake Huron and Lake Ontario　苏必利尔湖、密歇根湖、伊利湖、休伦湖和安大略湖
38. St. Lawrence River　圣劳伦斯河,源于五大湖,注入大西洋。
39. Niagara Falls　尼亚加拉大瀑布,地处美国和加拿大边界,伊利湖和安大略湖之间。
40. Florida　佛罗里达州
41. Oregon　俄勒冈州
42. Washington　华盛顿州
43. the Mojave Desert　莫哈韦沙漠
44. Arizona　亚利桑那州
45. California　加利福尼亚州
46. the Midwest　中西部
47. Gold Rush　淘金热
48. Butte, Montana　蒙大拿州的比尤特
49. New Mexico　新墨西哥州
50. Bingham, Utah　犹他州的宾厄姆城
51. Washington, D. C.　华盛顿市

52. the United States Capitol　美国国会大厦
53. the White House　白宫，常用作美国政府的代称。
54. the Pentagon Building　五角大楼，常用作美国国防部的代称。
55. New York City　纽约市，美国第一大城市。
56. Manhattan, Brooklyn, the Bronx, Queens and Richmond　曼哈顿、布鲁克林、布朗克斯、昆斯和里士满区，纽约市区。
57. the Erie Canal　伊里运河
58. the Statue of Liberty　自由女神像
59. Chicago　芝加哥，美国中西部第一大城市，美国第三大城市。
60. Los Angeles　洛杉矶，美国西部太平洋海岸第一大城市，美国第二大城市。
61. Philadelphia　费拉德尔菲亚/费城，位于特拉华河岸，曾为两次大陆会议的所在地，美国宪法和独立宣言在此起草并通过。
62. the Continental Congress　大陆会议，美国独立战争时期的中央领导机构。
63. the Delaware River　特拉华河
64. Pennsylvania　宾夕法尼亚(州)
65. the Independence Hall　独立大厅，美国独立宣言和 1787 年的宪法均在此起草并通过的。
66. American Declaration of Independence　美国独立宣言
67. Constitution of the United States of America　美利坚合众国宪法
68. Detroit　底特律，美国北部城市，以汽车制造而闻名于世，号称美国“汽车城”。
69. Houston　休斯敦，美国南部城市，因为有载人宇宙飞行控制中心，有美国“宇宙城”之称。
70. San Francisco　旧金山，亦译为“三藩市”或“圣佛兰西斯科”。
71. Chinatown　唐人街/华人城(不宜译为“中国城”)
72. Boston　波士顿，美国东北部海岸的大城市和海港，是美国东海岸港口中距离欧洲最近的一个，是美国的文化中心。
73. the Boston Tea Party　波士顿倾茶事件
74. Bunker Hill　邦克山
75. Harvard University　哈佛大学，美国最有名的大学。
76. Massachusetts Institute of Technology　麻省理工学院
77. Boston University　波士顿大学

78. Pittsburgh 匹兹堡，美国东部城市，曾有美国“钢铁城”之称。

Questions for Discussion

1. Point out the location, size and the administrative areas of the United States.
2. Describe the geographic features of the three basic landform regions of the continental United States.
3. What mountain ranges constitute the Cordillera Mt System?
4. What natural wonders can be found in the Far West of the US?
5. What do you know about the two youngest states: Alaska and Hawaii?
6. Point out the names of the important rivers in the United States.
7. Put down the names of the five Great Lakes and describe their location.
8. Point out the factors that affect the US climate. Describe the climate in New England, the Middle Atlantic States, the South, the Midwest, the Great Plains, the Rocky Mountains and the Pacific Coast respectively.
9. What natural resources is the United States rich in?
10. What important public buildings can be found in Washington, D. C.?
11. What are the basic characteristics of New York City?
12. Point out Chicago, Los Angeles, Philadelphia, Detroit, Houston, San Francisco, Boston and Pittsburgh on the map and tell what you know about these cities.

Exercises

Ⅰ. Choose the best answer and circle the letter before it.

1. The continental United States is situated in the ________ part of North America.

   A. northern　　B. southern

   C. western　　D. eastern

2. The United States is the ________ largest country in the world in terms

of area.

A. third　　B. fourth

C. fifth　　D. sixth

3. ________ is the largest state of the United States in area.

A. Hawaii　　B. Texas

C. Alaska　　D. Pennsylvania

4. Which of the following is NOT the Cordillera Range?

A. the Appalachian.　　B. the Coast Range.

C. the Cascades.　　D. the Rocky Mountains.

5. The ________ Mountains form the continental divide of the United States.

A. Appalachian　　B. Rocky

C. Sierra Nevada　　D. Cordillera

6. The highest peak in the continental United States is contained in the ________ Mountain Range.

A. Rocky　　B. Sierra Nevada

C. Appalachian　　D. Cascade

7. Alaska was bought by the United States from Russia ________.

A. during the War of American Independence

B. when Abraham Lincoln was the President

C. during the American Civil War

D. after the end of the American Civil War

8. The international rivers of the United States do not include ________.

A. St. Lawrence　　B. Rio Grande

C. River Columbia　　D. River Mississippi

9. River ________ flows through New York City.

A. Missouri　　B. St. Lawrence

C. Colorado　　D. Hudson

10. Of the five Great Lakes, Lake ________ is wholly within the US.

A. Superior　　B. Michigan

C. Huron　　D. Erie

11. Niagara falls is located on the US-Canadian boundary between ________.

A. Lake Michigan and Lake Huron

B. Lake Huron and Lake Erie

C. Lake Erie and Lake Ontario

D. Lake Superior and Lake Michigan

12. Southern Florida has a ________ climate.

A. cold B. tropical

C. temperate D. semitropical

13. The coasts of ________ are among the rainiest places in the world.

A. California B. Oregon and Washington

C. Florida D. New England

14. The Midwest of the United States has a ________ climate.

A. cold B. warm

C. dry D. temperate

15. The Rockies are cooler or colder than other regions in the same latitude because of their ________.

A. high latitude B. high altitude

C. longitude D. distance from the ocean

16. The greatest wonder is found in the forests of sequoia and fir trees on the ________ coast of the United States.

A. eastern B. southern

C. northwest D. southwestern

17. The deposits of ________ in the US rank the first in the world.

A. coal B. copper

C. gold D. natural gas

18. About three quarters of the iron ore in the United States comes from ________.

A. the Lake Superior region

B. the Appalachian Highlands

C. places in the West

D. the area near Pittsburgh

19. The ________ are rich in nonferrous metal deposits in the US.

A. Western mountain ranges

B. Great plains

C. Central Lowland

D. Appalachian mountain range

20. Which of the following is NOT in Washington, D. C.?
    A. The US Capitol. B. The White House.
    C. Pentagon Building. D. The UN Headquarters.

Ⅱ. Fill in the following blanks with appropriate words or expressions.

1. The United States covers a total area of ________ square kilometers.
2. The state of ________ is the largest in area of all the 50 states.
3. The eastern part of the US consists of highlands formed by the ____________ Range, the highest peak of which is Mount ________.
4. The Cordillera Range consists of the R ________ Range, the C ________, The Sierra-________ and the C ________ Mountains.
5. The two great plateaus west of the Rockies are: the ________ Plateau and the ________ Plateau.
6. Mount ________ is the highest peak in the US outside Alaska. ________ Valley is the lowest point in North America.
7. The central part of the US is composed of vast ________.
8. Alaska includes the mainland and the ________ Islands.
9. Of the five great Lakes, Lake ________ is wholly within the United States.
10. The famous ________ Falls are located on the US-Canadian boundary between Lake Erie and Lake Ontario.
11. New England states have a ________ climate. The Middle Atlantic states have a ________ climate and the South has a ________ climate.

Ⅲ. Explain the following in English.

1. Alaska
2. the Mississippi River
3. the Hudson River
4. "Gold Rush"
5. Hawaii
6. the "Motor City"
7. the "Space City, USA"
8. the Appalachian Mountains
9. the Cordillera Range
10. Niagara Falls

Ⅳ. **Match the names of the states in Column A with their major features in Column B.**

	Column A	**Column B**
1. ____	Washington	a. the leading state in the production of coal
2. ____	Texas	b. the leading state in the production of copper
3. ____	Arizona	c. the leading state in growth of trees of commercial value
4. ____	Pennsylvania	d. the leading state in the production of oil

Ⅴ. **Match the names of the cities in Column A with their features in Column B.**

	Column A	**Column B**
1. ____	Washington, D. C.	a. the third largest city of the US
2. ____	New York	b. the film center of the US
3. ____	Chicago	c. the seat of the federal government
4. ____	Los Angeles	d. the largest city in the US
5. ____	Philadelphia	e. "Space City, USA"
6. ____	Detroit	f. the largest leather, shoe and wool market
7. ____	Houston	g. the seat of the Continental Congress
8. ____	San Francisco	h. "Motor City, USA"
9. ____	Boston	i. one of America's top steel-making areas
10. ____	Pittsburgh	j. the city that has the largest Chinatown

Lesson 12 Geography: The People

Major Points

The United States has long been known as a " **melting pot.** "

The first colonial people were WASPs, who still constitute the dominant ethnic group in America.

Black people constitute the largest ethnic-racial minority group in the United States.

Hispanics constitute the second largest ethnic minority in the United States.

Asian Americans have always been a small community.

In the United States today immigrants still have to face discriminations both racial and religious or political.

According to the 1990 census, the population of the U. S totals 249 million.

The population center of gravity has been moving westward.

Today three out of four Americans live in towns, cities or suburbs.

English is the official language in the US and one of the five "working languages" of the United Nations.

Every major religion known to the world is represented in the United States.

Class is an objective reality in the American society, and there exists a strikingly wide gap between the wealthy and the poor. The fundamental social problem facing America in the 20th century is not mass poverty, but grave inequality in the distribution of wealth.

Main Contents

1. The "Melting Pot"

The United States has long been known as a "melting pot," because it is a country of many ethnic groups from different parts of the world. Many of its people are descended from settlers who came from all over the world to make their homes in the new land, which had sparsely been populated by native Indian tribes. Most Americans are of European origin, but many came from Latin America, Asia, Africa, Australia, Mexico and Canada. Therefore, there are many different Americans, who have been dissipating their different ethnic cultures toward some "standard" by living and working together in the "melting pot" of the United States and gradually forming a new nation. According to the 1990 census, the population of the United States has reached 249 million, compared with 226.5 million in 1980. The population of the United States is estimated to have reached 301.1947 million by 2007, compared with 249.5 million in 1990, with a growth rate of 0.9% and a birth rate of 1.42%.

Originally, North America was sprinkled with more than 300 tribes of **American Indians** who totaled about 8 million in the 18th century. The whites pursued the policy of genocide of these native peoples actively in the 19th century. Consequently, the number of Indians dwindled to a little over one million in the present-day United States, and after being robbed of their land, they were driven into barren desert regions, the so-called "**Indian Reservations.**" Indians total 2.475 million, and now represent less than 0.9% of the total population of the United States.

The first colonial people were White Anglo-Saxon Protestants (**WASPs**) from England, Northern and Western Europe. Attracted by reports of great economic opportunities and religious and political freedom, immigrants from many other countries flocked to the United States in increasing numbers, reaching a peak in the years between 1880 and 1914. In the 19th century there was a great influx of immigrants of various other ethnic groups from Europe, such as Irish peasants fleeing famine at home, political refugees from

Germany, and impoverished Italian tenant farmers, and in the early 20th century large numbers of Eastern European Jews were forced by pogroms to leave their countries. Between 1820 and 1980 the United States admitted almost 50 million immigrants. 300, 000 are admitted annually. Today Americans of European origin make up about 70% of the total population, but White Anglo-Saxon Protestants (WASPs) still constitute the dominant ethnic group in America.

Black people are descended from Negro slaves imported from Africa. Slave trade began almost as early as the WASPs set foot on the land of the New World, and in the 18th century slave labor was the mode of production in the southern colonies. Abraham Lincoln's **Emancipation Proclamation** declared them free initially in 1863, but slavery was not abolished irrevocably until ratification of the 13th Amendment to the Constitution in 1865, following **the Civil War.** Today their descendants make up about 12. 3% of the population and constitute the largest ethnic-racial minority group in the United States. They once lived mainly in the agricultural South but now are scattered throughout the nation, with some 60% of them concentrated in the 12 big industrial centers, such as New York, Detroit and Chicago.

2. Population and Settlement

Because Mexico had owned vast regions of the West and Southwest until the 1840s and 1850s, **Hispanics** originally settled large areas of the US. For generations more Hispanics, not only including **Mexican-Americans** but also Cuban refuges in Florida and **Puerto Ricans** now living in the slums of New York City, have been entering the US both legally and illegally. The Census Bureau estimated in 2007 that more than 35. 3 million persons of Hispanic descent were living in the United States. Today they constitute the largest ethnic minority in the United States, accounting for over 12. 8% of the total population.

Though Asian Americans have always been a small community until very recently, a large number of Chinese were tricked and shipped to America in the 19th century by slave traders as "coolies," who contributed largely to the building of the railways across the continent. In addition, Filipinos, South Koreans, Vietnamese, Laotians, Cambodians and overseas Chinese have been migrating in a small but noticeable trickle. Now Asian Americans total over 10. 2 million, accounting for 3. 5% of the total population of the country.

In the United States today immigrants still face discrimination because of their ethnicity or race and also because a general pattern has emerged: the first generation immigrant always takes the worst jobs unless that person is a WASP. In contemporary American speech the word ethnicity denotes a social group differentiated from others by country of origin, language or religion. A typical example of ethnicity is the Irish-American community, which is white, but suffered severe discrimination in jobs and housing throughout the 19th century. The reason for this is their religion, Catholicism, and country of origin, Ireland, which the WASP's considered an inferior country. Race is obviously different from ethnicity because its basis is skin color.

In America individuals encounter not only class oppression but also discrimination based on ethnicity and race. Some elements of the dominant WASP elite object to everyone who is not a WASP. Non-WASP European ethnics (Italians, Greeks, Irish, etc.) often reject Hispanics, Asians and blacks because these groups are not white. The blacks are at the very bottom of the society. They are the members of the working class and make up the bulk of the permanently impoverished. Despite the progress made by racial minorities since the 1960s, social inequality remains a stubborn fact in America today.

The United States makes a complete census, or count, of its people every 10 years. When the first count was made in 1790 the new nation had fewer than 4 million people, almost all living along the East Coast. Today, according to the 2007 estimation, the population totals 301. 139947 million people.

Population density in the United States varies from 4 persons per square kilometer to the higher density of about 100 persons or more per square kilometer with 85 people per square miles on average. Almost the whole eastern half of the country is thickly inhabited. But since 1790, the "population center of gravity" (that point at which the country would balance if only the weight of the population were considered) has been moving westward. Good climate and fertile soil in the Pacific Coast region and the discovery of gold in California in 1848 and later in the Rocky Mountains attracted the pioneers. Now California, on the Pacific Coast, is the largest state in population, with the state of New York second. Another western state, **Colorado**, is growing almost twice as fast as the nation as a whole. Some other western states have had spectacular booms: Arizona has more than doubled its population since 1960 while **Nevada** has almost tripled its population in the same period. The principal reason for the population movement today is the growth of new industries, especially in the West and the South.

In 1820 there were only 61 towns and cities in the United States, claiming merely 7.2% of its population. By 1970 there were 6,435 towns, cities and metropolises, embracing 76.1% of the population. Today three out of four Americans live in towns, cities or suburbs; about 54 million live in rural areas.

In the early decades of the 20th century, because of the development of public transportation in cities, population inside the cities began to move outward. Especially after the Second World War, the wealthy and even the **middle class** began to live in suburbs, leaving wretched ghettos behind in the city centers. Thus the boundaries of the urban area have continued to expand into previously rural areas. The great metropolitan area, a city and its suburbs that encircle it, is now the "real city" in every region of the country, and covers about one-fifth of the nation's total area.

3. Language

As the United States is a multinational country, many languages are spoken there. But English is its national language and is spoken as the mother tongue. In general, most of the black people speak English, but the Hispanics speak Spanish. Though efforts have been made by the American Indians to revive and preserve their own languages, there are not many Indian languages any more.

There is no doubt that English is one of the world's widely used languages. It is used as a native language by over 300 million people and as a native language in a great many countries such as India, Pakistan, Nigeria, Singapore, and the Philippines. It is one of the few "working languages" of the United Nations and is more frequently used than the others. Besides, it has actually become the language of international trade and transport, and the language of international co-operation in science and technology.

Since English has developed in different countries, there is a slight difference between the two international dialects-American English and British English—in vocabulary, spelling, intonation and pronunciation, and in syntax. However, both Americans and Englishmen can understand each other promptly without many problems.

Even in the United States, several different regionalisms of English have developed in different regions such as the South, the North and the Midwest. Linguists also recognize **Black English** as a separate dialect of English.

From a linguistic point of view, an ethnic language variety such as Black English is simply a nonstandard dialect of American English. Like other varieties of English, Black English has some vocabulary of its own. It has a number of distinctive features in its phonological, morphological and syntactic systems that are rule-governed and systematic. For example, Black English is phonetically characterized by the frequent simplification of consonant clusters at the end of words when one of the two consonants is an alveolar /t/ and /d/. Syntactically, Black English is characterized by the feature of the frequent absence of various forms of the copula "be" and the use of double negation constructions, such as "I ain't afraid of no ghosts." to mean in standard English "I'm not afraid of any ghost."

4. Religion

Since the United States is a multinational country and every American has the right to choose his own church and faith to worship, there are as many as over 333,000 local church groups, with some 253 religious sects throughout the country.

Between 1950 and 1970 church membership in the United States increased almost 55%. Today about 90 of every 100 Americans are members of a church or temple.

Protestants outnumber other religious groups. There are **Lutherans**, Anglicans (**Methodists**, **Congregationalists**, Quakers), **Calvinists** (**Baptists** and **Presbyterians**), etc., making up 52% of the population. They list themselves as Protestants, so as to be distinguished from the Roman Catholics.

Roman Catholics make up about 24% of the population (2002), the members of Mormon account for 2% and the members of Jewish faith account for 1%, and nearly 4 million **Eastern Orthodox** Church members. Many immigrants, particularly those from Mexico and the Philippines were Roman Catholics, but Asian immigrants were Buddhists, **Sikhs**, or **Hindus**, and immigrants from Turkey, Egypt and Pakistan were mostly **Moslems**. And the Native American religions are still practiced. It is, therefore, safe to say that every major religion known to the world is represented in America.

According to **the principle of "separation of church and state,"** the government of the United States gives no direct subsidies to any faiths, but exempts them from paying taxes on income and property.

5. The American Society

Class is an objective reality in the American society, in which despite huge national wealth some citizens live in luxury and others in great poverty. There is a strikingly wide gap between the wealthy and the poor.

Much of the nation's wealth is owned and controlled by a small number of the monopoly capitalists. In 1877 one percent of Americans owned 33% of all private wealth in the nation. And the top 20% controlled 77% of private wealth. The "super-rich" of the 20% form the apex of the class pyramid. The living standard of this class is unimaginably high and its influence over the nation is out of line with its numerical strength. The monopolies like **the Rockefeller Interest Group** and **the Morgan Interest Group** not only control the national economy but also exert much influence over the American government and policy-making activities.

At the bottom of the society are the poor, who constitute 29% of the population. In absolute terms, 12% of the population is so poor that they lack adequate nutrition (24.3 million in 1975). These Americans receive little or no medical attention, education or job training, and most of them suffer from an inadequate diet. Particularly among the aged, many poor people have been found subsisting on a diet of canned dog food. The **Washington Post** newspaper has estimated that the elderly poor consume more dog food than is eaten by dogs. The "relative" poor are those who are living in the state of poverty in which "income is not adequate for the necessities of life."

The poor exist not because the nation cannot generate the wealth to support them adequately, but because distribution of wealth is fundamentally unequal. The capitalists, not to say the monopolists, do little but gain much. They live in luxury. They own luxurious homes, collect valuable works of art, maintain private yachts, planes and cars, while the poor have to live in ghettos in urban areas, in shacks, eating food made for dogs. Poverty tends to breed ignorance, and lack of nutrition leads to bad health. Impoverished parents raise unhealthy children. As a consequence, the impoverished remain poor generation after generation.

Sandwiched between the wealthy and the poor is a large group of middle income wage or salary earners who are often referred to as the "middle-class." People of this class usually lead a rather comfortable life. Many have their own homes, cars, some form of medical insurance and enough money to prepare their children for middle class jobs. However, the **solvency** of the middle class depends on a combination of personal income and credit borrowing. Frequently they are heavily in debt because their style of life depends on cash outlay larger than what their salaries bring in. the middle class is the greatest bloc of consumers in America. They not only go into debt buying essentials but also incur debts buying non-essentials such as expensive clothing and furniture, vacation trip, stereo equipment, and second automobiles. The combination of **economic recession** with price inflation in 1982 led to the deterioration of the middle-income worker's position. Both husbands and wives must work now; yet even with two salaries, middle-income families find themselves unable to maintain their former standards of living.

Social inequality in the United States has persisted throughout the 20th century. Despite the pervasive myth of social mobility (anyone who works hard can get rich), statistics prove over and over again that the gap between the wealthy and the poor is not diminishing. It is, in fact, rapidly widening. Social inequality founded on class is further complicated by sex and race. Even within the same class, women and minorities consistently earn less than white men. Statistically, women at the same job as men earn only 60% of the male wage. For black men and women the situation is getting worse. In 1970 the national average black income was 61.3% of that of whites. By 1980 it had fallen to 57.9%.

The fundamental social problem facing America in the twentieth century is not mass poverty, but grave inequality in the distribution of wealth.

Notes

1. melting pot　大熔炉，常用来比喻美国。
2. American Indian　美洲印第安人
3. Indian Reservation　印第安人居留地
4. WASP　盎格鲁—撒克逊白人新教徒，是 White Anglo-Saxon Protestant 的缩略形式。
5. Emancipation Proclamation　《解放黑奴宣言》，林肯总统于 1862 年 9

月发表，于 1863 年 1 月 1 日生效。

6. the Civil War　美国南北战争/美国内战(1861～1865)
7. Hispanic　拉丁美洲人
8. Mexican-American　美籍墨西哥人
9. Puerto Rican　波多黎各人
10. Colorado　科罗拉多州
11. Nevada　内华达州
12. middle class　中产阶级，一般指美国的工薪阶层。
13. Black English　黑人英语
14. Protestant　新教徒
15. Lutheran　路德派教友
16. Methodist　卫理派教徒
17. Congregationalist　公理派教徒
18. Calvinist　加尔文派教徒
19. Baptist　浸礼派教徒
20. Presbyterian　长老会教友
21. Eastern Orthodox　东正教
22. Sikh　锡克教教徒
23. Hindu　印度教教友
24. Moslem　伊斯兰教教徒
25. the principle of "separation of church and state"　"政教分离"的原则
26. the Rockefeller Interest Group　洛克菲勒财团
27. the Morgan Interest Group　摩根财团
28. Washington Post　华盛顿邮报
29. solvency　偿付能力
30. economic recession　经济衰退

Questions for Discussion

1. Why has the United States long been known as a "melting pot"?
2. What do you know about the history and the present social status of the American Indians, WASPs, the Black people, the Hispanics and Asian Americans living in the United States?

3. Why has the population center of gravity of the United States been moving westward since 1790?
4. In what aspects does American English differ from British English? Give some examples.
5. What accounts for the fact that every major religion known to the world is represented in the United States?
6. Analyze the American society in terms of class, and describe the strikingly wide gap between the rich and the poor.
7. What do you think are the major causes of the wide gap between the rich and the poor in the United States?
8. What are the fundamental social problems facing America in the 20th century?

Exercises

Ⅰ. Choose the best answer and circle the letter before it.

1. The dominant ethnic group in the United States today is ________.
   A. the Black people　　B. WASPs
   C. Asian Americans　　D. Hispanics
2. The ________ constitute the largest ethnic-racial minority group in the United States.
   A. American Indians　　B. Hispanics
   C. Blacks　　D. Asian Americans
3. Race is different from ethnicity because its basis is ________.
   A. country of origin　　B. religion
   C. language spoken　　D. skin color
4. The ________ are at the very bottom of the society in the United States.
   A. Blacks　　B. Hispanics
   C. non-WASPs　　D. Asians
5. The state of ________ is the largest in population today.
   A. New York　　B. Colorado
   C. Arizona　　D. California
6. People in the US have kept moving westward for reasons except

________.

A. religious freedom

B. fertile soil in the West

C. good climate in the west

D. discovery of gold in the West

7. Hispanics in the US speak ________.

A. English

B. Spanish

C. French

D. their native languages

8. Today about ________% of Americans are church members in the United States.

A. 50 B. 90

C. 70 D. 80

9. ________ outnumber other religious groups in the United States.

A. Methodists B. Congregationalists

C. Quakers D. Protestants

10. The poor exist in the United States because ________.

A. the nation cannot generate the wealth to support the poor

B. there are regular economic depressions

C. its distribution of wealth is fundamentally unequal

D. the country is densely populated

11. The solvency of the middle class in the US depends on ________.

A. personal income

B. credit borrowing

C. cash outlay

D. the combination of personal income and credit borrowing

Ⅱ. Fill in the following blanks with appropriate words or expressions.

1. Most Americans are of ________ origin.

2. Originally, North America was sprinkled with more than 300 ________ of American Indians.

3. The first colonial people in present day United States were ________ from England, Northern and Western Europe.

4. Between 1820 and 1980 the US admitted almost ________ million

immigrants.

5. Black people in the US are descended from ________ slaves imported from ________.
6. Black people were declared free initially by Abraham Lincoln's __________ in 1863.
7. ________ people constitute the largest ethnic-racial minority group in the US today, and ________ form the second.
8. In the 19th century a large number of Chinese were shipped to America as "________."
9. The residents in Hawaii are mainly of ________ descent, ________ and ________ background.
10. In America individuals encounter not only class ________ but also discrimination based on ________ and race.
11. According to the 2007 estimation, the total population of the United States is ________ million.
12. Since 1790, the US population center of gravity has kept moving ________.
13. Most of the Black people in the US speak ________, but the Hispanics speak ________.
14. In the US ________ outnumber other religious groups.
15. Much of America's wealth is owned by a small number of the ________ capitalists. The poor exist because distribution of wealth is fundamentally ________.

Ⅲ. Match the names of the ethnic or racial groups with the percentage of the total population they make up at present in the United States.

1. ____	American Indians	a. 70%
2. ____	White people	b. 12.8%
3. ____	Black people	c. 0.9%
4. ____	Hispanics	d. 12.3%

Ⅳ. Explain the following in English.

1. melting pot
2. WASP
3. ethnicity
4. population center of gravity
5. Hispanic

Lesson 13 American Economy

Major Points

The development of the American economy has experienced three stages: commercial capitalism, industrial capitalism and corporate capitalism.

The three important industrial regions of the US are the Northeast, the South and the West.

Most of the important crop-growing areas in the US are in the central plain region, the Atlantic coast plain and the great basins west of the Rockies.

The staple crops in the United States are corn, wheat, oats, barley and rice.

The economic crops are cotton and tobacco.

The airplane provides Americans with the fastest means of travel.

Railways are important for carrying goods in the US.

The US trades with most of the nations in the world. The American government began to pursue a protectionist policy in trade in the 1970s in an attempt to eliminate the unfavorable balance of trade.

The US has played a dominant role in the world capitalist economy since the end of World War Ⅱ.

Main Contents

1. Corporate Capitalism (Imperialism)

The United States is a highly industrialized and monopolized country. The development of its economy has experienced three stages: commercial capitalism, industrial capitalism and corporate capitalism or imperialism.

Commercial capitalism was established as the dominant mode of production in the British colonies in the 17th century. Industrial capitalism

lasted from the late 18th century to the early 20th century. Its capitalist economy developed rapidly in this stage. By the 1870s, the total value of its industrial products had surpassed that of its agricultural products. It had surpassed Britain in industrial production and become the most powerful nation in the world by the 1880s. With the formation of the **trust corporations** in the late 19th century and the early 20th century, the United States entered the last stage in the development of capitalism—imperialism. In this stage large corporations have centralized capital and established ownership over the means of production, though actually the economy still includes a competitive free market sector.

When the United States got its independence in 1776, it was an agricultural country. It would remain so for another century, but some early decisions by American social and political leaders planted the seeds of industrial growth. Under the reign of George Washington, for example, Alexander Hamilton, the then Secretary of the Treasury, persuaded Congress to establish a protective tariff to protect national industries. This and his other measures gave great encouragement to business in general.

One key development was the introduction of the factory system. The first factory in the United States is generally dated to 1793 when a cotton textile mill was set up in Rhode Island. The same year saw the establishment of a cotton cloth factory by an Englishman named Samuel Slater. A second development was the "American system" of mass production that originated in the firearms industry about 1800. The new system required precision engineering to create parts that were interchangeable. This, in turn, allowed the final production to be assembled in stages, each worker specializing in a specific operation. The invention of cotton gin by Eli Whitney made cotton production more efficient. In 1913, Henry Ford introduced the "moving assembly" line. This variation on the earlier practice of continuous assembly made possible a major saving in labor costs. A third development was the application of new technologies to industrial tasks. The textile industry completed the switch from water to stream power after the 1860s. A fourth development was the emergence of new forms of business organization, namely the bank and the corporation. The construction of railroads beginning in the 1830's marked the start of a new era for the United States. The railroads

provided transportation for industries and promoted the economic activities. By 1913, over one-third of the world's industrial production came from the United States.

Development of the American corporations began in the 1870s. At that time production took place in single function businesses, usually owned by individual families and operated by an entrepreneur without reference to other businesses engaged in the same sort of production. Markets were still local and regional. However, trust corporations emerged in the late 19th century and the early 20th century, as a consequence of the process in which the smaller companies were purchased, merged with or destroyed by the more powerful ones. In these giant corporations management was rationalized and centralized, a central office controlled the activities of **subsidiary branches**. They produced for and sometimes monopolized not only local but national markets. The management systems of the modern corporations include functional departments, such as finance, personnel, purchasing, engineering, and sale. The division of labor in management meant that corporations were no longer concerned primarily with problems of production but with problems of planning strategies for maintaining or establishing monopolistic power, and ways of encouraging consumption of new products. To ensure continuing economic growth, giant monopoly corporations had to diversify (i. e. produce many different sorts of products), exploit international resources and markets. That is why Lenin once said that imperialism is the source of war. Now the enormous, diversified, **multinational monopolistic corporations** dominate the US economy, such as International Telephone and Telegraph (ITT), **International Business Machines** (IBM), **Dupont Chemical**, General Electric and **General Motors**.

2. Industry

The main industries of the United States are coal mining, iron and steel, aircraft, automobile, machine tool, electronic and electric equipment, textile, chemical and munitions.

The last century has seen the rise and decline of a succession of industries in the United States. The auto industry has had to struggle to meet the challenge of foreign competition. However, over the years, many new industries have appeared. Their products range from airplanes to television

sets; from microchips to space satellites; from microwave ovens to ultra-high speed computers. Many of the currently rising industries are among "high-tech" industries because of their dependence on the latest developments in technology. The GDP of the United States in 2005 is estimated to be $12.41 trillion, $42,000 per capita. Its real growth rate was 3.5% and it had a rate of inflation of 3.2% and an unemployment rate of 5.1% the same year.

There are three industrial regions where important industries are located: the industrial Northeast, the South and the West.

1) The Industrial Northeast

This region lies to the north of the Ohio River and the Potomac River and to the east of the Mississippi River. With 95% of the nation's iron and steel, and machine-making industries, it is the oldest and most important industrial region in the United States. The other important industries include ship building, coal mining, textile and chemical industries. Many industrial big cities such as New York, Philadelphia, Boston, Detroit, **Cleveland**, Pittsburgh, **Baltimore** and Chicago are located in this region.

2) The South

The South has historically been rather backward in industry. The situation remains so even to this day. Today, about 3/5 of the people in the South live on farms or in small towns, and make their living from the land. However, in recent decades a great deal of industry has been moved into the South from the North for cheap labor. Today much of the cotton grown in the South is sent directly to the textile plants in the southern cities. Other industries such as oil extracting and oil refining, shipbuilding, munitions and chemical industries have also been established in many sections of this region. The South has now become the newly developed industrial region of the United States.

3) The West

The West is an important mining area. Large quantities of important minerals such as iron ore, coal, oil, copper, gold, silver, lead, and tin come from the western states. The main industries in this region are electronic equipment, aerospace, aircraft manufacture and oil refinery, concentrated mainly in such big industrial cities as Los Angeles, San Francisco and **Seattle**. The West is at present the most rapidly growing section of the country.

Canned fish and lumber are the chief manufactured products of Alaska, and sugar and canned pineapples are the chief manufactured products of Hawaii.

The high degree of mechanization and computerization has brought about many changes in contemporary life, thought and culture in the United States. Many Americans do their banking and shopping with the aid of computers and many people are issued their paychecks by computers. Science fiction books and movies about robots or computerized worlds are very common. But there is also resentment at the dehumanizing trends in overly mechanized America. The growing use of machines to perform routine tasks in every field has exacerbated unemployment in the United States as a great number of workers have inevitably been displaced because of automation. The inherent capitalist economic law has never ceased its operation. Depressions cycle periodically. The American economy was badly hit by the depression of 1982, with its unemployment rate as high as 10.87%.

3. Agriculture

The United States is blessed with fertile soil, and a good climate for its agriculture. About one-fifth of the land area is farmed. Some 394 million acres are harvested cropland, and about 890 million acres are permanent pastureland.

Most of the important crop-growing areas in the United States are in the central plain region between the Appalachians and the Rockies. Others are in the Atlantic coast plain and the great basins west of the Rockies.

The staple crops are corn and wheat, with oats, barley and rice ranking next in importance. The wide **Corn Belt**, south of the Great Lakes, accounts for about 30% of the total cultivated area. **Iowa** in this region is the leading corn state, followed by Illinois, **Indiana** and Ohio. The other principal agricultural products of this region are wheat, cattle, and dairy goods. The wheat-land is mostly in the prairie region, and the state of **Kansas** leads the whole country in the production of wheat, followed by **North Dakota**, **South Dakota**, and **Oklahoma**. Rice is grown in the Gulf Plains in the South. Cotton and tobacco are the economic crops in the South. Other cash crops are beets, sugarcane and fruit such as oranges, lemons, and pineapples grown in Florida, the Pacific coast strip and Hawaii. The stock raising areas are scattered in the neighborhood of the Great Lakes and in the Corn Belt, on the eastern slopes of

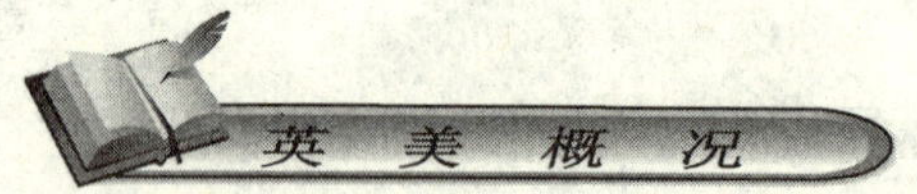

the Rocky range. Cattle and pigs are the most important livestock and sheep are raised on the ranches in the west highlands. Fishing, trapping, timbering and oil extracting have become the main industries in Alaska.

American agriculture is highly mechanized and operated on a large scale. Both farming and raising stock have become an industry. American agriculture is, by any standards, big business. Indeed, the term, "agribusiness" has been coined to reflect the large-scale nature of agricultural enterprise in the modern US economy. The farm population has decreased in the past few decades. In 1987, there were slightly more than 2 million farms in the United States—down by about 7% from the number just 5 years earlier. About 67,000 farms, or 3.2% of the total, are owned by corporations, but most of those corporations are owned by families. Although family farms are not disappearing, as some people fear, smaller farms are disappearing. People who farm small pieces of land find they cannot invest in the modern equipment they need to make the farms pay. According to the Department of Agriculture, the number of small farms—those with under $50,000 in annual sales—dropped by 120,000 between 1982 and 1987. There are only no more than 8 million persons who still live on farms today. Many farm owners, especially owners of smaller farms, do not work on the farm full-time. About 45% of farmers actually have other occupations. Nevertheless, there has been a tremendous increase in production. Both American and foreign consumers benefit from the American farmers' low-cost output. About one-third of the cropland in the United States is planted in crops destined for export—to Europe, Asia, Africa and Latin America.

The readiness of many farmers to adopt new technology has been one of the strengths of American agriculture. Computers are but the latest in a long time innovations that have helped American farmers to cut costs and improve productivity.

While the high productivity of American agriculture has kept food prices low for consumers, farmers have been perhaps too successful. Crop surpluses and low prices have made it hard for many farmers to make a profit.

The American farmer is not quite his own master in every thing. He often owes money on his land, his house and his machines. He has to borrow heavily from the bank each spring to buy seeds, fertilizer, oil and so on, and even has

to go into debt to see his family through the year with clothes and food. After he has sold his grain and paid his debts at the end of the year, he usually has not much left because the cost of the products farmers buy—tractors, fertilizers, pesticides—has risen faster than the prices they receive for their crops and high rates of loan interests have added to the farmers' burden. A slight fall in the price of grain may bring him ruin.

Critics accuse both corporate and family farmers of damaging the environment. American farmers have multiplied their use of artificial fertilizers and chemicals designed to kill weeds and insect pests and to protect against crop diseases. Such farming aids have played an indispensable role in increasing crop output, but they have caused problems of air and water pollutions. Toxic farm chemicals, some linked to cancer and other disease, have at times found their way into the nation's water, food and air, although constant vigilance by government officials at the state and federal levels is taken to protect these resources.

4. Transportation

The automobile is the most popular means of transportation in the United States. One in seven of all workers makes cars or serves them. Up to eight million new cars are made each year; four households out of five own at least one car, and more than a quarter own two. About 110 million cars and 15 million trucks run throughout the country along some 6.334 million kilometers of highways and 3.7 million kilometers of paved roads. A huge 68,000-kilometer interstate system of freeways crisscrosses the country linking all major cities. The automobile has brought many changes in American life. The remarkable growth of the suburbs in the past few decades and the creation of roadside businesses of various kinds such as the building of outdoor movie theaters and **motels** with parking spaces both have much to do with the good roads and the use of the automobile.

Although the automobile has provided Americans with a comfortable and convenient means of transportation, it has brought disasters to Americans as well. Over 125 million cars and trucks on the nation's roads have constantly caused huge **rush-hour traffic jams** and accidents. The high concentration of air pollution has jeopardized the health and even the very life of city dwellers.

The airplane provides Americans with the fastest means of travel. No other common means of transportation can take a person across the continent in six hours, and several companies competing with one another in quality of service join all major cities to one another. There are more than 12,700 civil airports, dozens of scheduled airlines and control centers that direct air traffic between cities.

Railways are still important for carrying goods. They were built by private enterprises and are still operated by commercial companies, each of which operates only in part of the country. In many cases two or more rival railways were built parallel with one another; even here competition has operated. Some of the railway companies still manage to make a profit from their operations of carrying freight, but for a long time they have all lost money on their passenger services. Year by year, these services are reduced, and now, except for commuter lines around big cities, the passenger network has only a few routes still working.

Inland waterways are also very important to transportation in the United States. The country has over 41, 000 kilometers of navigable inland channels, exclusive of the Great Lakes. The important port and harbors include Anchorage, Baltimore, Boston, Charleston, Chicago, Duluth, Honolulu, Houston, Jacksonville, Los Angeles, New Orleans, New York, Philadelphia, Portland, San Francisco, Seattle, etc.

5. Foreign Trade

The United States trades with most of the nations in the world. Its total value of foreign trade in 2005 was estimated $ 9275 millon fob. Its leading exports are machinery, automobiles, aircraft, textiles, iron, coal, petroleum products, chemicals and munitions and agricultural products. Canada and Mexico buy about one-fifth of the total.

The United States is also a great importer. It imports large quantities of coffee, sugar, petroleum, metals, paper and paper products from Europe, Latin America, Asia and Canada.

There has been **an unfavorable balance of trade** since the 1970s. So the American government began to pursue **a protectionist policy in trade** in the 1970s in an attempt to encourage its export and limit its import.

The major trading partners of the United States are Canada, Mexico, Japan, the United Kingdom, China and Germany.

6. American Economic Interests Abroad

The United States has played a dominant role in the world capitalist economy since the end of World War Ⅱ. It has the markets and raw materials of the third world. For example, in 1971 the total value of all investment abroad by all nations was estimated conservatively at 165 billion US dollars, of which American-based, multinational corporations owned more than 50%. The rapid growth of US private investment abroad since 1945 was facilitated by the economic, political and **military hegemony** established by America as a consequence of its victory in World War Ⅱ. Diplomatic pressure, **economic sanctions**, covert operations and outright military interventions are all part and parcel of the policy through which the US government has been able to maintain a favorable international situation.

Notes

1. trust corporation　托拉斯公司
2. subsidiary branch　辅助分公司
3. multinational monopolistic corporation　跨国垄断公司
4. International Business Machines (IBM)　(美国)国际商用机器公司
5. Dupont Chemical　杜邦化学公司
6. General Motors　通用汽车公司
7. Cleveland　克里夫兰,地处芝加哥和底特律之间,是美国中西部的主要工业城市之一。
8. Baltimore　巴尔的摩,美国东部城市
9. Seattle　西雅图,美国西北部 Washington 州海港城市。
10. Corn Belt　玉米带
11. Iowa　艾奥瓦州
12. Indiana　印第安纳州
13. Kansas　堪萨斯州
14. North Dakota, South Dakota　北达科他州,南达科他州
15. Oklahoma　俄克拉何马州
16. motels　备有汽车停车场的旅馆,是 motor ＋ hotel 的混成词。
17. rush-hour traffic jams　交通高峰期的汽车阻塞
18. an unfavorable balance of trade　贸易逆差,贸易顺差应为"a favorable balance of trade"。
19. a protectionist policy in trade　贸易保护主义政策

20. military hegemony 军事霸权
21. economic sanction 经济制裁

Questions for Discussion

1. In what aspects does corporate capitalism differ from commercial and industrial capitalism?
2. Why is it said that imperialism is the source of war?
3. In what ways are the three industrial regions of the United States important?
4. Tell what you know about the American agriculture, transportation and foreign trade.
5. What a policy in trade has been pursued by the American government since the 1970s? Why?
6. What a role has the United States played in the world capitalist economy since the end of World War Ⅱ? Why is it said so?

Exercises

Ⅰ. Choose the correct answer and circle the letter before it.

1. The last stage that American economy has experienced is ________.
   A. colonial stage B. corporate capitalism
   C. industrial capitalism D. commercial capitalism
2. Commercial capitalism was established as the dominant mode of production in the British colonies in the ________ th century.
   A. 17 B. 18 C. 19 D. 20
3. In the ________ stage American economy developed rapidly.
   A. commercial capitalism B. industrial capitalism
   C. colonial D. corporate capitalism
4. Trust corporations first emerged in ________ in the United States.
   A. the late 17th century and the early 18th century
   B. the late 18th century and the early 19th century

C. the late 19th century and the early 20th century

D. the late 20th century and the early 21st century

5. The division of labor in management meant that corporations were no longer concerned primarily with problems of ________.

A. production

B. planning strategies for maintaining monopolistic power

C. planning ways of encouraging consumption new products

D. diversification

6. Modern corporations in the United States are anything but ________.

A. diversified　　B. multinational

C. competitive　　D. monopolistic

7. The oldest and most important industrial region in the US is ________.

A. the Northeast　　B. the South

C. the Midwest　　D. the West

8. The South of the US has now become ________ developed industrial region.

A. the newly　　B. the oldest

C. the most rapidly　　D. the well

9. The West of the United States is an important ________ area.

A. agricultural　　B. mining

C. oil extracting　　D. crop-growing

10. Which of the following cities is NOT on the Pacific coast?

A. Baltimore.　　B. Los Angeles.

C. San Francisco.　　D. Seattle.

11. At present, ________ is the most rapidly growing section of the United States.

A. the Northeast　　B. the South

C. the West　　D. the Midwest

12. Canned fish and lumber are the chief manufactured products of ________.

A. Hawaii　　B. Alaska

C. Florida　　D. New Mexico

13. The growing use of machines to perform routine tasks in every field has exacerbated ________.

A. unemployment B. employment
C. inflation D. economic depression

14. About ________ of the land area is farmed in the United States.
A. one fourth B. one fifth
C. one third D. half

15. All states except ________ of the following are in the Corn Belt.
A. Iowa B. Illinois
C. Ohio D. Arizona

16. The state of ________ leads the US in the production of wheat.
A. North Dakota B. South Dakota
C. Oklahoma D. Kansas

17. Automobile has provided Americans with ________.
A. a comfortable and convenient means of transportation
B. fastest means of transportation
C. huge rush-hour traffic jams and air pollution
D. all of the above

18. The rapid growth of US private investment abroad since 1945 was facilitated by all the following except ________.
A. diplomatic pressure B. military interventions
C. economic depression D. economic sanctions

Ⅱ. Fill in the following blanks with proper words or expressions.

1. The three stages that the American economy has experienced in its development are ________ capitalism, ________ capitalism and ________ capitalism.
2. The United States had surpassed ________ in industrial production by the 1880s.
3. Development of the American corporations began in ________. In these giant corporations management was ________ and ________.
4. The division of labor in management meant that corporations were no longer concerned primarily with problems of ________ but with problems of planning, ________ for maintaining or establishing monopolistic power, and ways of encouraging ________ of new products.
5. Now the United States economy is dominated by ________, ________,

__________ monopolistic corporations.

6. The oldest and most important industrial region in the United States is the industrial ________.
7. The newly-developed industrial region of the US is the ________.
8. The West is an important ________ area.
9. ________ and ________ have virtually brought about another revolution in American industry in the 20th century.
10. Most of the important crop-growing areas of the US are in the ________ region.
11. The staple crops grown in the US are ________ and ________, with ________, ________ and ________ ranking next in importance.
12. The stock raising areas of the United States are scattered in the neighborhood of the ________, in the ________ and on the eastern slopes of the Rocky Range.
13. The ________ is the most popular means of transportation in the United States.
14. The airplane provides Americans with the ________ means of travel.
15. In the United States, railways are still important for carrying ________ and are still operated by ________ companies.
16. The United States government began to pursue a ________ policy in trade in the 1970s.

Ⅲ. Match the names of the states or regions with their chief agricultural or industrial products.

1. ____	Iowa	a. rice
2. ____	Kansas	b. corn
3. ____	the Gulf Plains	c. iron and steel manufacture
4. ____	the West	d. wheat
5. ____	the Northeast	e. mineral ores

Ⅳ. Explain the following in English.

1. corporate capitalism
2. ITT
3. IBM
4. the Corn Belt
5. the Wheat Belt

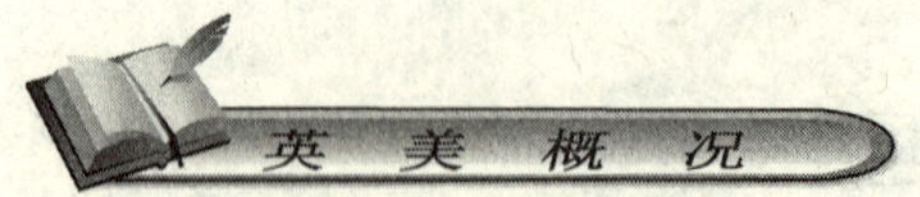

Ⅴ. Translate the following into Chinese.

1. Dupont Chemical
2. General electric
3. General Motors
4. Cleveland
5. Baltimore

Lesson 14 Political System: Government

Major Points

The Constitution of the United States of America follows two principles: the federal system and the "separation of powers."

The constitution gives the executive power to the President alone. The powers enjoyed by the President are larger than those given by the Constitution. All the executive departments and independent agencies are responsible to the President, who is not bound to be responsible to Congress.

Congress consists of the Senate and the House of Representatives.

Congress has the power to make any laws that are considered "necessary and proper."

There is a division of power between the two Houses of Congress. Much of the work of Congress is done in committees.

There are two separate systems of laws and courts: the federal system and the state system.

The federal court system consists of one Supreme Court, eleven courts of appeal and 91 district courts.

The three branches of the federal government are supposed to be independent of each other, each checking the other two so that no one can get all the power.

Main Contents

1. The Constitution

The United States is a federal union of 50 states. The system of government is laid down in the Constitution of the United States, which was framed in Philadelphia in 1787 and ratified in 1789.

The Constitution follows two principles: the federal system and the "**separation of powers.**" The federal system means that the states have the right to self-government. In other words, there is a division of powers between the federal government and the state governments. There is also a division of powers among the three branches of the federal government: the legislative branch, the executive branch and the judicial branch. **Congress** exercises the legislative power, the President, the executive power, and **the Supreme Court**, the judicial power. They are supposed to be independent of each other, but each checks the other two so that no one can get all the power. This arrangement is known as the "separation of powers," which calls for "**checks and balances.**" The principle sounds fine, but in practice, there is no, and cannot be, any "separation of powers," as the federal government tends to direct or influence the policies of the states and the power of the President has kept enlarging.

2. The President

The President of the United States is both the head of state and the head of government. The Constitution gives the President wide powers. Today his powers are far greater than those given in the Constitution.

The Constitution gives the executive power to the President alone. All the government departments, agencies and offices are led by the President and are responsible to him. But the President is not bound to be responsible to Congress as he is neither appointed nor elected by it. The **Cabinet**, made up of the heads of the government departments, only advises the President and does not make any decisions. The President is free to consult or ignore their advice.

As head of the executive branch, the President must carry out the government programs enacted into law by Congress. He recommends programs and laws to Congress and requests money for Federal Government operations. He has **a veto power** over bills passed by Congress. If a bill is vetoed by the President and returned to Congress, it can be passed again by a two-third vote of the full membership of both houses of Congress. With this power he can easily reject any bill he dislikes. The President has the power of appointing as many as thousands of officers, such as heads of the government departments, ambassadors and judges of the Supreme Court, with the consent of **the Senate.** He has the power to conduct foreign affairs. Important officers in the

diplomatic service are appointed by the President and confirmed by Congress. But the President can send out personal agents to represent him without the approval of the Senate, and they can take any action that a regular diplomatic representative does. Under the Constitution, the President can make treaties with foreign countries, but the treaty must be approved by a two-thirds vote of the Senators before it goes into effect. However, the President can make **executive agreements** with other countries without the approval of the Senate. And the Constitution does not make a clear distinction between a treaty and an agreement. In fact, they have the same force. The President is the **Commander-in-Chief** of the armed forces. The **Secretary of Defense** and the **Chairman of the Joint Chiefs of Staff** have to carry out his orders. The Constitution says that only Congress has the power to declare war upon other nations, but actually the President can start and fight a war if he wants to in a limited period of time. Many wars in the American history, such as Spanish-American War of 1898, the Korean War of 1950, the War in Vietnam in the 1960s and **the Gulf War** in the 1990s, were all started and fought by President rather than Congress.

3. Executive Departments and Agencies

The executive branch headed by the President is vast bureaucratic machinery. There are a dozen of departments and over a hundred independent agencies.

The Department of State, headed by the **Secretary of State**, advises the President on foreign relations. It handles all peaceful dealings with other countries, and issues passports to American citizens who wish to travel abroad, and visas to visitors to the United States.

The Treasury Department manages government finances, collects taxes, and mints coins and prints paper money. **The Secret Service**, which protects the President, Vice President and other dignitaries, is also part of the Department.

The Department of Defense is responsible for the nation's security. The Secretaries of the Army, Navy and Air Force assist the Secretary of Defense. It is the largest of all the departments, employing about 3.7 million people, of whom about 2.4 million are in the armed forces.

The Department of Justice is led by **the Attorney General**, who acts for the government in legal matters and moves against violators of federal laws. **The Federal Bureau of Investigation** (FBI) and federal prisons are among his responsibilities.

The Department of the Interior protects and develops the nation's natural resources and manages the national parks. It also enforces federal hunting and fishing laws, checks on the safety of mines and is responsible for the welfare of the Indian tribes.

The Department of Agriculture aids food production and looks after the interests of farmers. It issues reports on the supply and prices of farm products, conducts scientific studies of agriculture, and lends money to build rural electric systems.

The Department of Labor is concerned with the working conditions, safety and welfare of the nation's non-farm workers. It also renders a mediation and conciliation service to help employers and workers to settle labor disputes.

The Department of Commerce helps develop domestic commerce and trade with other countries. One of its branches issues patents for new inventions; another branch tests products to be sure they meet high standards; still another reports on weather conditions.

The Department of Health and Human Services (HHS) administers many of the nation's social service programs on a federal level.

The Department of Education administers and coordinates more than 150 federal aid-to-education programs.

The Department of Housing and Urban Development was established in 1965 to help provide adequate housing, and to coordinate and foster large-scale urban renewal programs.

The Department of Transportation was created in 1966 to coordinate transportation activities.

The Department of Energy, created in 1977 to address the nation's growing energy problems, is responsible for research, development and demonstration of energy technology; the marketing of federal power; energy conservation; the nuclear weapons program; regulation of energy production and use; pricing and allocation; and a central energy data collection and analysis program.

The Department of the Security of the National Territory and Resources was established soon after the event of September 11th of 2001, formed by the

combination of forces from the Department of National Defense, Department of Treasury, Department of Interior, National Security Council and CIA, mainly for the purpose of enhancing anti-terrorist activities, and keeping security of national territory and resources.

The powers of the President have been greatly enlarged as a result of the establishment of more executive agencies. There are numerous **independent agencies** charged with special functions. The largest of these is **the Postal Service**, which was created in 1970 to operate post offices. **The National Aeronautics and Space Administration** (NASA) maintains space program; **the United States Information Agency** (USIA) maintains information offices and libraries in most countries, operates the Voice of America (VOA) and conducts international cultural exchange programs. The most important agencies are **the White House Office**, **the National Security Council** (NSC), **the Central Intelligence Agency** (CIA), **the Bureau of the Budget** and **the Office of Emergency Planning.**

The National Security Council was set up in 1947 to advise the President on all matters related to national security. The council is composed of the President, the Vice President, the Secretary of State, the Secretary of Defense, the Secretary of the Treasury, the Director of the Office of Emergency Planning, and the Director of the CIA, the Chairman of the Joint Chiefs of Staff and the Special Assistant to the President for National Security. The Council does not make decisions; it makes suggestions to the President. Since it was set up, it has played a very important role in forming foreign policies of the US government. Whenever a serious situation arises, the President may first call a meeting of the council rather than the Cabinet.

The Central Intelligence Agency was also set up in 1947. Its activities have included instances of subversion, interference, and attempting to control other countries. Its organization, budget and personnel are kept secret.

4. Congress

Congress, the legislative branch, consists of the Senate and **the House of Representatives.**

Each of the 50 states elects two Senators. The term for Senators is six years, but one-third of them are elected every two years. A Senator must be over 30 years old and must have been an American citizen for at least nine years.

The number of representatives from each state is fixed according to the size of the population the state has. At present there is one Representative for over 500,000 people, but a state with a population less than that should elect one Representative. The total number of Representatives has been fixed at 435. Every ten years the membership of the House is redistributed among the states to make it suit the changes in population. All representatives serve a term of two years, and are elected every second year. A representative must be at least 25 years old and must have been an American citizen for no less than seven years.

Under the Constitution, Congress has the power to make any laws that are considered "necessary and proper." It has the power to impose and collect taxes, decide the expenditures of the government, control trade with foreign nations and among the states, establish and protect a monetary system and borrow money on the credit of the United States. It also has the power to raise and maintain an army and a navy and declare war upon other countries. Congress may admit new states into the Union and propose Amendments to the Constitution.

There is a division of power between the two houses of Congress. The Senate has the power to ratify all treaties with foreign countries, and approve the President's nominees for high-level official positions, while Representatives may propose bills for raising money. Impeachments should be proposed by the House but decided on by the Senate.

It is laid down in the Constitution that the Vice President of the United States is the president of the Senate, while the House elects a **Speaker** as its presiding officer.

In both houses there are a large number of officers, clerks, assistants, experts and secretaries. Today the real work of both houses is done in their committees. There are special committees, which are set up from time to time for a special purpose: investigating committees, sometimes appointed by Congress to investigate a certain matter; and joint committees, appointed by both houses to deal with special matters in which both are interested. The most important committees are the standing committees, which are considered the main parts of the legislative machinery. They deal with foreign affairs, taxation, appropriations, armed services, banking and money, commerce, labor, government operations and the law courts.

When a bill is introduced, it is passed on to a standing committee dealing with the subject for discussion. The committee, after considering it, may pass it or make some changes in it, or reject it. If it is accepted, it will be sent to the Senate or the House of Representatives for debate. After it is passed in one house, it is sent to the other to go through similar procedures. After both houses have passed it, it is sent to the President, who should sign it or veto it within ten days. If he vetoes the bill, it goes back to Congress; his veto may be overruled by a two-thirds vote of both houses of Congress and the bill then becomes a law. If he holds it for ten days without signing it, the bill also becomes law if congress remains in session. The single exception to this rule is that when Congress adjourns after sending a bill to the President and before the 10-day period has expired, his refusal to take any action then negates the bill. This process is known as **the "pocket veto."**

5. The President and Congress

In theory, Congress and the President are independent of each other. Their relationship is one of "checks and balances," that is, the powers of one limit those of the other. But in reality, there is close cooperation between the two branches of government. Only when they have different tactics or measures, may they sometimes find themselves in conflict with each other.

Under the Constitution a sitting President may be removed from office before his term expires only by an **impeachment** process whereby the House of Representatives, upon sufficient evidence, brings a "bill of impeachment" approved by two-thirds of its membership. Next comes a trial in the Senate, with the **Chief Justice of the Supreme Court** as the judge and the Senators as the jury. This power has been used only twice and no President has ever been actually impeached. In 1868 Congress tried to impeach President **Andrew Johnson** but failed. In 1974 a proposal was passed in a committee of the House to impeach President **Nixon** over the **Watergate Scandal.** But before the proposal went to the House for debate, Nixon resigned office, and **Gerald R. Ford**, the then Vice- President, succeeded him.

6. The Federal Court System

There are two systems of laws and courts: federal system and state system. Each is relatively independent of the other. The state courts enforce the state laws, and the federal courts enforce federal laws.

The Judicial Branch of the government is headed by the Supreme Court, which consists of the Chief Justice and eight Justices. All cases affecting ambassadors, ministers and consuls of foreign countries, and those in which a state is involved, can go straight to the Supreme Court. In other cases it acts as a court of final appeal. It has won for itself the power to interpret the Constitution and declare a law passed by Congress to be "**unconstitutional,**" and therefore, null and void, when the case in which the law is involved is put before it. By exercising this power of judicial review, the Court has actually won the power to say what the law is.

The second highest level of the federal judiciary is made up of 11 courts of appeal, which review the decisions of district courts. The decisions of the courts of appeal are final except when they are reviewed by the Supreme Court.

Below **the courts of appeal** are the district courts. At present there are 91 district courts, which serve as the trial courts.

The judges of all the federal courts are appointed for life. Only the Senate can remove them from office for misconduct and after a trial.

Notes

1. separation of powers 三权分立
2. Congress 国会，立法机关，分为参众两院。
3. the Supreme Court 最高法院
4. checks and balances 制衡
5. Cabinet 内阁
6. a veto power 否决权
7. the Senate 参议院
8. executive agreements 行政协定
9. Commander-in-Chief 总司令
10. Secretary of Defense 国防部长
11. Chairman of the Joint Chiefs of Staff 三军参谋长联席会议主席
12. the Gulf War 海湾战争
13. the Department of State 国务院
14. Secretary of State 国务卿
15. the Treasury Department 财政部

16. the Secret Service 特务局,主要负责总统、副总统和其他政府要员的安全。
17. the Department of Defense 国防部
18. the Department of Justice 司法部
19. the Attorney General 总检察长/司法部长
20. the Federal Bureau of Investigation 联邦调查局
21. the Department of the Interior 内政部
22. the Department of Agriculture 农业部
23. the Department of Labor 劳工部
24. the Department of Commerce 商业部
25. the Department of Health and Human Services 卫生及人类服务部
26. the Department of Education 教育部
27. the Department of Housing and Urban Development 房屋及城市发展部
28. the Department of Transportation 交通部
29. the Department of Energy 能源部
30. independent agencies 独立机构
31. the Postal Service 邮政总局
32. the National Aeronautics and Space Administration 国家航空航天局
33. the United States Information Agency 美国新闻总署
34. the White House Office 白宫办公厅
35. the National Security Council 国家安全委员会
36. the Central Intelligence Agency 中央情报局
37. the Bureau of the Budget 预算局
38. the Office of Emergency Planning 紧急计划委员会
39. the House of Representatives 众议院
40. Speaker 众议院议长
41. the "pocket veto" 搁置否决权
42. impeachment 弹劾
43. Chief Justice of the Supreme Court 最高法院的首席法官
44. Andrew Johnson 安德鲁·约翰逊(1808～1875),美国第17任总统,任期为1865～1869年。
45. Nixon 尼克松(1913～1994),1969～1974年任美国第37任总统,是美国第一位辞职的总统。

46. Watergate Scandal　水门事件
47. Gerald R. Ford　杰拉尔德·R·福特，于1973～1974年任美国副总统，1874～1978年任美国第38任总统。
48. unconstitutional　违宪的
49. the courts of appeal　上诉法院

Questions for Discussion

1. Tell what you know about the Constitution of the United States.
2. What powers does the President of the United States have?
3. Name some of the executive departments and point out their functions.
4. Name some of the important independent agencies under the President of the United States and tell what you know about each of them.
5. Give some examples to show that the powers of the President have been enlarged.
6. Describe the organization and the working of Congress, and the law-making procedures.
7. What powers does each of the two houses of Congress have?
8. Give an account of the federal court system of the US.

Exercises

Ⅰ. Choose the best answer and circle the letter before it.

1. The Constitution of the United States was framed in ________ in 1787.
   A. Washington　　B. Boston
   C. New York　　D. Philadelphia
2. The President of the United States exercises the ________ power.
   A. legislative　　B. executive
   C. judicial　　D. veto
3. The power of the US President has ________.
   A. remained the same as prescribed in the Constitution
   B. kept enlarging

C. kept belittling

D. remained the same from generation to generation

4. ________ has the veto power in legislation in the United States.

A. President　　B. Vice President

C. Secretary of State　　D. Speaker

5. Congress can veto the President's veto by a ________ vote of the full membership of both houses.

A. two-fifths　　B. two-thirds

C. three-fourths　　D. three-fifths

6. Under the US constitution, the President has the power to ________ without the consent of the Senate.

A. appoint high officials

B. sign a treaty with other nations

C. declare war upon other nations

D. sign an executive agreement with other nations

7. The Constitution of the United States says that only ________ can declare war upon other nations.

A. the President

B. Congress

C. Department of Defense

D. the National Security Council

8. The Department of ________ advises the President on foreign relations.

A. Defense　　B. State

C. Commerce　　D. Labor

9. The Secret Service is part of the ________ Department.

A. Treasury　　B. Defense

C. Interior　　D. Justice

10. FBI and federal prisons are among the responsibilities of the Department of ________.

A. State　　B. Defense

C. Justice　　D. Commerce

11. The largest of independent agencies is ________.

A. the NASA　　B. USIA

C. NSC　　D. the Postal Service

12. A Senator must be ________.
    A. over 25 years old and must have been an American citizen for at least nine years
    B. over 30 years old and must have been an American citizen for at least seven years
    C. over 30 years old and must have been an American citizen for at least nine years
    D. over 25 years old and must have been an American citizen for at least seven years
13. The number of Representatives from each state is fixed according to the size of ________ the state has.
    A. the territory　　B. the economy
    C. the voters　　D. the population
14. Representatives in the United States are elected ________.
    A. annually　　B. every two years
    C. every three years　　D. every four years
15. Impeachment of the President should be ________.
    A. proposed by the Senate and decided on by the House
    B. proposed by the House and decided on by the Supreme Court
    C. proposed by the House and decided on by the Senate
    D. proposed by Senate and decided on by the Supreme Court
16. In the process of an impeachment, the ________ serve as the Jury.
    A. Representatives
    B. Senators
    C. Judges
    D. Justices of the Supreme Court

Ⅱ. Fill in the following blanks with proper words or expressions.

1. The Constitution of the United States follows two principles: the ________ system and the "________ of powers."
2. The Constitution gives the executive power to the ________ alone.
3. The Cabinet of the American government is made up of the heads of ________.
4. In legislation the President has a ________ power over bills passed by Congress.

5. In the United States treaties signed by the president with other countries and officials appointed by him must be confirmed by the ________.
6. The Constitution says that only ________ can declare war upon other nations.
7. The Department of State is headed by the ________.
8. The Department of Justice is headed by the ________.
9. The national parks in the United States are managed by the Department of ________.
10. Congress consists of the ________ and the House of ________.
11. Congress has the power to make any ________ that are considered "necessary and proper."
12. The president of the Senate is the ________ and the presiding officer of the House is ________.
13. The number of Representatives is fixed at ________.
14. Today the real work of both houses of Congress is done in their ________.
15. The President's veto may be overruled by a ________ vote of both houses of Congress.
16. the Judicial branch of the US government is headed by the ____________.

Ⅲ. Match the names of the departments or agencies with their corresponding duties or responsibilities.

1. ____ Department of State	a. national security
2. ____ Department of Interior	b. government finances
3. ____ Department of Defense	c. foreign affairs
4. ____ Department of Labor	d. welfare of Indians
5. ____ Department of Justice	e. issuing patents
6. ____ Department of Commerce	f. settling labor disputes
7. ____ Treasury Department	g. federal prisons
8. ____ US Information Agency	h. operating post offices
9. ____ Department of Energy	i. operating the VOA
10. ____ Post Service	j. energy conservation

Ⅳ. Explain the following in English.

1. separation of powers
2. the National Security Council
3. the Central Intelligence Agency
4. "pocket veto"
5. Congress
6. the United States Information Agency
7. the Supreme Court
8. judicial review

Lesson 15 Political System: State Government and Party Politics

Major Points

The state government is made up of three branches: the legislative, the executive and the judicial.

The most important part of a state government is the legislature. The chief executive of a state is the governor. The state court system is by no means subordinate to the federal judiciary. Trial by jury is guaranteed to the accused.

There are three kinds of local governments under a state government: the county government, the city, town or village government and the governments of districts set up for special purposes.

The Constitution of the US says nothing about political parties. The oldest parties in the American history are the Federal Party and the Democratic-Republican Party.

The two principal parties in the US today are the Democratic Party (formed in 1828) and the Republican Party (formed in 1854).

The two parties have almost the same basic organization.

The presidential elections which take place every four years in the US have been controlled by the two principal parties: the Democratic and the Republican.

The presidential election is conducted in five stages.

Main Contents

1. State Government

The Constitution of the United States says that all powers not granted to the federal government are to be kept by the individual state. The federal powers are enlisted powers, those enlisted in the Constitution, while state powers are residual powers. The states enjoy much autonomy. Each state has its own constitution. It generally includes voting requirements, the organization of the state government, the state and local courts, taxation, impeachment, etc.

Like the federal government, a state government is also made up of three branches: the legislative, the executive and the judicial.

The legislature is the most important part of a state government. It usually consists of two houses: the Senate and the House of Representatives, with the exception of **Nebraska**, which has a single-chamber legislature. The functions of the two houses are similar to those of the national Congress. They collect taxes, elect their officers, approve state government officials and pass state laws.

The chief executive of a state is the **governor**, elected by popular vote, typically for a four-year term (in a few states the term is two years). The powers of a governor are outlined in the state constitution, and generally parallel to those of the President of the United States. Besides his administrative duties, the governor is the commander of **the National Guard** of the state, just as the President is the Commander-in-Chief of the national armed forces.

The state court system is in no way subordinate to the federal judiciary. It consists of a group of courts roughly parallel to the federal pattern. It begins with purely local jurisdictions, followed by a series of intermediate trial courts, then by appellate courts and finally, at the top of the pyramid, by the state's supreme court.

Judges are usually elected officials though in some states the governor or state legislature appoints judges. In higher courts, terms of office range from 6 to 15 years, and are shorter in the lower courts. Trial by jury is guaranteed to those accused of committing a crime. As in the federal system, two types of juries are utilized: the **grand jury** and the **petit jury**. The grand jury indicts or refuses to indict accused persons. If a majority of the grand jury decides there is sufficient evidence for a trial, the case passes to a court where guilt or innocence is decided by a petit jury, which is usually made up of 12 persons. In

most states, the petit jury must reach a unanimous agreement on guilt, or the defendant is acquitted or mistrial declared.

2. Local Governments

Each of the 50 states has created units of local governments. Generally speaking, there are three kinds of local governments under a state government:

1) Country governments.

There are over 3,000 county governments. The sheriff is the chief law enforcement officer of the county, and is also an officer of the courts.

2) City, town, or village governments.

Most large cities have an elected mayor as head of the local government and an elected council to help him. This mayor-council system is the most popular kind of local government. The city-manager type is the second most popular kind of city government, in which an elected council hires a professional manager to administer and watch over the city business, while the elected council keeps the legislative power. Some smaller cities choose a commission form of government, in which five men are elected to take care of the city's economic and political affairs.

3) Local governments of school districts or districts set up for special purposes.

All these administrative areas are not systematically divided; in many places, counties and cities overlap, so do villages and towns, school districts and fire districts and water districts. As a result, a person may find himself living under many different government bodies, and having to pay many different kinds of taxes. **The US Bureau of the Census** has identified no less than 78,218 local governmental units in the United States.

3. Political Parties

The Constitution of the United States says nothing about the role of political parties, but two parties emerged immediately after the establishment of the first federal government in 1789: **the Federal Party** and **the Republican Party**. The Federal Party, headed by **Alexander Hamilton**, represented the interests of the commercial capitalists, who were in favor of a strong central government and the development of commerce and industry and tried to maintain friendly relations between the United States and England. The

Republican Party, later called the Democratic- Republican Party, led by **Thomas Jefferson**, represented the interests of the southern slave-owners and the middle classes in the North, who were in favor of a weak central government, the maintenance of state powers and the development of agriculture. And in foreign relations, they wanted to be friendly with France. These two parties broke up during the early part of the 19th century, after the "Second American War of Independence," a war fought between the United States and England from 1812 to 1814, in which the English took over the capital city Washington and burned down many of its public buildings, including the White House.

When the question of slavery was being debated in the middle of the 19th century, **the Democratic Party** (formed in 1828) wanted to keep the slave system, while the new Republican Party (formed in 1854) tried to abolish it. The Civil War broke out when **Abraham Lincoln**, the Republican candidate, was elected President in 1860. Since then the two parties have begun to control the political life of the country, and have taken terns at ruling the country. The two parties are both bourgeois in nature. Whichever party is in power, the same basic policies are followed. But during the election year, they attack each other fiercely, and the newspapers are full of news about the fight between the Elephant (symbol of the Republican Party) and the Donkey (symbol of the Democratic Party).

The two parties have almost the same basic organization. At the national level, there is **the national convention** and the national committee. At the state level conventions are held in a few states, while each state has a state committee. Below the state committee, there are county and city committees. At the bottom are **precincts**, which are small divisions of wards. In each precinct there is one election station. The party leader of a precinct is often called the precinct captain, whose job is to get the voters to vote for his own party on the Election Day.

National conventions of both parties are held every four years to choose the candidates for the Presidency and Vice Presidency of the United States, and decide the party's policy and program. These conventions are generally held in June, July or August of the election year.

The highest permanent organization of each party is the national

committee, made up of one man and one woman from each state and territory. The committee serves for four years from convention to convention. Its main task is to direct the election campaign and raise money for it. If the party wins the election, the committee sees to it that the "spoils" (public offices to be appointed) are properly distributed.

The leader of the national committee is the chairman, but he is not the real leader of the party. The real leader of the party in office is the President. The leader of the defeated party is the defeated presidential candidate, or the retired President, or both.

State committees of both parties direct election campaigns in the state. The party that has won a state election can distribute the public offices of the state government. Election campaigns of members of both houses of Congress were also organized by state committees of the two parties.

Generally, some men of a great influence in the area control state and local (county, city, ward, etc.) committees of each party. They often lead such committees for a long time though there is an election every two years.

Election campaigns are very expensive in the United States. It has been reported that the two parties spent over several hundred million dollars for the campaigns of a single election year. The two parties depend on monopoly capitalists for their election money.

4. Presidential Election

For over two hundred years, the presidential elections, which take place every four years, have been controlled and managed by two political parties: the Democratic Party and the Republican Party. The method of choosing a President is so complicated that even ordinary Americans find it puzzling. Generally speaking, there are five steps.

1) The Primary

This is the election of delegates to the national conventions of the two parties in each state from February to June of the Election Year.

2) The National Conventions

The national conventions of the two parties are held in July or August. Convention business usually begins with the discussion and acceptance of **the party platform**, a very general statement of the party's policy for both domestic and foreign affairs. The next business of the convention is to choose the presidential and vice presidential candidates.

3) The Election Campaign

The election campaign is conducted from September to November. In this period the **presidential candidates** of the two parties travel all over the country, trying to win the support of the voters in the election with the help of the machinery of their party. They use every possible means to influence the voter: radio and television talks, newspaper statements and interviews, public rallies, party dinners, newspaper advertising, and so on.

4) The Election Day

On the first Tuesday after the first Monday in November in an election year, voters cast ballots for President and Vice President. Some members of Congress and many state and local officials are also elected at the same time. Because of the use of voting machines and computers, the results of the elections are usually known by late evening of the same day.

The voters do not vote directly for the President and Vice President. They vote for **electors** who are named by the two parties, and the electors will, in turn, vote for the President and Vice President. As the electors will certainly vote for the presidential candidate of their own party, the winning candidate is already elected when the electors are chosen on the Election Day.

The number of electors in each state is equal to the total number of representatives and senators the state sends to Congress. So states with larger populations have more electoral votes, or more electors. The party that has won a majority of the popular votes (votes cast by the voters for the election of presidential electors) in a state on the Election Day will get all **electoral votes** (votes cast by the Presidential electors for the election of the President and the Vice-President) of that state. For example, New York State elects 45 electors. Each party names 45 candidates. If one party receives more than a half of the popular votes on the Election Day, all the candidates of the party will be the electors of that state, while the other party will have none. Thus, whether a party wins or loses in the few states that have the largest populations is often decisive to the result of the election.

5) Casting the Electoral Vote

The process is simply a formality. On the first Monday after the second Wednesday of December in an election year, the electors meet in the capital of

their own state and vote for President and Vice-President. Then they mail their votes to the president of the Senate. The votes are counted before a joint meeting of the two houses of Congress. The presidential and Vice-Presidential candidates who get the majority of the electoral votes are elected President and Vice-President. The newly elected President takes up office on January 20th of the next year.

If no candidate receives majority of the votes of the electors, the House of Representative will choose President from **the top three candidates** and the Senate will choose the Vice-President from the top two candidates. In this case, a state has only one vote. The candidate who receives the majority of votes will be elected.

The president of the United States is elected for a four-year term and may be re-elected. From 1789 to 1940 it was the custom that a President should not serve more than two terms. But in 1940 and 1944 **Franklin D. Roosevelt** was re-elected President for the third and fourth times. In 1951 Congress passed an amendment to the Constitution, limiting a President to two terms or to ten years successively in office. According to the Constitution of the United States, if a President dies or resigns or is removed from office before the end of his term, the Vice-President succeeds him.

The President of the United States must be a native-born citizen at least 35 years old. His salary is $200,000 a year, and he also gets an extra $50,000 for expenses; but he must pay **income tax** on the whole amount. He gets up to $100,000, tax free, for travel and entertaining, and is provided a home and extensive office space at the White House.

Notes

1. Nebraska 内布拉斯加
2. governor 州长
3. the National Guard 国民警卫队
4. grand jury 大陪审团
5. petit jury 小陪审团
6. The US Bureau of the Census 美国人口普查局
7. the Federal Party 联邦党
8. the Republican Party 共和党，亦称“反联邦党”（Anti-Federalists），成立于1854年。

9. Alexander Hamilton　亚历山大·汉密尔顿，美国第一任财政部长。
10. Thomas Jefferson　托马斯·杰斐逊(1743～1826)，于1801～1809年任美国第三任总统。
11. the Democratic Party　民主党，成立于1828年。
12. Abraham Lincoln　亚伯拉罕·林肯，于1861～1865年任美国第16任总统。
13. the national convention　全国代表大会
14. precincts　选区
15. the Primary　预选阶段
16. the National Conventions　(两党分别召开)全国代表大会阶段
17. the party platform　党的竞选纲领
18. the Election Campaign　竞选阶段
19. presidential candidate　总统候选人，由各党提名。
20. the Election Day　大选日，定为大选年11月份的第一个星期一后的第一个星期二。
21. elector　总统选举人，各州总统选举人数目与该州在国会参众两院的议员人数等同，由该州大选中获胜的政党(即获得多数普通选票的政党)的党员充任。
22. electoral vote　总统选举人所投的选总统的票
23. Casting the Electoral Vote　总统选举人投票选总统
24. the top three candidates　得票最多的三位候选人
25. Franklin D. Roosevelt　富兰克林·D·罗斯福(1882～1945)，1933～1945年任美国第32任统。
26. income tax　所得税

Questions for Discussion

1. What does a state constitution usually include?
2. Is the state government parallel to the federal pattern? In what ways?
3. Tell what you know about the local governments under the state government.
4. Describe the basic organization of the two principal parties in the United States.

5. How do Americans choose their President and Vice President?
6. Why is it said that whether a party wins or loses in the few states which have the largest populations is often decisive to the result of the election?
7. How are the President and Vice President of the United States chosen if no candidate receives a majority of the votes of the electors?
8. What is the relationship between the President and the Vice President of the United States?

Exercises

Ⅰ. Choose the correct answer and circle the letter before it.

1. ________ is the most important part of a state government.
   A. The executive　　B. The legislature
   C. The Judicial　　D. The governor
2. The state legislature usually consists of two houses except the state of ________.
   A. North Dakota　　B. South Dakota
   C. Nebraska　　D. Oklahoma
3. The chief executive of a state is the ________.
   A. governor　　B. sheriff
   C. Supreme Court　　D. council
4. Judges of state courts are usually ________.
   A. appointed officials　　B. elected officials
   C. hired officials　　D. life officials
5. The most popular kind of city government in the United States is the ________ system.
   A. city-manager　　B. city-council
   C. mayor-council　　D. mayor-manager
6. The Federal Party was led by ________.
   A. George Washington　　B. Alexander Hamilton
   C. Thomas Jefferson　　D. James Madison
7. The Federal Party was in favor of ________.

A. a weak central government

B. the maintenance of state powers

C. the development of agriculture

D. friendly relations with England

8. Two political parties emerged in the middle of the 19th century United States over the issue of ________.

A. slavery

B. the Constitution

C. admission of new states

D. the economic development

9. The party leader of a precinct is often called the precinct ________.

A. secretary B. captain C. officer D. chairman

10. The highest permanent organization of each party is the national ________.

A. convention B. committee

C. Congress D. campaign

11. The General Election in the United States is held every ________ years.

A. three B. four C. five D. six

12. The national conventions of the two parties usually begin with the discussion and acceptance of the ________.

A. party candidates

B. party policy for domestic affairs

C. party platform

D. strategies of the election campaign

13. The US Election Day is set on ________.

A. the first Tuesday after the first Monday in October

B. the first Tuesday after the first Monday in November

C. the first Monday after the first Tuesday in November

D. the fist Monday after the first Tuesday in October

14. The number of electors in each state is equal to the total number of ________ the state sends to congress.

A. Representatives B. Senators

C. Congressmen D. popular votes

15. The newly elected President takes up office on ________.
    A. January 10th
    B. January 20th of the next year
    C. March 10th
    D. April 20th of the next year

Ⅱ. Fill in the following blanks with proper words or expressions.

1. Like the federal government, a state government is made up of ________ branches.
2. The ________ is the most important part of a state government. It usually consists of ________ houses.
3. The chief executive of a state is the ________, elected by ________ vote. He or she is the commander of the ________ of the state.
4. The state court system begins with purely local ________, followed by a series of intermediate ________, then by appellate courts and finally by the state's ________ court.
5. The two types of juries utilized in the US are the ________ jury and the ________ jury. The decision for a trial is made by the ________ jury, while the ________ jury decides guilt or innocence.
6. The three kinds of local governments under a state government are ________ governments, city, town, or ________ governments and local governments of districts set up for special ________.
7. The two political parties that emerged in 1789 were the ________ Party and the ________ Party. They both broke up during the early part of the ________ th century.
8. The two parties that have taken turns at ruling the US since the middle of the 19th century are the ______ Party (formed in 1828) and the ______ Party (formed in 1854).
9. National conventions of the two parties are held every ________ years to choose the ________ and ________ candidates and decide the party ________.
10. The national committees of the two parties serve from convention to convention to direct the ________ and raise ________ for it.
11. The two parties depend on ________ for their election money.
12. At the primary stage of the general election, the voters elect ________

to the national conventions of the two parties in each state.

13. The convention business usually begins with the discussion and acceptance of the party ________.
14. The American voters do not vote directly for the President but vote for presidential ________.
15. The number of electors of each state is equal to the total number of ________ and ________ that the state sends to ________.
16. The party that wins a ________ of the popular votes in the state on the Election Day will get all the electoral votes of that state.
17. The Presidential candidate who gets the majority of the ________ votes is elected President of the United States.
18. If no candidate receives a majority of the votes of the electors, the ________ chooses the President and the ________ chooses the Vice-President.
19. In 1951 Congress passed an amendment to the Constitution to limit a president to ________ terms or to ________ years successively in office.
20. If a President dies or resigns or is removed from office, ________ succeeds him.

Ⅲ. Explain the following in English.

1. the grand jury and the petit jury
2. the mayor-council system of city government
3. the city-manager type of local government
4. the Federal Party
5. the Democratic-Republican Party
6. the "Second American War of Independence"
7. popular vote
8. electoral vote
9. party platform
10. the Election Day

Lesson 16 History: The Early Colonization

Major Events

1492 Columbus discovered the New World.
1497 Amerigo Vespucci sailed for the New World.
1606 the Virginia Company of Plymouth and the Virginia Company of London were formed.
1607 Jamestown was set up.
1620 Puritans founded Plymouth.
1623 The Dutch founded New Netherlands.
1634 The English set up Maryland.
1646 The English conquered the Dutch settlement.
1682 Pennsylvania was set up.
1733 Georgia was set up.

Main Contents

1. The American Indians

The earliest inhabitants in North and South Americas were the **American Indians**, who had lived and labored there for thousands of years before Christopher Columbus, an Italian navigator, discovered the New World in 1492. Some scientists believe that they had come over from Asia about 25,000 years ago when Asia and North America, separated by **the Bering Strait** today, were tied together by a land bridge and it was possible to walk from Asia to America because much ocean water was frozen in glaciers and the sea level was lower than it is today. The grass-eating animals were among the first to leave Asia, followed by flesh-eating animals, and thus, in search of their food supply, the hunters tracked the animals across northern Alaska into Canada and south along **the Mackenzie River**. They then followed the animals south along the eastern edge of the Rocky Mountains, and gradually spread all over North and South Americas. For these early immigrants America was no melting pot. The American Indians were divided into hundreds of tribes, enormously varied in physical appearance, language and civilization. Some tribes made their living by hunting, others by fishing, herding, farming or gathering rye seeds. Later, the sea covered the land bridge from Asia to America and separated the two Americas from the rest of the world. The Indians and the people of the rest of the world knew little about each other until the New World was discovered in 1492.

2. The Discovery of the New World

The fifteenth century saw great changes in Europe. A feudalist society was finally established in Britain. The bourgeoisie was just beginning to grow and came up to the historical stage in Europe. This was the time in history when the growing bourgeoisie began to look for new markets, and it was an age of discovery for new lands.

Influenced by **Marco Polo's** famous travel book, in which China, India and other countries were described to be very rich in gold and jewelry, kings, lords and merchants in Western Europe were eager to get hold of the treasures from the east. But at that time going by land was both expensive and dangerous and so they tried to explore sea routes to **the Far East**.

An Italian navigator named **Christopher Columbus** believed that the earth was round and that he could reach the Far East by sailing westward. He offered his services to **Queen Isabella** of Spain, who decided to take a chance and persuaded her husband **Ferdinand Ⅱ** to pay for an expedition of three ships and give Columbus authority, under Spain, over any lands he might discover on the way.

On August 3rd, 1492, Columbus started sailing from the harbor at **Palos**, Spain, with 87 sailors in three ships. They sailed westward. Columbus, their admiral, expected to find a new route to India, had with him a compass, an astrolabe, a globe and some maps. He also carried books and charts. By using a sandglass he figured his speed at about four miles an hour. Columbus kept a journal (daily record) of the voyage. The crews on the three ships become more frightened as they sailed on. Columbus feared they might turn back to

their homeland.

Finally after many weeks of sailing, Columbus and his men saw flocks of birds, then floating logs, then plants and trees. At last on October 12, 1492, a beautiful island stretched before them. Columbus stepped ashore, thanked God for their safe arrival and took possession of the land in the name of the King and Queen of Spain.

The people Columbus met in the new land were a new race, copper-colored, strongly built, with straight black hair. Their houses were simple and crude and they used bows and arrows as weapons. Columbus called them Indians because he then believed the islands to which he had come to be off the coast of India.

Columbus and his men spent many days sailing around the nearby islands. They reached Cuba and **the Island of Hispaniola**.

On March 15, 1493, Columbus returned to Spain, Isabella and Ferdinand received him warmly. Columbus brought with him ten Indians, some parrots, and other birds and animals they had captured.

Columbus eagerly told the king and the queen of the beautiful land he had discovered. They, too, thought he had found an all-water route to India.

But people gradually doubted if the land was real India, for they did not find as much gold, perfume or spices as they had imagined or expected previously. On the other hand, the natives were very primitive, not a bit so rich and advanced as they had thought. So, after Columbus brought back to Europe news of the new route to the "East," many other sailors followed him. Among them was **Amerigo Vespucci**, an Italian sailor, who sailed for the new continent in 1497. He wrote lots of reports back and proved it a big continent, and indicated that India could be reached by crossing another ocean. In 1507, a German professor published a map of the New World on the basis of Amerigo's voyage and called it America. The continent was thus named after the explorer Amerigo Vespucci.

Ferdinand Magellan, a Portuguese navigator, set out from Spain in 1519. Like Columbus, he hoped to reach India by sailing west. After crossing the Atlantic, he sailed along the coast of South America and around the southern tip of the continent and on to the broad Pacific Ocean. Two of Magellan's ships were able to go on northwest across the unknown Pacific. They reached the

Philippines where the natives killed Magellan. At last only one of his ships was able to keep going. It finally sailed around Africa and on to Spain, the country from which it had started. The long voyage took three years, and proved that India could be reached by sailing west.

What Columbus and those who followed him "discovered" and explored was a great and rich world. North and South Americas together made up an area almost as large as Africa and Europe combined. In America there were all those resources necessary for agricultural and industrial development: fertile land, seas full of fish, great forests, all the essential metals and minerals, huge coal and oil supplies, and rivers rich in water-power.

The discovery of this rich new world was one of the great events of world history. As Karl Marx and Engels say in ***The Manifesto of the Communist Party***, it "opened up fresh ground for the rising bourgeoisie." It helped to undermine feudalism and speed up the growth of capitalism in Europe.

3. The Colonization in North America

The ruling classes of Europe fell upon this rich world greedily. Only fifty years after Columbus's first voyage had the Spanish and Portuguese already overrun the vast land of what is today called Latin America. For about a hundred years after Columbus's crossing of the Atlantic, only explorers and traders visited North America. But at the beginning of the 17th century, European settlers began to arrive. Portugal set up colonies in Brazil, while Spain explored and colonized much of South America and Mexico.

The settling of the present-day United States and Canada by the English and French went more slowly. The French built settlement along the St. Lawrence River and in the Great Lakes region. They founded Montreal and **Quebec** in Canada. As they traveled down the Mississippi River, they started **the City of St. Louis**, and farther down, the city of **New Orleans**.

Although English explorers made attempts to settle North America, the 16th century closed without any English colony there. But, impelled by greed and **Chauvinism**, the attempts to colonize the New World never ceased. In 1606 a number of English noblemen, gentlemen and merchants joined to petition the King, James I, for authority to establish colonies in America. The joint-stock company was chosen as a means of undertaking large and dangerous enterprises without risking financial ruin. It was designed for participants to profit or

suffer in proportion to the number of shares they purchased. The king gave the two groups of petitioners a charter incorporating two companies—**the Virginia Company of Plymouth** by the group from Plymouth and **the Virginia Company of London** by the group from London—for the colonization of North America. The companies planned to finance the emigration of settlers who would agree to give up the fruits of their labors to the investors for the first seven, or ten, or even fifteen years; after that the settlers could enrich themselves. Such settlers were called **indentured servants.** Those who paid their own passage were freemen. The Plymouth group founded a colony survived only one winter. The Virginia Company of London sent over its first settlers in December 1606. In May 1607 they sailed up a river they called the James and landed on a peninsula they called **Jamestown**, where they set up the first permanent colony. This region was soon to develop a flourishing economy from its tobacco crop, which found a ready market in England. By 1620, when women were recruited in England to come to Virginia to marry and make their homes, great plantations had already risen along **the James River**, and the population had increased to a thousand settlers.

In 1620 the first group of **Puritans** arrived from England. They were so called because they represented the rising bourgeoisie of the time and wished to "purify" the Church of England, the established church, with the king as its head. In order to escape from religious persecution at home, a group of Puritans set sail for America on a ship called the ***Mayflower***. This group of "pilgrims," as they called themselves, went to the New World in search of religious freedom. They began their journey in September with 102 men, women and children on board. Before they landed, they signed an agreement called the ***Mayflower Compact***, in which they promised to obey the rules and laws of the colony. This was the worst season of the year for crossing the Atlantic. The crossing was rough, and many people died on the ship. It took the Mayflower 65 days to reach Cape Cod, Massachusetts. They had sailed to America under the auspices of the London (Virginia) Company and were intended for settlement in Virginia, but their ship made its landfall far to the north. After some weeks of exploring, the colonists decided not to make the trip to Virginia but to remain where they were. They chose the area near **Plymouth** harbor as a site for their colony and put up simple houses of logs.

They called their small village Plymouth after the port in southwest England from which they had sailed. Later more Puritans arrived and altogether they set up four colonies, which they called collectively New England.

The pilgrims were not well prepared for living in such a wild place. During their first winter in the new world, they suffered a great deal. Poor food, hard work, epidemic diseases and bitterly cold weather killed almost half of them.

At first the American Indians treated the newcomers well on the whole. They helped them in many ways. They introduced them to Indian foods, utensils, clothing and means of transportation, and guided them through the wild forests on Indian paths. All this made it possible for the settlers to live in their strange new homes.

By the mid-18th century practically the whole of North America had been divided out among the European colonialists. Most of the east coast south of the St. Lawrence River, north of Florida and stretching inland as far as the Appalachians in the west was in the hands of the British. Along this stretch of coast were thirteen British colonies. **Connecticut**, **Rhode Island and New Hampshire** were founded by people from both Massachusetts and England. Some came for religious freedom, others wanted to govern themselves. **Maryland** was founded in 1634 by people from England seeking religious freedom. It was to be a refuge for Catholics who were unhappy in England. **North Carolina and South Carolina** were founded by colonists from **Virginia**. The North and South Carolinas were owned by proprietors, men who were friends of the King of England. The colonists were not happy because they wanted to help make their own laws instead of being governed by England. **Delaware** was settled by people from Sweden and was soon taken over by the Dutch governor of **New Netherland**. New Netherland, founded by the Dutch in 1613, finally became the English colony called New York. Pennsylvania was set up by a group of people from England called Quakers headed by William Penn in 1682. The Quakers wanted to worship God in their own way and have a voice in their own government. **Georgia** was set up in 1733 by Colonel **James Oglethorpe** to provide homes for poor people from England who, because they could not pay their debts, had been thrown into prison.

4. The Thirteen British Colonies

By the time when Georgia was set up, the thirteen British colonies had had a population of 629,000. By 1750 it increased to 1,171,000. In terms of their political administration, the thirteen colonies can be divided into three types: the proprietary colonies, which belonged to a person or a group of persons; the Royal colonies, those controlled directly by the King of England and the English government; and self-governing colonies, which were ruled by the colonists living in them. Most of the proprietary colonies soon became royal ones. Only Connecticut and Rhode Island were self-governing colonies.

Later, owing to geographical, economic and social factors, the thirteen colonies developed in different directions.

1) The New England Colonies (Massachusetts, New Hampshire, Connecticut and Rhode Island) became a center for lumbering, shipping and fishing. With generally thin, stony soil, relatively little level land, short summers, and long winters, New England was inferior farm country. So the New Englanders turned to other pursuits. They harnessed waterpower and established gristmills and sawmills. Good stands of timber encouraged shipbuilding. Excellent harbors promoted trade, and the sea became a source of great wealth. In Massachusetts, the cod industry alone quickly furnished a basis for prosperity. From the middle of the 17th century onward, it grew prosperous, and Boston became one of America's greatest ports.

2) The Central Colonies (New York, **New Jersey**, **Pennsylvania**, Delaware and **Maryland**) became a region of small farms. Society in these colonies was far more varied, cosmopolitan, and tolerant than New England. The Quakers' talent for successful business enterprise soon made Philadelphia one of the thriving centers of colonial America. Mixed, as were the people in Pennsylvania, it was in New York that the polyglot nature of America was best illustrated. By 1646, in which the Dutch settlement was taken by conquest, the population along the Hudson River included Dutch, **Flemish**, **Walloons**, French, Danes, Norwegians, Swedes, English, Scots, Irish, Germans, Poles, **Bohemians**, Portuguese and Italians. In rich valleys great estates flourished. Cattle and sheep, horses and pigs were raised, and tobacco and flax planted.

3) The Southern Colonies (Virginia, North and South Carolinas and

Georgia) developed a plantation system with the exploitation of slave labor. The discovery of a method of curing Virginia tobacco to make it palatable to the European taste in 1612 revolutionized the economy of Virginia. The first shipment of this tobacco reached London in 1614, and within a decade it had become Virginia's chief source of revenue. By the late 17th and early 18th centuries, the southern planters, supported by slave labor, held most of the political power and the best land, built great houses, adopted an aristocratic way of life, and kept in touch with the world of culture overseas. In terms of the political and social system, the southern colonies remained a society in which slavery was combined with feudalism.

Society in the thirteen British colonies was like a **pyramid**, the top of which was made up of foreign merchants and landlords, and the base refugees from Europe, black slaves from Africa and the American Indians. The Africans were out-and-out slaves, who were sold like animals. As for the Indians, they would not put up with slavery. If any Indian were enslaved, his fellow tribe members would fight to free him. So the colonialists soon gave up the attempt to use them as slave labor. Instead they seized the land of the Indians and drove them away or kill them.

Slaves, indentured servants and workers who found themselves unable to bear their conditions used to run away to the frontier where they cleared the forests and opened up farms of their own. Uprisings or rebellions often took place against the royal government of the colonies.

Notes

1. American Indian 美洲印第安人
2. the Bering Strait 白令海峡
3. the Mackenzie River 马更些河
4. Marco Polo 马可·波罗
5. the Far East 远东
6. Christopher Columbus 克里斯托弗·哥伦布
7. Queen Isabella （西班牙）伊莎白拉女王
8. Ferdinand Ⅱ 斐迪南二世
9. Palos 帕拉斯，西班牙港口
10. the Island of Hispaniola 西斯班尼拉岛
11. Amerigo Vespucci 亚迈里哥·维斯普奇

12. Ferdinand Magellan　菲迪南德·麦哲伦
13. *The Manifesto of the Communist Party*　《共产党宣言》
14. Quebec　魁北克
15. the City of St. Louis　圣路易斯城
16. New Orleans　新奥尔良，美国南方城市，位于密西西比河口。
17. Chauvinism　沙文主义
18. the Virginia Company of Plymouth　普利茅斯的弗吉尼亚公司
19. the Virginia Company of London　伦敦的弗吉尼亚公司
20. indentured servant　契约仆人，曾译"契约奴"。
21. Jamestown　詹姆士城
22. the James River　詹姆士河
23. Puritan　清教徒
24. *Mayflower*　五月花号船
25. *Mayflower Compact*　五月花公约
26. Plymouth　普利茅斯，英国西南部港口。
27. Connecticut, Rhode Island and New Hampshire　康涅狄格、罗德岛和新罕布什尔，各为英国北美13块殖民地之一。
28. Maryland　马里兰，英国北美13块殖民地之一。
29. North Carolina and South Carolina　北卡罗来纳和南卡罗来纳，各为英国北美13块殖民地之一。
30. Virginia　弗吉尼亚，英国北美13块殖民地之一。
31. Delaware　特拉华，英国北美13块殖民地之一。
32. New Netherland　新尼德兰，1613～1664年，荷兰人在哈得逊河和特拉华河边建立的殖民地，1664年为英国人夺得。
33. Georgia　佐治亚，英国北美13块殖民地之一。
34. James Oglethorpe　詹姆士·欧格绍普（1696～1785），英国将军，美国佐治亚之建设者。
35. New Jersey　新泽西，英国北美13块殖民地之一。
36. Pennsylvania　宾夕法尼亚，英国北美13块殖民地之一。
37. Maryland　马里兰，英国北美13块殖民地之一。
38. Flemish　佛兰德人
39. Walloon　瓦龙人
40. Bohemian　波希米亚人
41. pyramid　金字塔

Questions for Discussion

1. How did Columbus discover the New World?
2. Who was the New World named after?
3. Why is it said that the world discovered by Columbus was a great and rich world?
4. Give a brief account of the colonization in North America in the 17th century and early 18th century.
5. Who were Puritans? Which of the 13 colonies did Puritans set up?
6. How did the American Indians at first treat the newcomers on the whole?
7. What were the three types of the English colonies in terms of their political administration?
8. Give a brief account of the New England colonies, the central colonies and the southern colonies in terms of their economy.
9. Describe the society of the thirteen British colonies.
10. How did the British colonists treat the American Indians?

Exercises

Ⅰ. Choose the correct answer and circle the letter before it.

1. Christopher Columbus was a(n) ________ navigator.
   A. English B. French C. Italian D. Spanish
2. The New World discovered by Columbus was named after ________.
   A. Amerigo Vespucci B. Christopher Columbus
   C. Ferdinand Magellan D. Marco Polo
3. The earliest British settlement on North America was ________.
   A. Plymouth B. Jamestown
   C. Quebec D. St. Louis
4. The Puritans' first settlement on North America was ________.
   A. Jamestown B. Plymouth

C. New Orleans　　D. Virginia

5. Which of the following was NOT a New England colony?

A. Connecticut　　B. New Hampshire

C. Massachusetts　　D. Maryland

6. ________ was the colony set up by Colonel James Oglethorpe in 1733.

A. North Carolina　　B. South Carolina

C. Georgia　　D. Virginia

7. In 1682, a group of ________ headed by William Penn set up the colony of Pennsylvania.

A. Puritans　　B. Methodists

C. Quakers　　D. Prisoners

8. Delaware was first settled by people from ________.

A. Denmark　　B. Sweden

C. Holland　　D. England

9. Of the 13 British colonies only ________ were self-governing colonies.

A. Massachusetts and Connecticut

B. Connecticut and Rhode Island

C. Massachusetts and Rhode Island

D. New Hampshire and Connecticut

10. Which of the following expressions is NOT for the description of the Central Colonies?

A. Inferior farm country.

B. A region of small farms.

C. Cosmopolitan.

D. Tolerant in religion.

11. The Southern Colonies developed a ________ system with the exploitation of slave labor.

A. industrial　　B. small farm

C. plantation　　D. slavery

12. In the 13 colonies, ________ people were enslaved.

A. the native　　B. the Black

C. the indentured servants　D. the Dutch

Ⅱ. Fill in the following blanks with proper words or expressions.

1. The earliest inhabitants in America were ________, who had come over

from ________ by crossing the land bridge across the present ________ Strait.

2. Influenced by ________ 's famous travel book, kings, lords and merchants in Western Europe were eager to find sea routes to the Far East.
3. Christopher Columbus discovered the New World in the year of ________. He called the natives Indians because he believed the island to which he had come were off the coast of ________.
4. America was named after ________.
5. In the early colonization of Americas, Portugal set up colonies in ________, while Spain explored and colonized much of ________ and ________. The French built settlements along the ________ River and in the ________ region.
6. The two joint-stock companies set up in England in 1606 were: ________ and ________.
7. The first English colony set up in May 1607 was called ________.
8. In 1620 a group of ________ sailed for America on a ship called the *Mayflower*. They called themselves ________. Together with those who arrived later, they set up four colonies, which they called ________.
9. In terms of their political administration, the thirteen British colonies can be divided into three types: the ________ colonies, the ________ colonies and the ________ colonies.
10. The New England colonies became a center for ________, ________ and fishing. The central colonies became a region of ________. And the southern colonies developed a ________ system with the exploitation of ________ labor.

Ⅲ. Match the names of the British colonies in Column A with the corresponding people who founded them in Column B.

	Column A	Column B
1. ____	Massachusetts	a. Catholics
2. ____	Maryland	b. colonists from Virginia
3. ____	Carolinas	c. Puritans
4. ____	Pennsylvania	d. colonists from Massachusetts

5. ____ Connecticut e. Quakers

Ⅳ. Explain the following in English.

1. American Indian
2. Christopher Columbus
3. Ferdinand Magellan
4. Indentured Servant
5. Mayflower Compact
6. Jamestown
7. New England
8. Proprietary Colonies
9. Royal Colonies
10. self-governing colonies

Lesson 17 History: American Revolution

Major Events

1689—1697	King William's War
1702—1713	Queen Anne's War
1744—1748	King George's War
1756—1763	the French and Indian War
1764	the passage of the Sugar Act
1765	the passage of the Quartering Act and the Stamp Act
1765	The Stamp Act Congress was held.
1770	"Boston Massacre"
1772	The Committees of Correspondence were set up.
1773	"Boston Tea Party"
1774	the First Continental Congress
1775	the battle at Lexington and Concord and the Second Continental Congress
1776	The Declaration of Independence was adopted.
1777	the battle at Saratoga
1781	the battle at Yorktown
1783	the peace treaty in Paris
1786	Daniel Shays' Uprising
1787	the Constitutional Convention in Philadelphia
1789	the establishment of the first federal government

Main Contents

1. Toward Independence

1) The French and Indian War

In the 17th century, England found itself fighting against France for world leadership in many parts of the world after having defeated **the Spanish Armada** in 1588 and taken the place of Spain as a world power. Its contest with France for the North American Continent never ceased. As early as 1613, local clashes occurred between English and French colonists. Eventually, three wars were fought between the English and the French from 1689 to 1748, namely, **King William's War** (1689—1697), **Queen Anne's War** (1702—1713) and **King George's War** (1744—1748), which corresponded respectively to **War of the League of Augsburg**, **War of the Spanish Succession** and **War of the Austrian Succession** in Europe.

In the 1750s, the conflict was brought to a final phase. An armed clash in 1754 between Virginian militiamen under the command of George Washington and a band of French regulars ushered in the French and Indian War (1756—1763), which paralleled to the wider **"Seven Years' War."** It began in the Ohio Valley, a large territory claimed by both the French and the English, and was fought by the English against the French and their Indian allies.

The war went badly for England till 1757. The English managed to advance in both Canada and the Ohio Valley in 1758, and in the following year they took over the important French city of Quebec. Finally the English won the war. A peace treaty was signed in Paris in 1763, in which the French were forced to agree to these terms: (1) France ceded to England all her Canadian lands; (2) France ceded to England all her lands east of the Mississippi River, except for New Orleans; and (3) France gave New Orleans and all her lands west of the Mississippi River to Spain.

As a result of the War, France ceased to be a major power in North America, but England became an important world power. At the same time, the English colonists no longer faced the danger of French enemies and the Indian raids. So they wanted more freedom in politics, trade and commerce.

Meanwhile, England wanted more money and more taxes levied on the colonists because the mother country found herself badly in need of money as a result of the long war. It was clear that the desire of England to levy more taxes on the colonies and the desire of the colonists to have more right made the colonies and their mother country pull in different directions.

2) The Enlightenment

In the 18th century, along with the development of science, people in Europe began to believe that the universe created by God was guided by natural laws, which were left to be discovered and enforced by man.

John Locke, an English materialist philosopher, furnished the century with a theory about reason. Locke, rejecting innate knowledge, believed that man's knowledge was acquired from the experience of five senses, from observation and experiment, and from the reflection by the mind. Civil government was instituted by mutual agreement for the purpose of enforcing natural laws. The most important natural law was that no man should take away the life, liberty, or property of another. The purpose to establish a government is to protect these natural laws. A government that failed to protect life, liberty, and property lost its reason for existence and deserved being altered or overthrown by the people it governed.

Reason led Locke to condemn absolute government and led the bourgeoisie to advocate free trade, free speech, and free thought. This confidence in reason, which animated the European philosophers of the 18th century, came to be known as the Enlightenment.

The Enlightenment in Europe had a wide and profound influence in America. College students learned **Newton**'s physics and Locke's psychology. Politicians cited Locke to support their arguments. Intellectuals formed clubs to discuss philosophy. As a son of the Enlightenment, **Benjamin Franklin** played an important role in exemplifying the Enlightenment to his countrymen. The Enlightenment sang the praises of intellectual freedom, Franklin, as a printer and writer, defended his right to publish and write what he pleased. The Enlightenment encouraged scientific experiment; Franklin made significant observations on a wide variety of scientific subjects. His achievements in both science and literature won him world fame.

The Enlightenment in America provided the colonists with a theoretical and philosophical weapon against the British rule and marked the formation and maturity of the new nation, which was bound to be independent of its mother country.

3) The British Mercantilist Policy and the Colonists' Resistance

In an attempt to solve its economic problems and achieve economic superiority over its European rivals, the British government practiced **the policy of mercantilism** in the colonies after the end of French and Indian War. According to this policy, the colonies existed to enrich the mother country by providing England with raw materials and buying back manufactured goods, which were much more expensive than raw materials. The result of this policy was that the colonies usually wound up owing money to the mother country owing to an unfavorable balance of trade. By practicing such a policy, the British ruling class tried to monopolize the markets in the colonies, to hold back the development of manufacturing there, and to control everything and keep all profits for themselves. For example, the British government now strictly enforced **the Navigation Acts**, one of which provided that only British-owned ships could carry colonial goods to British possessions. This Act hurt colonial merchants, who had to pay higher rates for using British ships than they might pay to foreign ship-owners. Another of the Navigation Acts was one that enumerated certain articles that could be exported only to England. These articles included sugar, tobacco, wood, cotton and naval supplies. This Act aided the British merchants who needed raw materials, but deprived the colonists of the right to sell these raw materials for a better price to other nations.

Having triumphed over France, British overseas territories expanded enormously; in North America alone, they had more than doubled. Therefore, the British government needed huge sums of money and increased personnel to support the growing empire. Obviously, the "old colonial system" embodied in the Navigation Acts and in the Act of 1696 was inadequate. New measures had to be taken.

To put a new system into effect, to tighten control over the colonies, one of the first things attempted by the British was the royal proclamation in 1763, which reserved all the western territory between the Alleghenies, the Floridas, the Mississippi, and Quebec for the use of the Indians; for the British government feared that the colonist farmers migrating into the new lands would provoke a series of Indian wars.

More serious in the repercussions of the new system was the new financial policy of the British government. The first step was the passage of **the Sugar Act** of 1764, under which all molasses entering the colonies from lands other than the British **West Indies** would be taxed. Later in the same year, the Parliament enacted a **Currency Act** to prevent the colonies from making their paper money legal tender. To the colonists, equally objectionable was **the Quartering Act** of 1765, which required colonies to provide quarters for the royal troops. Although opposition from the colonists to these acts was strong, the British Parliament passed **the Stamp Act** of 1765, which required that a stamp, purchased from the British government, be placed on all legal documents, newspapers and other printed materials. This Act aroused the hostility of the most powerful and articulate groups in the population. Soon leading merchants organized for resistance and formed non-importation associations. Prominent men organized as **"Sons of Liberty,"** and political opposition soon flared into rebellion. What was more significant was that delegates from the assemblies of nine colonies met at New York in October 1765 (**the Stamp Act Congress**) to discuss the Stamp Act menace and to concert their opposition to the Parliamentary taxes. The reaction from the colonies was so violent that the British government was forced to repeal the Act, but the British government issued the **Declaratory Act**, declaring that the government had the right to pass any economic laws it desired.

After the failure of the program of internal taxation, the British government developed a system of **external taxation** to levy taxes on items that were shipped into the colonies. The shipper would pay such taxes first, and then they would add them to the price of the item. In this way the colonists had to pay the taxes in an indirect way. The items on which the taxes were levied were glass, paper, paint, lead, and tea. However, the colonists wanted no taxes at all, neither internal nor external.

In order to enforce tax laws and stop the heavy smuggling going on there, the British issued special search warrants, called **writs of assistance**, which allowed British officers to search anywhere at any time. To enforce the laws, thousands of British soldiers were sent to restrict the colonists' political

activities. People in the colonies grew more and more dissatisfied with their English rulers. On March 5, 1770, violence broke out in Boston. A group of about fifty Boston citizens were jeering at the British soldiers and tempers ran high. Some of them threw snowballs with stones inside at the British soldiers. As the tension mounted, the soldiers fired at the crowd and killed five men. This incident came to be known as the **"Boston Massacre."**

Soon after the Boston massacre, the British repealed almost all the Acts. Only the tax on tea was kept as the symbol of the British right to levy taxes. Nevertheless, the political and economic conflicts between the colonies and their mother country were far from cease. Protests of the colonists were organized and led by such men as **Samuel Adams**, **John Dickinson** and Benjamin Franklin. They organized protest meetings, boycotts and other forms of action against the English. By 1772, Samuel Adams had organized **the Committees of Correspondence**, which made possible the cooperation of colonists all over the thirteen colonies.

In 1773, the British government passed the **Tea Act**, which permitted the British East India Company to sell tea directly to its agents in the colonies. The dumping of the British tea in the colonies would be ruinous to some colonial merchants who were not agents of the company and to some tea smugglers. This Act made many merchants angrier than ever with the British. On December 16, 1773, a group of Boston citizens, who disguised themselves as Indians, boarded three British ships in the harbor and tossed a cargo of tea worth £17,000 overboard. This was the famous **"Boston Tea Party."**

Faced now with a crisis, the British Parliament decided to demonstrate its authority to control the colonies; it responded with new laws in 1774, which the colonists immediately dubbed **the Intolerable Acts**. The first one, **the Boston Port Act**, ordered the Boston port closed to shipping until the colonists made restitution for the tea. The **Massachusetts Government Act** required that the king should appoint the governor's council, and that the town meetings be held once a year except by permission of the governor. **The Administration of Justice Act** provided that any government or customs officer indicted for murder could be tried in England, beyond the control of local juries. A new Quartering Act authorized the quartering of troops within the town whenever their commanding officer thought it desirable. And **the Quebec Act**, though not a punitive measure, threatened to interfere with the westward movement and seemed to hem them in to the north and northwest by a Roman Catholic-dominated province. All these acts, instead of subduing Massachusetts, rallied her sister colonies to her aid. To coordinate action against the Intolerable Acts, an inter-colonial congress was organized.

In September 1774, fifty-five representatives from all the colonies except Georgia held a meeting in Philadelphia to talk about their troubles with their mother country. The meeting was called **the First Continental Congress.** As the majority of the representatives were capitalists or landowners, who still thought they could settle their quarrel with Britain by compromises, nothing important was done at the meeting. They only drew up a petition asking the King to grant self-government to the colonies. The motto of the colonies was "No taxation without representation." They agreed not to import any goods from England until England repealed all the unfair laws.

Neither Parliament nor King George listened to the petition of the First Continental Congress, Matters grew rapidly worse as England planned to send more soldiers to enforce the laws. The towns in the colonies began drilling fighters or "minutemen" and collecting guns and ammunition. Secret revolutionary organizations were set up, such as the Sons of Liberty. In Boston, political activity had almost wholly replaced trade.

General Thomas Gage, the then commanding officer of the garrison at Boston, was assigned there to enforce the laws. When he was informed that the colonial militia was assembling arms and ammunitions at the interior town of **Concord**, he decided, on instructions from the British government, to take offensive against the rebellious colonists. On April 19, 1775, Gage sent seven hundred British soldiers to Concord to capture the supply of arms reportedly stored there. Although the force got started in the dark of early morning, the whole countryside of Concord had been warned that the British soldiers were coming. A group of minutemen met the British at **Lexington**, where the first shots of the revolution were fired. The British marched on to Concord, where they met attacks again by the embattled colonists at North Bridge. When the British partly accomplished their purpose—they had burned a few gun carriages, they began their return march to Boston. All along the road, behind stone walls, hillocks, rocks, trees, and houses, militiamen from villages and

farms made targets of the bright red coats of the British soldiers. The British losses were three times as heavy as those sustained by the colonists.

2. Fight for Independence

1) The Second Continental Congress

The news of Lexington and Concord flew from one local community to another, from Maine to Georgia. Within 20 days, it evoked a common spirit of patriotism throughout the thirteen colonies. And immediately after the conflicts at Lexington, the Second Continental Congress was called in May 1775. Representatives from all the thirteen colonies met in Philadelphia to discuss the situation. One of the first decisions it made was to establish a regular army, with George Washington as commander-in-chief.

On July 4, 1776, the Second Continental Congress adopted **the Declaration of Independence**, which Marx calls the "first declaration of the rights of the individual." Thomas Jefferson, who, in spite of the fact that he was a slave-owner, became one of the outstanding spokesmen for bourgeois democracy, drew up the declaration. The main ideas of the Declaration of independence were that all men are created equal and have certain inalienable rights, among which are life, liberty, and the pursuit of happiness; that governments get their powers from the consent of those they govern; and that a government that does not live up to the purposes for which it was created can be abolished by the people. The Declaration also listed ways in which the colonists had been mistreated, so as to make the American Revolution sound reasonable.

2) The War of the American Revolution

The war did not go well for Americans at first, because the British army was the finest and strongest in the world. The British had a navy to control the sea and a highly-developed industry and commerce to keep the army well supplied, while the American army was composed mainly of farmers, craftsmen, and small traders, who were poorly trained and equipped. What is more, there was no strong central government to raise money to support the American army. As a result, they were constantly driven back. George Washington had taken Boston in May 1775, but then he had to move his army to New York. Later he was forced to withdraw from the city, too, with the British army following close behind. On Christmas Day, 1776, the Americans won a brilliant victory in **the battle of Trenton**, defeating enemy forces much

bigger than their own.

The victory at Trenton raised the spirits of the Americans, so the war went on. They won a great victory at **Saratoga** on October 17, 1777, which was a turning point of the war. But then the American army was still not strong enough to beat the British; it won some battles but lost others. Washington withdrew his army to **Valley Forge**, Pennsylvania, where, in spite of the bitter conditions, Washington went ahead with military training. Finally in 1781, after several more years of fighting with the aid of the French, the Americans won a decisive victory at **Yorktown**, Virginia. Then English army led by **General Cornwallis** was forced to surrender on October 19, 1781, and the war came to an end. A peace treaty was signed in Paris on September 3, 1783. England acknowledged the independence of the former thirteen colonies.

The American War of Independence was an event of great historic importance. By smashing the fetters of British rule, it gave the colonies their right to national independence and assured US capitalism of a free development. It was the first large-scale revolutionary movement of a colonial people against national oppression—for political and economic emancipation. The revolution shook the foundation of feudalism all over Europe. It directly led to the French Revolution in 1789 and some fifty years later, to the revolutions in the Spanish colonies in America.

3. The Constitutional Convention

The American Revolution was bourgeois in character. It did not solve the problem of land demanded by the laboring people. In addition, the heavy costs of the war were placed on their shoulders. There was great dissatisfaction among the people. No sooner had the war ended than a number of demonstrations and uprisings took place. The famous 1786 uprising took place in Massachusetts, where Daniel Shays led 1,200 men in an armed uprising.

The news of **Shays' Rebellion** came as a terror to the capitalists and the plantation owners, who thought the Confederation government provided by **the Articles of Confederation** (the Constitution of the thirteen colonies adopted in 1781) was too weak to protect their lives and property. In desperation, some of the leaders called for a meeting to see if some changes could be made.

In May 1787, **the Constitutional Convention** met in Philadelphia. When the convention met, it soon gave up the idea of changing the Articles of

Confederation. Instead it drew up a new constitution, for the purpose of setting up a strong central government. After four months of hard work, the Convention was finished. Wise, patriotic men such as George Washington and Benjamin Franklin had found ways to meet the many difficult problems of writing the Constitution. Another great leader, **James Madison**, did much work on the writing of the Constitution. For this he was known as the "Father of the Constitution." The Constitution was ratified in 1789. In 1791, the first ten Amendments to the Constitution, or **Bill of Rights**, were added. Among the more important rights guaranteed to the US citizens are freedom of religion, freedom of speech, freedom of the press, the right to assemble, and the right to petition for what a citizen may think is needed from the government.

After the Constitution was ratified, a President and Congress were elected under its provisions. George Washington was elected the first President of the United States and took office in 1789. He organized the first administration under the new Constitution.

Notes

1. the Spanish Armada 西班牙无敌舰队
2. King William's War 威廉王战争
3. Queen Anne's War 安妮女王战争
4. King George's War 乔治王战争
5. War of the League of Augsburg 奥格斯堡联盟战争
6. War of the Spanish Succession 西班牙王位继承战争
7. War of the Austrian Succession 奥地利王位继承战争
8. Seven Years' War 七年战争
9. the Enlightenment 启蒙运动
10. John Locke 约翰·洛克(1632～1704),英国唯物主义哲学家。
11. Newton 牛顿(1642～1727),英国科学家。
12. Benjamin Franklin 本杰明·富兰克林(1706～1790),美国政治家、剧作家和发明家。
13. the policy of mercantilism 重商主义政策
14. the Navigation Acts 航海条例
15. the Sugar Act 糖税法
16. West Indies 西印度群岛

17. Currency Act 货币法案
18. the Quartering Act 驻兵法案,亦译为“驻兵条例”。
19. the Stamp Act 印花税法
20. Sons of Liberty 自由之子社
21. the Stamp Act Congress 反印花税大会
22. the Declaratory Act 宣告令
23. external taxation 外部征税
24. writs of assistance 特别搜查令
25. Boston Massacre 波士顿屠杀案
26. Samuel Adams 塞缪尔·亚当斯(1722～1803),美国革命家。
27. John Dickinson 约翰·狄勤生
28. the Committees of Correspondence 通讯委员会
29. Tea Act 茶叶法案
30. “Boston Tea Party” 波士顿倾茶事件,亦译“波士顿茶党事件”。
31. the Intolerable Acts 不可容忍法案
32. the Boston Port Act 波士顿港口法案
33. the Massachusetts Government Act 马萨诸塞政府法案
34. the Administration of Justice Act 司法行政法案
35. the Quebec Act 魁北克法案
36. the First Continental Congress 第一次大陆会议
37. Concord 康科德
38. Lexington 莱克星顿
39. the Second Continental Congress 第二次大陆会议
40. the Declaration of Independence 独立宣言
41. the Battle of Trenton 特伦顿战役
42. Saratoga 萨拉托加
43. Valley Forge 富奇谷
44. Yorktown 约克镇
45. General Cornwallis 康沃利斯将军
46. Shays' Rebellion 谢司起义
47. the Articles of Confederation 邦联条例
48. the Constitutional Convention 制宪会议
49. James Madison 詹姆斯·麦迪逊(1751～1836),于1809～1817年任美国第四任总统。

50. Bill of Rights 权利法案,亦即美国宪法的头十条修正案。

Questions for Discussion

1. Give a brief account of the background, the process and the consequences of the French and Indian War.
2. What do you know of the John Locke's theory about reason? What influence did it exert on the American Revolution?
3. What a policy did the British government pursue in the thirteen colonies in the years just before the outbreak of the American Revolution?
4. What acts were passed by the British Parliament in the 1760s to levy taxes on the thirteen colonies? Which of these acts directly led to the outbreak of the American Revolution?
5. To offer resistance against the British rule over the colonies, what revolutionary organizations were set up by the colonists?
6. Relate the process of the battle at Lexington and Concord.
7. What important decisions did the Second Continental Congress make?
8. What are the main ideas of the Declaration of Independence?
9. Describe the process of the War of American Independence, and point out its significance.
10. In what circumstances was the Constitution of the United States of America framed or drafted? What a central government was provided by the Constitution?

Exercises

Ⅰ. Choose the correct answer and circle the letter before it.

1. The French and Indian War was a war fought between ________.
   A. the French and Indians
   B. the English and Indians
   C. the French and the English

D. the English and the Spanish

2. As a result of the French and Indian War, the ________ lost all their land in North America.

   A. English   B. French   C. Indians   D. Spanish

3. In the 18th century, people in Europe began to believe that ________ guided the universe.

   A. God   B. natural laws

   C. Man   D. natural forces

4. Which of the following about knowledge is NOT what John Locke's belief?

   A. Man's knowledge is innate.

   B. Man's knowledge is from observation and experiment.

   C. Man's knowledge is from the reflection by the mind.

   D. Man's knowledge is acquired from experience of five senses.

5. Reason led Locke to condemn ________.

   A. free trade   B. free thought

   C. weak government   D. absolute government

6. ________ played an important role in exemplifying the Enlightenment in America to his countrymen.

   A. Benjamin Franklin   B. George Washington

   C. Thomas Jefferson   D. Samuel Adams

7. The ________ and the ________ passed by British Parliament in 1765 directly led to the outbreak of the American Revolution.

   A. Quartering Act, Stamp Act

   B. Currency Act, Quartering Act

   C. Sugar Act, Stamp Act

   D. Declaratory Act, Quartering Act

8. Which of the following is NOT a name given to an American revolutionary organization?

   A. Sons of Liberty.

   B. Committees of Correspondence.

   C. the Stamp Congress.

   D. Boston Tea Party.

9. The Intolerable Acts do not include ________.

A. the Boston Port Act
B. the Massachusetts Government Act
C. the Administration of Justice Act
D. the Tea Act

10. The Second Continental Congress was held in ________.
    A. New York City   B. Boston
    C. Philadelphia   D. Valley Forge
11. Karl Marx called The Declaration of Independence ________.
    A. the first decision made by the Second Continental Congress
    B. the first declaration of the rights of the individual
    C. the first Bill of Rights
    D. the first Constitution of the United States
12. The victory at ________ was a turning point of the American War of Independence.
    A. Trenton   B. Saratoga
    C. Valley Forge   D. Yorktown
13. The Constitutional Convention was held in ________ in May 1787.
    A. Boston   B. New York
    C. Philadelphia   D. Washington, D. C.
14. ________ was known as the "Father of the Constitution."
    A. George Washington   B. Thomas Jefferson
    C. James Madison   D. Benjamin Franklin

Ⅱ. Fill in the following blanks with proper words or expressions.

1. The French and Indian War was a war fought between the ________ and the ________, who were contending for the ________ Valley.
2. After the French and Indian War, the English colonists in North America wanted more ____________ in politics, trade and commerce, while England wanted more ____________.
3. John Locke furnished the 18th century with a theory about ________. He believed that civil government was instituted by mutual ________ for the purpose of ________ natural laws, and that a government failed to do so lost its ________ for existence and deserved being ________ by the people it governed.
4. As a son of the Enlightenment, ________ played an important role in

exemplifying the Enlightenment to his countrymen-Americans.

5. The Enlightenment in America provided the colonists with a ________ and ________ weapon against the British rule.
6. After the French and Indian War, the British government practiced the policy of ________ in the colonies. By practicing such a policy, the British ruling class tried to monopolize the ________ and to hold back the development of ________ in the colonies.
7. One of the Navigation Acts provided that only ________ owned ships could carry colonial goods to British possessions.
8. The Declaratory Act passed by the British government declared that the British government had the right to pass any ________ laws it desired.
9. The British government developed a system of ________ taxation after the failure of the program of internal taxation on the thirteen colonies.
10. The motto of the colonies was "No taxation without ____________."

Ⅲ. Match the historical events in Column A with the years in which they took place in Column B.

	Column A	Column B
1. ____	Boston Tea Party	a. 1786
2. ____	Boston Massacre	b. 1774
3. ____	Daniel Shays' Rebellion	c. 1770
4. ____	the First Continental Congress	d. 1773
5. ____	the battle at Trenton	e. 1787
6. ____	the battle at Yorktown	f. 1776
7. ____	the battle at Saratoga	g. 1777
8. ____	the Constitutional Convention	h. 1781
9. ____	the adoption of the Declaration of Independence	i. 1789
10. ____	the ratification of the Constitution	j. 1776

Ⅳ. Explain the following in English.

1. the French and Indian War
2. John Locke
3. Mercantilist policy
4. the Stamp Act
5. the Sugar Act

6. Boston Massacre
7. Boston Tea Party
8. Sons of Liberty
9. the Second Continental Congress
10. the Declaration of Independence
11. Committees of Correspondence
12. Bill of Rights

Lesson 18 History: American Civil War

Major Events

1803	Louisiana Purchase
1807	The American Industrial revolution began.
1819	The U. S. "purchased" Florida.
1823	Monroe Doctrine
1845	The US annexed Texas.
1846—1848	Mexican-US War
1867	The US purchased Alaska.
1820	Missouri Compromise
1828	the formation of the Democratic Party
1850	Henry Clay's Compromise
1852	publication of Uncle Tom's Cabin
1854	the formation of the Republican Party
1860	Abraham Lincoln was elected President.
1861	The Confederate States of America was formed.
1861—1865	the American Civil War
1862	Lincoln issued the Emancipation Proclamation.
1865—1878	the Reconstruction of the South

Main Contents

1. The Background of the Civil War

1) The Territorial Expansion

When the United States was first founded, it consisted of only thirteen states, with a territory of about 900,000 square kilometers. The Treaty of Paris of 1783 defined its national territory as being to the east of the

Mississippi River. However, the territorial expansion proceeded hand in hand with the growth of US Capitalism.

In 1803, President Thomas Jefferson, by taking advantage of the war in Europe, made **Napoleon** Ⅰ agree to sell **Louisiana Territory** for \$15 million, at the price of 4 cents per acre. This was a vast region of more than 2.6 million square kilometers, stretching from the Great Lakes to the Gulf of Mexico. The Louisiana Purchase doubled the territory of the new nation.

In 1819, the United States "purchased" Florida (about 150,000 square kilometers in size) from Spain after having occupied it for several years.

On December 2, 1823, President **James Monroe** delivered to Congress his annual message in which he announced his **"Monroe Doctrine,"** which warned the European powers against any attempt at intervention in Latin American affairs with the aim of keeping Latin American countries for the United States itself. It came as a logical consequence of the early expansionist tendencies of US capitalism.

In 1845, the United States annexed the Mexican territory of Texas after the US settlers there had first formed an "independent government" with Washington's support. Further U.S. provocations on the border resulted in the **Mexican-US War** of 1846—1848. In consequence of **the Mexican War**, the United States added to itself a territory of approximately 2,446,000 square kilometers, embracing the present state of Texas, California, Arizona, Nevada, Utah, New Mexico, Colorado, and part of **Wyoming.**

In the same year, the United States forced England to cede **the Oregon Region**, which includes the present states of Oregon, Washington, **Idaho**, and part of **Montana** and Wyoming.

In 1867, the United States purchased from **Czarist Russia** the territory of Alaska and the off-lying Aleutian Islands for \$7.2 million. This territory is twice as large as the original thirteen colonies.

By the middle of the 19th century, the national territory of the United States had reached over 9 million square kilometers, about ten times the size of the total area of the original thirteen states.

2) The Economic Expansion

After the War of Independence the American national economy was growing rapidly. Its industrial revolution began in 1807 with its textile industry. New equipment and technology were introduced from Europe, and modern industries were established. Its total value of the industrial production in 1860 increased by about ten times that of 1810.

In the 1820s there came a flood of new immigrants from Europe to the United States because labor was needed with the rapid development of industry in America and most European countries were in a very bad state. The immigrants played an important role in promoting the rapid expansion of the American capitalist economy.

3) Economic Antagonism between the North and the South

As a result of the rapid growth of capitalism, the center of the American economy had definitely shifted from the agrarian areas to the industrial centers in the North by the time **Andrew Jackson** came to the presidency in 1829. By the mid-19th century, the North had been industrial because it had rich resources, while the South had been agricultural because farming was very profitable there. The swiftly growing industries in the North required the restriction of slavery as well as an expanding territory so as to provide capitalist production with raw materials, markets and an abundant labor supply. The slave economy of the South was an obstacle to industrial growth and expansion. **Economic antagonism** between the two sections grew to an alarming extent during the period of some 20 years before the outbreak of the Civil War.

The South was agricultural and had a large number of plantations, which were making huge profits out of tobacco and cotton with slave labor. The South insisted that slavery be kept, and furthermore, that more states in the Union should be turned into slave states. Meanwhile the South exported each year plenty of cotton to England and Europe and imported a large quantity of manufactured goods from abroad. So the Southerners wished to have a low **tariff**, as a high tariff would raise the prices of imported goods. On the contrary, the North had a different interest. The northern industrialists wanted a high tariff to protect the industries in the North. Besides, the North had a growing shipping industry. The Northerners wanted the federal government to provide money to aid this young industry. Since the South had no such interest, the Southerners wanted to abolish the subsidies. The interest conflict between the two sections grew sharper as the economy developed. The

antagonism of the two social-economic systems led to increased **political conflict** between the North and the South and finally to the outbreak of the Civil War.

4) Disputes over Slavery

With the invention of the cotton gin by **Eli Whitney** of Massachusetts in 1793 and the growth of cotton production, the South needed slaves more than ever on its plantations. In order to protect their interest, southern leaders were determined to prevent the North from controlling Congress. As the population and wealth of the North grew more rapidly than those of the South, the South soon found itself outnumbered in the House of Representatives. In these circumstances, the Southerners tried to keep the number of slave states equal to that of free states so that the Northern Senators could not outvote the Southern Senators. In this case slavery became a political issue that seemed hardest to solve.

When **Missouri** was to be admitted to the Union as a new state in 1820, a compromise was made to keep the balance in the Senate by admitting Missouri as a slave state and **Maine** was created and admitted to the Union as a free state. **The Missouri Compromise** of 1820 also prohibited slavery in any other lands in the Louisiana Territory north of the 36° 30′ line. For a time the problem of slavery seemed to have been solved, but when California was ready to be admitted in 1850, the question arose once again whether it was to be a slave state of a free one. The question was resolved by **Henry Clay's Compromise** of 1850: California became a free state, while in the new territories of Utah and New Mexico the citizens were to decide for themselves on the issue of slavery, and a new, more strict **Fugitive Slave Act** was passed, which gave slave-owners the right to search for and seize runaway slaves in any free states. Beneath the surface, however, the tension grew. The new Fugitive Slave Law deeply offended the northerners, whose resentment brought new strength to the **abolitionists**, those who advocated and worked for the abolition of slavery. Meanwhile the publication of the novel ***Uncle Tom's Cabin*** by **Harriet Beecher Stowe** fueled a strong, widespread anti-slavery feeling in the North and the West.

In 1854 **the Kansas-Nebraska Act** extended the idea of "**popular sovereignty,**" a doctrine advocated by the moderates proposing respect for the American tradition of self-government and grant of permission to the people who actually settled in a territory to decide for themselves the question of slavery. But the Missouri Compromise of 1820 had closed to slavery the lands the Nebraska-Kansas Act referred to. Passage of the Kansas-Nebraska Act meant the Missouri Compromise of 1820 was in effect repealed. The flow of both southern slaveholders and the northern men into Kansas resulted in armed conflicts, hence "Bleeding Kansas."

In 1857, the Supreme Court ruled in the Dred Scott case that slaves were property and that the Missouri Compromise was **unconstitutional**. The Dred Scott decision stirred excitement throughout the North; the feeling against slavery rose higher than ever in the North. This and other events brought the nation closer to upheaval.

Politically, after the establishment of the federal government, the planters dominated the scene for many years. There was a whole line of Democratic presidents and congresses putting out laws to protect the planters' interests. Congress made a big cut in the tariff on imported goods in 1857. Two years later it wiped out ship subsidies for the North. These measures enraged all people except the planters. However, things took a different turn in the 1860 presidential election.

The Republican Party was formed in 1854. It won about one-third of the total popular votes in the general election of 1856 though it failed to win the Presidency. The Republican Party represented mainly the interests of the northern industrialists and supported the people's struggle for the abolition of slavery and distribution of land in the west to the small farmers.

In the election of 1860, the republican put up **Abraham Lincoln**, a northerner, for the presidency. Lincoln was thought to be an abolitionist. So the slave states almost immediately began to secede from the Federal Union when Lincoln was elected President. The Civil War became inevitable.

2. The Civil War

The American Civil War broke out on April 12, 1861 and ended on April 9, 1865.

Eleven days after the election of 1860, **South Carolina** seceded from the Union, and ten other slave states followed suit. In February 1861, six of the slave states that had seceded from the Union formed **the Confederate States of America** and elected **Jefferson Davis**, a planter, President of the Confederacy.

On March 4, A. Lincoln was sworn in as President. In his **inaugural address**, he refused to recognize the secession, considering it "legally void." His speech closed with a plea for restoration of the bounds of the Union. But the South turned deaf ears to what he said . On April 12, 1861, the rebels fired on **Fort Sumter**, a spot garrisoned by federal troops, and the Civil War began.

The North had many advantages over the South, such as more states, a larger population and almost all the industry of the United States, which could provide the North with abundant facilities for manufacturing arms and ammunition, clothing and other supplies. The network of railroads in the North contributed to federal military prospects. Most of the navy was in the Union's hands, which was used to blockade the southern coast. More important, Lincoln was supported by the great majority of the people. Yet despite its potential strength, the war went badly for the North in the first eighteen months. That was mainly because the North lacked the determination and will to fight the war. For nearly 18 months Lincoln hesitated on the question of slavery, because he was not a firm abolitionist. He had condemned slavery, but had never publicly said that slavery must be abolished. He once said in a letter, "My major object in this struggle is to save the Union. If I could save the Union without freeing any slaves I would do it; if I could save it by freeing some and leaving the others alone I would do that." To make matters even worse, pro-slavery capitalists sabotaged the war effort in the rear. The British and French governments supplied the Confederates with food and munitions. For a time things looked gloomy indeed to the Northerners.

In order to change the situation and win the war, several measures were taken by Lincoln's Administration in 1862: (1) In May 1862, Congress passed **the Homestead Act**, under which the land problem was solved in the interests of the small farmers; (2) On September 22, 1862 Lincoln issued **the Emancipation Proclamation**, which liberated some four million Negro slaves in the South. After it went into effect on January 1 of the following year, there were more slave revolts and strikes than ever in the South and as many as half a million Negroes fled the plantation, thus seriously disrupting production in the South; (3) Negroes were allowed to serve in the Union Army from August 1862. A large number of Negroes joined the Union Army. They fought bravely and many gave their lives to the cause of their people's emancipation.

With such mass support, the Union Army began to win decisive victories on the battlefield from the summer of 1863. It defeated the Confederate Army at **Gettysburg**, Pennsylvania. On April 9, 1865, after the fall of **Richmond**, the Confederate Capital, **General Robert E. Lee** of the South surrendered to **General Grant** of the North at **Appomattox Court House**, Virginia and the war was over.

The Civil War lasted for four years and cost at least a million lives.

3. The Significance of the Civil War

The Civil War is of great significance in American history. It preserved the Union. It solved the agrarian problem. It destroyed the feudal slavery—plantation system, which had been an obstacle on the path of the development of capitalism, so that American capitalism developed at a higher speed after the war. In this sense it is, therefore, also called the Second American Bourgeois Revolution. Since the war was not fought for the emancipation of the Negroes, they were not emancipated after the end of the war. When the war ended, the blacks had a very hard time, as they did not know how to take care of themselves. It was a difficult time in the South for the white people, too. Things were made more difficult because some Northern people called **Carpetbaggers** went to the South, hoping to control the blacks and the state governments.

Lincoln had had wise and kind plans to help the states that had seceded to re-enter the Union and have them rebuilt. After his death, the reconstruction of the South became slow and difficult. It lasted until 1878.

Notes

1. Napoleon Ⅰ　拿破仑一世(1769～1821),法国皇帝,在位期间为1794～1815年。
2. Louisiana Territory　路易斯安娜地区,北起五大湖南至墨西哥湾的大片领土,美国于1803年从法国拿破仑手中购买。
3. James Monroe　詹姆士·门罗(1758～1831),于1817～1825年任美国第五任总统。
4. Monroe Doctrine　门罗主义,门罗于1817～1825年任总统期间奉行的欧洲国家不干涉南北美洲事务的理论。
5. Mexican-US War/the Mexican War　美国对墨西哥的战争/墨西哥战争。
6. Wyoming　怀俄明州

7. the Oregon Region　俄勒冈地区
8. Idaho　爱达荷州
9. Montana　蒙大拿州
10. Czarist Russia　沙皇俄国
11. Andrew Jackson　安德鲁·杰克逊，1829～1837年任美国总统。
12. economic antagonism　经济对抗
13. tariff　关税
14. political conflict　政治冲突
15. Eli Whitney　伊莱·惠特尼
16. outvote　以票数胜过
17. Missouri　密苏里州
18. Maine　缅因州，根据1820年密苏里妥协案创立。
19. the Missouri Compromise　密苏里妥协案
20. Henry Clay's Compromise　亨利·克莱妥协案
21. Fugitive Slave Act　逃亡奴隶引渡法
22. abolitionist　废奴主义者
23. *Uncle Tom's Cabin*　《汤姆叔叔的小屋》，曾译《黑奴吁天录》。
24. Harriet Beecher Stowe　哈里特·B·斯托夫人
25. the Kansas-Nebraska Act　堪萨斯—内布拉斯加法案
26. popular sovereignty　人民主权论，主张由当地居民投票表决是否蓄奴。
27. unconstitutional　违宪的
28. Abraham Lincoln　亚伯拉罕·林肯
29. South Carolina　南卡罗莱纳州
30. the Confederate States of America　美国南部同盟
31. Jefferson Davis　杰斐逊·戴维斯
32. inaugural address　就职演说
33. Fort Sumter　萨姆特要塞
34. the Homestead Act　《宅地法》
35. the Emancipation Proclamation　《解放黑奴宣言》
36. Gettysburg　葛底斯堡
37. Richmond　里士满
38. General Robert E. Lee　罗伯特·E·李将军，南部同盟军总指挥。
39. General Grant　格兰特将军，北部联军总指挥。
40. Appomattox Court House　阿波麦托克斯镇政府所在地

41. Carpetbaggers　美国南北战争后利用南方不定局势谋私利的人。

Questions for Discussion

1. Describe the territorial expansion of the United States in the first half of the 19th century.
2. Relate the economic expansion of the United States along with its territorial expansion in the first half of the 19th century.
3. Interpret the cause of the American Civil War in terms of economy.
4. Interpret the cause of the American Civil War in terms of politics.
5. What historical events fueled an anti-slavery feeling in the North before the outbreak of the American Civil War?
6. What advantages did the North have over the South in the American Civil War?
7. Why did the Civil War go badly for the North in the first phase?
8. What important measures were taken by the Lincoln Administration in 1862 to win the War?
9. What was the significance of the American Civil War?
10. What do you know about the reconstruction of the South after the Civil War?

Exercises

Ⅰ. Choose the correct answer and circle the letter before it.

1. The United States purchased Louisiana Territory from ________ in 1893.

   A. Indians　B. Spain　C. France　D. Russia

2. The Mexican territories annexed by the United States as a result of the Mexican War include the following present states except ________.

   A. Texas　B. California　C. Arizona　D. Oregon

3. The Oregon Region includes the following present states except ________.

A. Washington B. Utah

C. Idaho D. Oregon

4. By ________, the United States had finished its territorial expansion in the Continent.

A. the late 18th century

B. the early 19th century

C. the middle 19th century

D. the late 19th century

5. The American Industrial Revolution began in 1807 with its ________ industry.

A. shipbuilding B. coal mining

C. textile D. machine-making

6. The Missouri Compromise of 1820 prohibited slavery in any other lands in the ________ Territory north of the 36°30′ line.

A. Louisiana B. Oregon

C. Mexican D. Spanish

7. Henry Clay's Compromise of 1850 was made to solve the problem aroused by the admission of ________ into the Union.

A. Missouri B. Maine

C. California D. Nebraska

8. The Supreme Court ruled in the Dred Scott case that the ________ was unconstitutional.

A. Missouri Compromise of 1820

B. Henry Clay's Compromise of 1850

C. Nebraska-Kansas Act

D. the idea of popular sovereignty

9. Which of the following is NOT the measure taken by the Lincoln Administration in 1862 to change the situation and win the Civil War?

A. The passage of the Homestead Act.

B. The issuing of the Emancipation Proclamation.

C. The allowance of Negroes to join the Union Army.

D. The ordering of the Union Army to take over Richmond.

10. At the end of the American Civil War, the Black people were ________.

A. completely emancipated

B. not emancipated at all

C. called Carpetbaggers

D. able to control the state governments

Ⅱ. Fill in the following blanks with proper words or expressions.

1. The United States purchased ________ territory from France in 1803.
2. In 1819, the United States "purchased" Florida from ________ after having occupied it for several years.
3. The United States annexed the Mexican territory of ________ in 1845.
4. The United States forced England to cede the ________ Region in 1846.
5. In 1867, the United States purchased the territory of Alaska and the Aleutian Islands from ________.
6. By the mid-19th century, the territory of the United States had reached over ________ million square kilometers, about ________ times the size of the total area of the original thirteen states.
7. The American industrial revolution began in the year of ________ with its ________ industry.
8. During the period of some 20 years before the outbreak of the Civil War, the industrial North needed ________ labor, while the South needed ________ labor. The northerners wanted a ________ tariff, while the southerners wanted a ________ tariff.
9. When the South found itself outnumbered in the House of Representatives, the southerners tried to keep the number of ________ states equal to that of ________ states so that the Southern senators could not be ________ by the Northern senators. So in this case slavery became a ________ issue.
10. The novel *Uncle Tom's Cabin* was written by ________.
11. The Kansas-Nebraska Act of 1854 extended the idea of ________ sovereignty.
12. In 1857, the Supreme Court ruled in the ________ case that the Missouri Compromise was unconstitutional.
13. The Republican Party was formed in the year of ________.
14. In February 1861, six of the slave states that had seceded from the

Union formed the ________ and elected ________ their president.

15. The American Civil War began on April , 1861 when the rebels fired on Fort ________.
16. On September 22, 1862 Lincoln issued the ________ Proclamation.
17. On April 9, 1865, after the fall of ________, General Lee of the South surrendered to General ________ of the North at ________ Court House, and the war ended.
18. The American Civil War is also called the Second American ________ Revolution.

Ⅲ. Match the following historical events with the corresponding year in which they took place.

1. ____ Louisiana Purchase — a. 1846
2. ____ Monroe Doctrine — b. 1823
3. ____ The US annexed Texas — c. 1803
4. ____ the outbreak of The Mexican-US War — d. 1867
5. ____ The US purchased Alaska. — e. 1845

Ⅳ. Rearrange the following historical events in the order in which they took place.

1. ____ a. Lincoln issued the Emancipation Proclamation.
2. ____ b. The rebels fired on Fort Sumter.
3. ____ c. The Union troops took over Richmond.
4. ____ d. The Confederate States of America was formed.
5. ____ e. Lincoln assumed office.

Ⅴ. Explain the following in English.

1. Louisiana Purchase
2. Monroe Doctrine
3. the Compromise of 1820
4. the Compromise of 1850
5. the Kansas-Nebraska Act
6. popular sovereignty
7. the Confederate States of America
8. the Emancipation Proclamation
9. the Homestead Act
10. Carpetbaggers

Lesson 19 History: US Imperialism

Major Events

1894	The US became the world leading industrial country.
1877	the Pennsylvania railway workers' strike
1886	the workers' strike in Chicago
1898	the Spanish-American War
1899	The "Open Door" policy was initiated.
1903	The Panama Canal Zone was leased to the US.
1914—1918	the First World War
1919	The Treaty of Versailles was signed.
1920s	the "roaring 20s"
1929	the advent of the worldwide economic crisis
1933	Franklin D. Roosevelt assumed office.
1936	Franklin D. Roosevelt was re-elected President.
1938	Munich Agreement
1941	The Japanese attacked Pearl Harbor.
1945	the end of World War Ⅱ
1947	The Taft-Hartley Act was passed.
1950	The investigation of un-American activities began, and the war in Korea broke out.
1972	President Nixon's visit to China
1973	The US withdrew its troops from Vietnam
1979	the establishment of diplomatic relations between China and the United States
1980	Reagan was elected President.
1988	George Bush (Sr.) was elected President.
1991	The Gulf War broke out.
1992	Clinton was elected President.

2000 Bush (Jr.) was elected President and terrorists destroyed the building of the World Trade Center.

2003 the Iraq War

Main Contents

1. The Formation of US Imperialism

1) Highly Developed Industry

The Civil War sped up the growing industrial revolution in the United States, which, in turn, brought about many changes in the nation. Towards the end of the 19th century the United States had already become a highly developed capitalist country and reached the stage of imperialism. Machinery steadily replaced the use of hand labor in the manufacturing of goods. Railways extended from coast to coast. Ships were built. Transportation and communications were greatly improved to meet the needs of an industrial society. Investments in business grew larger, and corporations replaced small privately owned firms in many industries. By 1894, America had become the world leading industrial country. Its total industrial production of manufactures was almost sevenfold more than that of 1860, accounting for one-third of the world total.

2) The Rapid Concentration of Capital

The rapid concentration of capital was also accelerated after the Civil War, with many small and medium-sized enterprises being swallowed up by bigger ones in the process. Big monopolies first appeared in the heavy industries. Industrial barons such as Rockefeller's, Morgan's and Ford's, controlled 80 to 95 percent of the nation's railways, the production of oil, steel and automobiles. The light industries and agriculture went through a similar process of concentration. Some powerful financial groups came into being. They began to dominate the country's economy, controlling numerous banks, insurance companies, manufacturing and railroad companies. Wealth was highly concentrated; a small number of men controlled a large part of the national economy. In 1913, the Morgan Group and the Rockefeller Group owned one-third of the wealth of the United States. The emergence of such trusts suggested the shift of the United States from competitive capitalism to monopoly capitalism.

Big business was not concerned with the public interest, but only with profit making. It was common practice for the corporations to sell impure foods and drugs, and to use unfair methods in advertising. Many writers wrote articles and books about the conditions in American life in the 1890s and early 1900s. One of them was **Upton Sinclair**, whose book ***The Jungle*** was a story about the meatpacking plants in Chicago, a vivid description of the dirt and disease in the meatpacking industry. The workers worked long hours under extremely bad conditions and were paid low wages. Hard times every few years brought long periods of unemployment. Child labor was common. They were paid less than men, and the result was that men's wages were kept down.

3) The Rise of the Working-Class Movement

A rising working-class movement accompanied the growth of monopoly capital. During the 1880s and 1890s, workers began for the first time to form unions on a large scale. The capitalists tried to sabotage the unions by enlisting the union workers on "blacklists," which would be sent to other companies in the industry with a warning not to hire them, and by forcing workers to sign **"yellow dog" contract** pledging not to join unions. In spite of all this, workers still formed unions and went on strikes, fighting against the strikebreakers. **The Knights of Labor** and **the American Federation of Labor** were organized in the 1880s. During the 1890s, a group of unions joined to form **the Congress of Industrial Organization**. In 1955, A. F. of L. and the CIO merged to form a single national union. In their battle for unionism they developed their own methods for gaining success, such as collective bargaining, strikes, boycotts and the **closed shop**, an agreement that requires the employer to hire only union members.

Strikes often took place in the industrial cities in those days. The Pennsylvania railway workers' strike of 1877 was the first large-scale struggle of its kind in the American history. On May 1, 1886, hundreds of thousands of workers went on simultaneous strikes in Chicago, Washington, New York and other large cities. They fought for an eight-hour working day, higher wages and better working conditions. Two days later, the police opened fire on the strikers at Chicago's **Haymarket**, inflicting many casualties. To pay tribute to the Haymarket martyrs, **the Second International Meeting** at Paris in 1889 adopted a resolution designating May 1 as International Labor Day to be observed by the workers of the world.

4) The Overseas Expansion

In the mid-19th century, the United States basically completed its territorial expansion on the continent. Now its great financial strength gave it the power to go abroad. It looked greedily at Asia and Latin America. It occupied **the Samoan Islands** in 1880, and convened the first **"Pan-American Conference"** in 1889 in an attempt to control Latin America. In order to grab Cuba, one of the Spanish colonies in Latin America, the United States went into war with Spain in 1898 when an American battleship, ***the Maine***, was blown up in Havana Harbor with a loss of 260 lives and the Spanish officials were accused of doing it though the real cause was never known. **The Spanish-American War** broke out in April, lasted for only 70 days and ended with the United States as victor. A peace treaty was signed in December 1898 in Paris. As a result of the war, Spain was forced to cede her former colonies Cuba, **Puerto Rico**, **Guam** and the Philippines to the United States; the United States agree to pay 20 million dollars for them in an attempt to put a good face on its foreign expansion. Cuba remained a US "protectorate" for some years, while the Philippines was not granted its independence until after the end of World War Ⅱ. The United States seized Hawaii from Spain after the Spanish-American War of 1898.

The Spanish-American War strengthened the US interventions in Americas. One of the most important interventions was in **Panama**. The United States felt the need of cutting a canal in Panama most keenly during the Spanish-American War. So in 1902, the US began to negotiate with **Colombia**, which owned the area, for the site of the Canal, but the terms proposed by the US were refused by Colombia in 1903. So the United States cooked a "revolution" in Panama against Colombia and sent a gunboat to prevent Colombian troops from trying to suppress the rebellion. Three days after the "revolution," the US government recognized the independence of the Republic of Panama. A treaty was signed between the United States and the new Republic, which leased to the United States the use of a canal zone ten miles wide for 99 years. The construction of the canal began in 1907, and was completed in 1914. The Panama Canal shortened the voyage between New York and San Francisco by about 8,000 miles. It promoted trade and made naval movements much easier.

In the Far East, China was the main objective of the US overseas expansion. In 1844, US imperialism invaded China and compelled the *Qing* Dynasty to sign the unequal **"Treaty of Wangxia."** The United States gained the privilege of settlement and consular jurisdiction in China. It imposed the **"Treaty of Tientsin"** on the Manchu government in 1858. It advocated an **"Open Door" policy** in 1899, in an attempt to seek equal trading privileges in China along with other foreign powers. In 1900, the United States and other powers sent troops to China to put down the ***Yihetuan* Uprising.** All this shows that the US imperialism tried to have the whole of China under its control.

2. America in World War Ⅰ and the Post-War Period

The outbreak of World War Ⅰ in 1914 came as an inevitable explosion of the major contradictions racking the capitalist world. The United States sought to remain neutral in the first few years of the War. It did not enter the war until April 1917 when it decided that the Germans were directly threatening American interests as the German submarines were used to sink American ships on the sea.

The United States played an important part in the war. Its troops were sent to Europe just at the time when the Central and the Allied Powers had been greatly weakened in the conflict. The entry of the United States into the war quickened Germany's defeat. By November 1918 the Allied forces had compelled the Germans to seek an armistice. The United States was now a fully recognized world power. President **Woodrow Wilson** personally attended the peace treaty meeting at **Versailles**, France, where he proposed a fourteen-point program, which included freedom of the seas, disarmament, and removal of international economic barriers and the establishment of **the League of Nations**. He wanted the peace terms to adhere to his fourteen-point program. The Treaty of Versailles was signed in June 1919. Germany was disarmed and lost all of its territorial possessions. However, the US Senate refused to ratify the treaty. With the rise of its economic position in the world it began to assume by itself a more and more important political role in world affairs.

US imperialism reaped a huge fortune out of the war by selling arms to both sides of the war in the first phase of the war and by doing well in the post-war division of spoils among the victorious allies. As the chief munitions maker of the world, American industry reached a degree of prosperity and concentration unparalleled in the past during the war period. It not only repaid all its foreign debts, but also granted loans and credit to the Allied countries to the extent of $10, 300 million. It had a favorable trade balance of 2, 500 million US dollars in 1915. The gold reserves of the US amounted to half the world's stock of the precious metal.

The United States flourished with great prosperity in the 1920s. The expression **"roaring 20's"** is often used to describe the period of American life. There was an industrial boom in this decade because material damage and shortages created by the war were to be repaired and filled. Meantime there was a great expansion of industries making consumer goods. Millions of people speculated in stocks and bonds and in real estate. For many people the main drive of the 1920s was to get some degree of personal wealth and comfort. As this materialism was widespread in the nation, organized gangsterism became a part of American life. The smuggling of liquor became a major business controlled by rival mobs of gangsters.

However, the post-war industrial boom and the prosperity were soon to vanish. In 1929, a deep, worldwide economic crisis broke out. The first outward sign of the depression was the collapse of the stock market in October 1929, followed by the closing of thousands of plants and banks. The depression kept growing worse from 1929—1932. At least 13 million workers, and possibly as many as 15 million, were out of work. At least two-thirds of the nation's banks had been closed down. The production of coal, iron, steel, and automobiles dropped by 40 to 80 percent. The farm crisis, in existence since 1921, was worse than ever.

President **Franklin D. Roosevelt** assumed office in early 1933. He put forward many emergency measures, known as **the New Deal**, trying to save the situation. The New Deal measures had two principal purposes. Internally, through a huge increase in government expenditure large-scale public works were launched to create employment, and crops were destroyed and agricultural production reduced in order to raise the sagging farm prices.

Externally, the **"Good Neighbor Policy"** towards Latin America was adopted. The United States even established diplomatic relations with the Soviet Union. Efforts were made to consolidate the old markets abroad and to conquer new ones.

The New Deal program had some initial remedial effect, but it failed to produce recovery, and solve the problem of unemployment. The crisis continued to deepen until a change was brought about by the outbreak of the Second World War.

3. America in World War Ⅱ

With the German and Italian fascists bent on war, the world situation was deteriorating rapidly when Roosevelt was reelected President in 1936. But the United States still remained neutral. It was actually colluding with the fascist aggressions by its policy of "non-entanglement" and its deep-seated hostility towards the Soviet Union. When Germany attempted to annex **Czechoslovakia** in 1938, the United States stepped in and urged England and France to sign an agreement with Germany and Italy, known as **Munich Agreement**, which was actually a conspiracy unfavorable to Czechoslovakia.

The Japanese attack on the American naval base of **Pearl Harbor** in Hawaii on December 7, 1941 brought the United States into the war. It tasted defeat in the first few months after it went into war. The Philippines and several other islands in the Pacific were taken by Japan. The US troops were forced to retreat to Australia. In 1943, the United States turned its strength to the Pacific war area and regained the Philippines and many islands nearer to Japan. By 1944 American troops and air forces were hitting the Japanese hard. The American navy smashed the Japanese fleet. The United States dropped atomic bombs on **Hiroshima** and **Nagasaki** in 1945.

Since it entered the war, the United States had played an important role in defeating the fascist powers. It had supplied the antifascist countries with great amounts of food and military materials. It had sent its own troops to open the second front in Europe and had done a lot in promoting the formation of the Anti-fascist united front. However, the nature of US imperialism had made itself felt during the whole period of the war. The US monopolists had no scruples about selling arms and ammunition to the aggressors. It was the course later taken by the war that made the United States the so-called "arsenal of democracy."

4. America in the Post-War Period

After the end of the war, US imperialism utilized its preponderant industrial and economic expansion abroad for establishing its sway over two vast intermediate zones separating itself from the Soviet: the zone of Western Europe and that of Asia, Africa and Latin America. Both the **Truman Doctrine**, which promised economic and military aid to any nation threatened by an outside power, and the **Marshall Plan**, which offered aid to Western European countries, were directed towards this aim.

The US military and economic aggressions against other nations and its attacks upon the people at home aroused the vigorous resistance of the world's people, the American people included. Immediately after the war, the Truman Administration had to face many problems, both at home and abroad: the problems rising in the **Cold War**, and other problems at home such as high prices, shortages of consumer goods and strikes. In 1947, Congress passed the **Taft-Hartley Act**, which outlawed the closed shop and put other restraints on labor unions, and a program was established to investigate the loyalty of the federal employees in the executive branch. Many innocent persons were charged with "disloyalty" and were persecuted. In 1950, **McCarthy**, a notorious Senator, suggested investigating so-called un-American activities in governmental establishments. Under the pretence of these investigations, the reactionary forces in the US intensified their persecution of communists and progressives. However, the American people went on with their struggles. Labor movements, student movements and black movements continue even at present.

American foreign policy changed a bit during the post-war period. In the first two decades after the war, the US government adopted a policy of Cold War and "**Containment**" in its relationship with the Soviet Union, as the US was superior to the Soviet both in its economic and political position and in military power. But because of the defeats it suffered in China, Korea and Indo-China, US imperialism soon began falling from the height of power it had attained during the war. The large-scale war of aggression in Vietnam cost the US over 120,000 million dollars and a total of hundreds of thousands of casualties. The United States was forced to sign the armistice agreement in

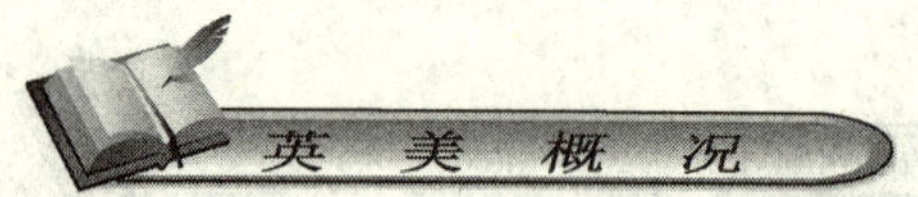

January 1973 and withdraw its troops from Vietnam. Before long the United States became weaker, while the Soviets posed a serious challenge to America's hegemonic position. Thus, the American foreign policy of Cold War and "Containment" began to be replaced by the policy of contention for world hegemony. This policy lasted until **the Gulf War** and the disintegration of the former Soviet Union in 1991.

The American economy has been afflicted with several repeated economic crises since the end of World War Ⅱ. There has been one economic crisis every five years on average, with a decline in production, millions of workers unemployed, huge financial deficits, serious inflation and soaring prices.

Nixon resigned in August 1974 and was succeeded by Gerald R. Ford, who soon gave Nixon a "full, free and absolute pardon."

Jimmy Carter became President in 1977. His administration experienced a eventful period. On the economy, the Carter administration's initial focus on unemployment was soon replaced by concern with the highest inflation rates. The inflation was caused mainly by rises in OPEC oil price, wage boosts, and large budget deficits. Carter formally recognized the People's Republic of China in 1979 and won approval of a treaty giving Panama sovereign control over the Panama canal by A. D. 2000. In the foreign affairs, he succeeded in his mediation efforts to bring Israeli Prime Minister Menachem Begin and Egyptian President Anwar El-Sadat to settle long-standing differences growing out of the 1973 Arab-Israeli war. However, his failure in dealings with the hostage crisis of the American embassy in Teheran spoiled his image among the American public. In the general election of 1980, Carter was defeated by his opponent, Ronald Reagan.

After he became President, Reagan proposed a wide-ranging program of legislation. His major goals were a reduction in federal spending and the size of government, cuts in taxes, and a strengthening of the US defense establishment. But in reality, government expenditures continued to rise. In 1988, the federal government spent more than $1,000 billion and about $4,500 for each individual. Tax cuts, designed to promote savings and to stimulate investment, had resulted merely in reduced revenues and huge federal deficits. Though Reagan had pledged in the 1980 campaign to balance the budget, by 1988 the gross federal debt was more than $2 trillion. Reagan dramatically

increased defense spending even as he slowed increase in other areas and cut the federal budget in still others. His "Star Wars" program, officially called the Strategic Defense Initiative (SDI), was envisioned as one of the biggest research projects in the American history, a five-year $26 billion undertaking. This project seeks to discover and construct a defensive "shield" against incoming nuclear missiles. The shield would be made laser and electronic devices that would destroy such missiles launched to attack the United States.

The foreign policy of the Reagan Administration could be called "protect American values by fighting communism." Under this policy the United States frequently intervened in the affairs of other countries in the world.

George Bush succeeded Ronald Reagan in 1989. During the Bush Administration, Iraq invaded Kuwait in August 1990 and the United States responded by sending troops to the Gulf region. In February 1991, the Gulf War broke out and in only 21 days the US troops almost completely destroyed the Iraqi troops and forced Iraq to withdraw its troops from Kuwait. Though George Bush won the war in the Middle East, he lost the general election in 1992, as a result of which Bill Clinton was elected President, who remained in office till the end of the 20th century.

In the election of 2000, Bill Clinton was defeated and was succeeded by George W. Bush. On September 11th, 2001, only a few months after George W. Bush was elected President, the World Trade Center Building was destroyed by terrorists and caused deaths of thousands of people. President George W. Bush declared the country in a state of war and made public his government's determination to wipe out terrorists. On the grounds of anti-terrorists, the United States then launched a war against terrorists hidden in Afghanistan, where many terrorist bases were destroyed.

On March 20th, 2003, the United States launched the Second Gulf War against Iraq, completely ignoring the Charter of the United Nations and the strong opposition of the people in most countries. The war, with both air and land attacks against Iraq, lasted for a little more than 20 days and presented to the world a completely new and modern war. It successfully overthrew the government of Iraq, but the US troops have fallen in great troubles in Iraq. The war has caused peoples' doubt about the role of the United Nations in preserving peace throughout the world.

5. Sino-American Relations

Problems both at home and abroad resulted in President **Nixon**'s visit to the People's Republic of China in February 1972. Liaison offices of the two countries were established in Beijing and Washington in May 1973. After consultations, the two countries agreed to establish diplomatic relations on January 1, 1979. Ambassadors of the two countries were exchanged on March 1, 1979. The establishment of the diplomatic relation between the two countries put an end to the abnormal state of relations between the two, and opened a new page in Sino-American relations. It is a favorable development to the people of the world in their struggle for world peace.

Notes

1. Upton Sinclair 厄普敦·辛克莱(1878～1968),美国作家及社会主义者。
2. *The Jungle* 《丛林》
3. "yellow dog" contract 工人向资方保证不参加工会的合同
4. the Knights of Labor 劳动骑士团
5. the American Federation of Labor 美国劳动者联盟,简称"劳联"。
6. the Congress of Industrial Organization 产业工会联合会,简称"产联"。
7. the closed shop 只招聘工会会员的工厂和商店或劳资双方达成的这样的协议
8. Haymarket (芝加哥的)干草市场
9. the Second International Meeting 第二国际大会
10. the Samoan Islands 萨摩亚群岛
11. Pan-American Conference 泛美会议
12. *the Maine* 缅因号(军舰)
13. the Spanish-American War 美西战争
14. Puerto Rico 波多黎各
15. Guam 关岛
16. Panama 巴拿马
17. Colombia 哥伦比亚
18. *Treaty of Wangxia* 《望厦条约》
19. *Treaty of Tientsin* 《天津条约》
20. "Open Door" policy "门户开放"政策

21. *Yihetuan* Uprising 义和团起义
22. Woodrow Wilson 伍德罗·威尔逊(1856～1924),美国第28任总统(1913～1921)。
23. Versailles 凡尔赛
24. the League of Nations 国际联盟
25. "roaring 20's" 喧嚣的20年代
26. Franklin D. Roosevelt 富兰克林·罗斯福(1882～1945),于1933～1945年任美国第32任总统。
27. the New Deal 新政
28. Good Neighbor Policy 友好睦邻政策
29. Czechoslovakia 捷克斯洛伐克
30. Munich Agreement 慕尼黑协定
31. Pear Harbor 珍珠港
32. Hiroshima 广岛
33. Nagasaki 长崎,日本九州岛西岸港市。
34. Truman Doctrine 杜鲁门主义
35. Marshal Plan 马歇尔计划
36. Cold War 冷战
37. Taft-Hartley Act 塔夫脱—哈特利法案
38. McCarthy 麦卡锡(参议员)
39. Containment 遏制政策
40. the Gulf War 海湾战争
41. Nixon 尼克松(1913～1994),1969～1974年任美国第37任总统,因水门事件辞职,成为美国第一位辞职的总统。

Questions for Discussion

1. What were the social, economic and political changes that marked the formation of US imperialism? Try to explain each.
2. How was the United States brought into World War I?
3. What do you know about the fourteen-point program?
4. How did the United States manage to reap a huge fortune out of World War I?

5. Describe the situation in the United States in the 1920's and the 1930's?
6. Give a brief account of the New Deal program and its effect on the economic crisis in the 1930's.
7. What a role did the United States play in World War Ⅱ? How did the United States manage to reap a huge fortune out of World War Ⅱ?
8. Give a brief account of the American foreign policy in the post-war period, and the relations between China and the United States.

Exercises

Ⅰ. Choose the correct answer and circle the letter before it.

1. The US imperialism was marked by all the following except ________.
   A. highly developed industry
   B. high concentration of capital
   C. free business competition
   D. overseas territorial expansion
2. Which of the following were used to restrict the formation of workers' unions?
   A. "Yellow dog" contract. B. Closed shop.
   C. Boycotts. D. Collective bargaining.
3. Which of the following lands was NOT ceded by Spain to the United States as a result of the Spanish-American War?
   A. Cuba. B. Puerto Rico.
   C. Guam. D. Hawaii.
4. The Spanish-American War strengthened the US interventions in ________.
   A. the Far East B. Americas
   C. Europe D. Africa
5. In the late half of the 19th century, ________ was the main objective of the US overseas expansion.
   A. India B. China
   C. Vietnam D. the Philippines
6. The establishment of The League of Nations was initiated by

________.

A. Franklin D. Roosevelt B. Woodrow Wilson

C. Harry S. Truman D. William Taft

7. Which of the following was NOT the characteristic of the "roaring 20's"?

A. Workers' strikes. B. Industrial boom.

C. Organized gangsterism. D. Smuggling of liquor.

8. Which of the following was NOT the measure of the New Deal?

A. Reducing the public expenditure.

B. Destroying crops.

C. Adopting the "Good Neighbor Policy" towards Latin American countries.

D. Launching public works.

9. The US foreign policy in the 1930's may be termed " ________. "

A. the policy of non-entanglement

B. separating itself from the Soviet Union

C. the policy of containment

D. the policy of contention for world hegemony

10. The United States and China established diplomatic relations in the year of________.

A. 1973 B. 1972 C. 1978 D. 1979

Ⅱ. Fill in the following blanks with proper words or expressions.

1. By the year of ________ the United States had become the world leading industrial country.

2. The emergence of trusts suggested the shift of the United States from ________ capitalism to ________ capitalism.

3. *The Jungle* was a story about the ________ plants in Chicago.

4. On May 1, 18 ________, workers went on simultaneous strikes in Chicago and other large cities.

5. The United States looked greedily at Asia and ________ after it completed its territorial expansion on the continent.

6. The first Pan-American Conference was convened in the year of ________.

7. In order to grab ________, the United States went into war with Spain

in 1898. As a result of the war, Spain ceded ________, ________, ________ and the Philippines to the United States.

8. In 1902 the United States began to negotiate with ________ for the site of the Panama Canal.
9. In 1844 US imperialism invaded China and compelled the Qing Dynasty to sign the unequal *Treaty of* ________.
10. In 1858 US imperialism imposed the *Treaty of* ________ on the Manchu government.
11. In 1899 US imperialism advocated an "________" policy, in an attempt to seek equal privileges in China along with other foreign powers.
12. The United States entered the First World War in April 19 ____.
13. The fourteen-point program proposed by President Wilson included freedom of the ________, disarmament and the establishment of the ________ of Nations.
14. The Japanese attacked ________ Harbor in Hawaii on December 7, 1941.
15. In the first two decades after World War Ⅱ the US government adopted a policy of ________ War and "________" in its relationship with the Soviet Union. This policy was later replaced by the policy of ________ for world hegemony.
16. President Nixon visited China in February 19 ____. In the year of ________ the United States established diplomatic relations with China.

Ⅲ. Explain the following in English.

1. "blacklists"
2. "yellow dog" contracts
3. A. F of L.
4. CIO
5. closed shop
6. Haymarket martyrs
7. the Spanish-American War
8. the New Deal
9. Truman Doctrine
10. Marshal Plan

Lesson 20 American Education

Major Points

1. History

American education, like all the other elements of American culture, is rooted in the Old World. Coming to the American wilderness with a belief that education was fundamental to religion and to service for the commonwealth, the settlers began their work in establishing an education system soon after their arrival. By the American Revolution, something of an American pattern of education was emerging.

With the achievement of independence, American education came into its own. Among the Founding Fathers of the United States, Thomas Jefferson made the most contribution to American educational philosophy and practice.

The Post-Civil War era was marked by the proliferating of compulsory education laws and the rapid expansion of public schools.

After the turn of the 20th century, a variety of federal programs exerted great influence on education. Racial segregation in education was declared unconstitutional.

2. Administration

Since the US constitution mentions nothing on education, all educational matters are left to individual states.

On the state level, educational policy is generally the responsibility of a state board of citizens. Yet there is no uniform pattern of state administration.

Most state boards are appointed, but a few are elected.

Local administration, too, varies tremendously. The general pattern is that local schools are governed by local school boards. There are, however, numerous exceptions.

Funds for schools come from 3 sources: local property taxes, state, and national government. Two extreme cases are Hawaii and New Hampshire.

Most colleges and universities are administered by separate university boards. Public higher education is financed at least two thirds by state and federal grants with the balance paid by students. Private colleges and universities support themselves, and levy high tuition charges.

3. Practices

American education mainly falls into 3 categories: elementary education, secondary education, and higher education.

Elementary education covers 12 years with a number of subdivisions.

Elementary education has experienced a shift in emphasis on its goals: from a sense of responsibility to the development of autonomous individuals.

Secondary education is identified with several different kinds of high schools: vocational and technical high schools, academic high schools, and comprehensive high schools, each having a somewhat different mission.

Higher education includes undergraduate study and graduate study. The former lasts for four years while the latter varies with different fields of study.

Professors teach undergraduates by giving lectures supplemented by class discussions between them, and give different examinations for different purposes.

In order to receive an undergraduate degree, students are required to complete successfully a minimum number of credits for their courses. Each course is worth a certain number of credits depending on how many hours of classes or other teaching activities they have each week.

Graduate work leads to the master's degree and, beyond that, the doctor's degree, both of which emphasize preparation for research or professional practice.

Assistantships are available in many graduate schools. Students awarded assistantships are expected to devote up to 20 hours each week for certain duties.

A central factor in the operation of higher education institutions is that it is the faculty that determines the students' recruitment, the length of study, the curriculum, and the selection of teaching staff.

One unique characteristic of American higher education is that colleges and universities, especially the land-grant universities and the public community colleges, offer a wide range of services to the communities they serve.

Main Contents

1. History

American education was rooted from the beginning in the Old World experience. When the Puritan settlers in Massachusetts came to the New World, they brought with them a belief that education was fundamental to religion and to service for the commonwealth, and a familiarity with English schools and universities. Quite a number of the early settlers of the Bay Colony were graduates of Cambridge and Oxford universities. The Puritans set up schools as instinctively as they set up churches: the Boston Latin School in 1635, and **Harvard College** in 1636. Not long after their arrival in the New World wilderness, they took their first step toward establishing a system of public schools. In 1642, the colony of Massachusetts passed a law assigning responsibility for the education of children to parents. In 1647, Massachusetts passed another, more radical law, which required every town to provide its children with schools and schoolmasters.

The New Englanders showed the greatest zeal for education. Yet everywhere the American colonists created schools and brought in schoolmasters. Following the lead of the settlers in New England, the American colonies set up schools, academies, and colleges by the hundreds all through the colonial period. By the time of the American Revolution, public schools, charity schools, church schools, and academies were teaching children, and nine colleges (among them were College of William and Mary in **Williamsburg**, Virginia in 1639 and **Yale** in **New Haven**, Connecticut in 1701) scattered through the American wilderness, most of them later becoming universities. Already something of an American pattern of education was emerging.

With the achievement of independence, American education came into its own. The Founding Fathers of the United States, who themselves were educators, laid down the principles and institutions of education which still flourish. Of all the Founding Fathers, it was Thomas Jefferson who contributed most to American educational philosophy and practice. It was

Jefferson who, in his old age, built, almost single-handed, the first great state university in America-the University of Virginia. He urged the Virginia legislature for more ventures into the support of education, which were replicated in one way or another by other states. And these early efforts were quickly supplemented by **the Northwest Ordinance** of 1787, which, again with Jefferson's strong support, mandated each township in the Northwest Territory to reserve at least a mile-square section of land for educational purposes. However, the movement for free public schools gained its greatest momentum in the 1830's. By 1850, every state had provided for a system of free public schools open to all and paid for by public taxes. By the same year, state-supported colleges and universities had already been established in many states. And in 1862, Congress passed a law (**the Morrill Land-Grant College Act**), which provided states with public (federal) lands to be used for higher education, especially for the establishment of agricultural and mechanical-art colleges. These new state-supported institutions joined the large number of older, well established, and well to do privately financed universities.

Before the Civil War in the 1860s, there was little taste for laws that coerced children to attend school. Americans often asserted that parents alone had the right and responsibility to determine the extent to which children needed formal schooling. Moreover, the limited involvement of children in schools was comfortably consistent with the needs for child labor in an expansive industrial nation. With the rapid rise of cities on the American landscape and the surge of Eastern and Southern European immigrants into the cities after the Civil War, fears arose that urban children would be the source of urban disorder and crime. Consequently compulsory educational laws proliferated at an astonishing rate, and public schools expanded rapidly. This was a period in which the main lines of the modern American education system were established and fundamental assumptions about the American education system were shaped. And by 1900, there were almost a thousand institutions of higher education in the United States.

Since then federal legislature and government have continued influence with education. There were relief programs during the economic depression of the 1930's, the work-study programs in the "War on Poverty" beginning in 1964, and large financial contributions to schools starting in 1965. What is more significant is that **racial segregation** in both schools and colleges was declared unconstitutional.

2. Administration

In America, there is not one but 50 educational systems. This is largely due to the fact that the US Constitution mentions nothing about education. Each state enjoys substantial freedom to develop a school system as extensive or as limited as it desires. Local communities in turn were given by most states substantial freedom to select teachers and administrators and to schedule the school year and day to meet the minimum standards by the states. In America, therefore, education is a national concern, a state responsibility, and a local function.

Nationally, there was not a federal organization for education until the establishment of the **US Office of Education** in 1867, which in 1953 became a branch of the then largest federal agency—the **Department of Health, Education, and Welfare**. However, before 1965 this office was largely a statistics-gathering organization with little authority to run any programs, despite that the federal role of this office increased between 1957 and 1965. Although a federal Department of Education was established in 1979, its function is merely to gather information, to advise, and to help finance certain educational programs.

Since the US Constitution is silent on education, all educational matters are left to the individual state. On the state level, educational policy is generally the responsibility of a **state board** of citizens. Yet there is no one uniform pattern of state administration. Most of the northern states govern education with a state board of education, which in turn appoints a state commissioner of education.

In most states, the state legislature or governor appoints state boards, but a few state boards are elected. Ohio, for example, has one board member elected from each of 24 districts. What is confusing is the variety of the patterns. California has a state **Superintendent** elected by the people and a board appointed by the governor. **Wisconsin** is the only state with an elected superintendent but no board. New York's board is chosen by both houses of the legislature, and exerts the most control over schools, colleges, and other cultural institutions. The trend, however, has been toward a board appointed by the governor.

Of all the states, only Hawaii has complete authority over local schools and administers a single system of education, and, at the other extreme, **New Hampshire** leaves 98% of the financing of schools up to the local communities and to their property taxes.

Many southern and western states also determine the textbooks used in schools. Yet many other states leave the textbook selection and purchasing generally to the local school officials.

As a general pattern, states issue specific rules by which local schools determine a minimum school year (generally 170—180 days), a minimum length of day (5—6 hours), and minimum standards for teachers. They may also specify detailed standards concerning other matters as the construction of new buildings and the maintenance of existing facilities.

The governor, the state legislature, state court decisions, and tradition all influence the size and shape of state educational agencies. New York has long emphasized a strong state leadership. **Vermont**, Maine, and New Hampshire have kept their staffs small and favored a strong local initiative and citizen controls at the community level. **The Midwest** and **the Far West**, which were settled by New Englanders, also believed in local control.

Local administration varies tremendously from small local districts to counties and cities. As a general rule, most communities in the North, Midwest, and West have local school boards, which hire a superintendent to recruit and evaluate the teaching staff. The board is usually composed of lay citizens chosen in non-partisan elections for a term of 2—5 years. There are, however, numerous exceptions. Many large cities, such as Chicago, Philadelphia, and Pittsburgh, have their citizen school boards appointed by the mayor. Several states have partisan nominations for school board positions. Teachers employed by the school system cannot serve on the board for which they work.

Southern states administer education on a county basis, which is the pattern from Maryland south to Florida and west to **Louisiana** (where counties are called "parishes"). Local control in the South is therefore usually through a country superintendent. Until the 1950s, the Midwest and Pacific states also used county superintendents, but since then, some have abolished the system of county superintendence and others have modernized it by creating a regional superintendent to coordinate specialized services.

Funds for schools come from 3 sources. Approximately 50% is raised through local property taxes by vote of local citizens or officials, an average of from 40%—50% comes from the states, and only 8%—9% is from the national government. As usual the pattern varies enormously. Hawaii finances schools exclusively with state funds, and New Hampshire only provides 2% of the money needed with the rest 98% coming from local funds.

Colleges and universities are administered in a way quite separate from that of schools. The federal government influences higher education and contributes financially to it but has no control over its substance and practice.

Most states have separate university boards for what is called "higher education" (usually degree-granting colleges) or "post-secondary" (beyond the 12th year of high school). There are, however, some important exceptions: State boards in New York, Rhode Island, and **Michigan** set policy for education for all levels.

Most states have **"land-grant" universities**, which began as agricultural and mechanical colleges after 1862. Later, states also transformed the old normal schools and teachers colleges into state or regional universities. Much more recent are the community colleges, which offer two-year programs with many technical options for students of all ages. This is important because American education does not require that students choose between a technical career and a college.

Most state systems of education find ways to provide coordination between the various levels of education through board members or staff serving on other boards or committees. Pennsylvania, for instance, has a board consisting of two councils, one on higher education and the other on "basic education" (primary and secondary schools), which meet periodically.

Public higher education (state-run universities) is financed at least two-thirds by state and federal grants with the balance being paid by students in the form of tuition and other fees. Out-of-state students generally pay more at these institutions. Private colleges and universities levy higher tuition charges, which is the cause of the gradual decreasing of the number of students attending these institutions.

3. Practices

In America, education is carried out at various levels, which are mainly divided into elementary education, secondary education, and higher education.

Elementary and secondary education covers 12 years from age 6 through 18, but a variety of subdivisions may be identified, with the most popular pattern being 8-4 (8 years for elementary school and 4 years for high school). Other common patterns include 6-2-4 (6 years for primary school, 2 years for junior high school, and 4 years for senior high school), 6-3-3 (6 years for elementary school, 3 years for junior high school, and 3 years for senior high school), 4-4-4 (4 years for primary school, middle school, and high school respectively), and 6-6 (6 years for elementary school and combined junior and senior high school respectively).

What is worth nothing is that most schools start at the kindergarten level from age 4 or 5. And there are school districts that do not have this beginning stage, and others have an additional "pre-school" phase.

Ever since the colonial period, there has been a shift in emphasis on the goal of elementary education. For more than 250 years, the primary purpose of elementary schools has been to develop a sense of responsibility—religious, familial, economic, and civic or national. In the 20th century, however, there arose controversy over whether the goal of elementary education should be the development of a sense of responsibility or the development of autonomous individuals. Nonetheless, the four sets of general goals—academic, vocational, social, and personal—stand side by side before both teachers and students.

Secondary education takes place in a variety of junior and senior high schools. There are several different kinds of high schools with somewhat different missions. Vocational and technical high schools generally provide for a variety of occupations and vocations; some of them specialize in a single vocational or technical area such as aviation, electronic, and automotive trades. Academic high schools emphasize their schooling in academic and intellectual disciplines. The majority of American high schools, however, call themselves secondary education for almost all high schools age children and are responsible for providing good and appropriate education, both academic and vocational, for all young people.

Higher education in America is, too, noted for its complexity. The terms "college" and "university" are confusing. Although the two terms are often used synonymously, "college" usually refers to an institution that concentrates on a four-year study leading to graduation with a bachelor's degree, while a university is usually larger and provides, in addition to four years of undergraduate work, advanced research and studies in academic areas and professional fields leading to doctoral degree. "College" also sometimes refers to academic units, within universities. "University" can refer to a public system of higher education within a state that includes many campuses.

Higher education includes undergraduate study and graduate study. Undergraduate study lasts for four years. Undergraduate students are classified according to their year of study. First-year students are called freshmen, second-year students, sophomores, third-year students, juniors, and fourth-year students, seniors. The first two years of a four-year college program are devoted to general learning. Students at this stage of study take survey courses, which are generally broad in scope, i. e. treat a vast area of subject matter, and are usually taken as introductory courses for more specialized courses. During the third and fourth years of college, students specialize in one subject by concentrating most of their courses in it. The field of concentration is called a major.

The method of teaching in most colleges and universities consists of lectures supplemented by reading assignments and class discussions between the professor and students. Assignments usually call for students to read a number of books and/or articles and to write essays, reports and/or term papers. They may also include individual research, laboratory experiments, field trips, etc.

Examinations are mostly written. There are quizzes or tests, which are short examinations consisting of short questions requiring short responses, questions requiring essay-type answers, multiple-choice questions, or true-false questions. Mid-semester (midterm) examinations, given in the middle of the school term, are usually longer than quizzes. Midyear exams are given at the end of a term when a course carries over to the next semester. Finals are examinations that cover the subject matter of an entire course.

Every course is worth a certain number of hours; credits or points, depending on how many hours of lectures; class meetings, laboratory work, etc. are offered each week. Most colleges and universities require each student to complete successfully a minimum of 120 credits in order to receive an undergraduate degree. To receive full credit for their courses, students must maintain a satisfactory standard on the five-letter scale denoting levels of achievement. An average of grade C is considered a satisfactory level of achievement work. Degree B denotes above-average or superior work and "A" indicates excellent achievement, "D" is a passing grade, but denotes lower-than average work. "E" or "F" symbolizes completely unsatisfactory work. When a student receives an unsatisfactory grade, he is said to have failed or, colloquially, flunked. Some colleges allow students who receive an "E" to take a second final examination, but a student who receives an "E" or an "F" as a final mark fails to receive credit for the course. Selective courses are often marked Pass or Fail.

Graduate work leading to a master's degree usually requires two years' study beyond the bachelor's degree. Typically, requirements for the master's degree include successfully completing 30 to 32 credits of graduate courses with 20 of them in the major field of study, maintaining a minimum average of grade "B", writing a thesis, and passing examinations in all required courses. A doctor's degree requires a minimum of two years' full-time study beyond the master's degree, but in most fields more is necessary. For example, completion of the requirements for a doctorate in the field of science usually takes 4 to 5 years of study beyond the master's degree. Requirements for a doctor's degree often include demonstrating a reading knowledge of one or more foreign languages. In general, advanced studies leading to a master's degree and those leading to a doctor's degree emphasize preparation for research or professional practice.

Many graduate schools have assistantships available to candidates for graduate degrees. Assistantships are in a sense paying jobs. Assistantship duties range from grading papers or serving as a laboratory technician to teaching freshmen courses or doing specialized research. Assistants are expected to devote up to 20 hours each week for their service.

What is central to American higher education is the fact that the actual substance of education and the way it is provided are determined by individual professors or by their own institutions through the collective judgment of the professors. It is the faculty of the college or university that decides who shall be taught and for how long, what shall be taught and how, and who shall have the right to teach.

Also important to American higher education is the dual system of public and independent (private) educational institutions. The public institutions are created and supported by the state government and are expected to carry out missions assigned by it. The independent institutions support themselves, set their own missions, and operate relatively freely from outside influence. Despite the fact that the percentage of all students served by independent institutions has been dropping, these institutions remain highly influential. In fact, certain independent universities, such as **Harvard**, Chicago, and **Stanford**, are disproportionately influential.

One of the unique characteristics of collegiate institutions in the United States is the wide range of services such institutions offer the communities that they serve. These may include offering advice for farming, helping to conduct public school systems, providing cultural events and mass entertainment, contracting with local government and business for many different kinds of services, and even using institutional funds to rebuild deteriorating part of the cities in which they are located. Of the many different types of higher education institutions, the land-grant state universities and the public community colleges explicitly claim to provide such services as a major purpose and receive public subsidies to do so.

In spite of the developments made in the course of the American history, the actual practice of higher education continues to be more based on tradition than on social science evidence. The organizational structure, for example, is based for the most part on tradition rather than on evidence concerning how organizations operate. There has been much research and experimentation, but the overall effects seem to be slight.

Notes

1. Harvard College　哈佛学院
2. Williamsburg　威廉斯堡，弗吉尼亚东南部城市。
3. Yale　耶鲁(大学)
4. New Haven　纽黑文

5. the Northwest Ordinance 西北条例
6. the Morrill Land-Grant College Act 莫里尔关于政府划拨土地兴办大学的法案。美国国会于1862年通过该法案，根据这一法案，联邦政府向各州划拨土地，以兴办高等院校，特别是农业学院和机械艺术学院。
7. racial segregation 种族隔离
8. US Office of Education 美国教育部，始建于1867年。
9. Department of Health, Education, and Welfare 卫生、教育和福利部
10. state board 州教育委员会
11. Superintendent 教育主管
12. Wisconsin 威斯康星州
13. New Hampshire 新罕布什尔州
14. Vermont 佛蒙特州
15. the Midwest 中西部
16. the Far West 大西部
17. Louisiana 路易斯安那州
18. Michigan 密歇根州
19. "land-grant" universities 由政府划拨土地而建起来的大学
20. Harvard 哈佛(大学)
21. Stanford 斯坦福(大学)

Questions for Discussion

1. Why is it said that American education is rooted in the Old World?
2. What is the general pattern in which individual states administer education?
3. How are schools and colleges and universities financed?
4. What are the main categories of American education?
5. Describe the subdivisions of elementary and secondary education.
6. What are the different kinds of high schools? Give a brief description of their missions.
7. What is the central factor in the operation of American higher education institutions?
8. Why was it necessary for the US Congress to pass laws enforcing

compulsory education after the Civil War?

9. How is "college" different from "university"?
10. What are the different kinds of examinations for undergraduate students? Describe them briefly.
11. Give a brief description to the five-letter grading system.
12. What are students required to do in order to receive a master's degree or a doctor's degree?

Exercises

I . Choose the correct answer and circle the letter before it.

1. American education was rooted from the beginning in ________.
   A. the Old World experience
   B. the New World experience
   C. the early colonization
   D. the American Civil War
2. The settlers set up Harvard College in ________.
   A. 1635　B. 1636　C. 1642　D. 1647
3. American education came into its own with the achievement of ________.
   A. independence　B. economic development
   C. science and technology　D. industry
4. Of the founding fathers, ________ contributed most to American educational philosophy and practice.
   A. George Washington　B. Alexander Hamilton
   C. Thomas Jefferson　D. James Madison
5. The Morrill Land-Grant College Act passed by Congress in 1862 provided states with federal lands to be used for ________ education.
   A. elementary　B. secondary
   C. private　D. higher
6. The main lines of the modern American education system were established after ________.
   A. the Independence

B. the Constitution was drawn up

C. the Civil War

D. the turn of the 19th century

7. The Supreme Court declared ________ unconstitutional in 1965.

A. relief programs

B. the work-study programs

C. War on Poverty

D. racial segregation in Education

8. In the United States, education is a ________ responsibility.

A. federal　　B. state

C. local　　D. county

9. ________ has an education board member elected from each district.

A. Wisconsin　　B. California

C. Hawaii　　D. Ohio

10. Of the 50 states, only ________ has complete authority over local schools and administers a single system of education.

A. Ohio　　B. California

C. Hawaii　　D. New Hampshire

11. Most state "land-grant" universities began as ________ colleges after 1862.

A. medical

B. regional

C. agricultural and mechanical

D. teachers

12. ________ is the cause of the gradual decreasing of the number of students attending private colleges and universities.

A. Higher tuition charge　　B. Low academic standards

C. Racial segregation　　D. Poor prospect for word

13. The most popular elementary and secondary education pattern in the US is ________.

A. 8-4　　B. 6-2-4

C. 6-3-3　　D. 4-4-4

14. For over two and half centuries, the primary purpose of elementary schools had been to develop ________.

A. intelligence of the pupils B. academic level

C. a sense of responsibility D. physical conditions

15. Undergraduate students in the US are classified as freshmen, sophomores, juniors and seniors, according to their ________.

A. academic levels B. year of study

C. sexes D. economic conditions

16. The method of teaching in most US colleges and universities consists all the following except ________.

A. lecture B. class discussions

C. assignments D. collective research

17. ________ are examinations that cover the subject matter of an entire course.

A. Finals B. Midyear exams

C. Mid-semester exams D. Quizzes

18. Every course is worth a certain number of credits or points, depending on ________.

A. degree the students get

B. the difficulty the course has

C. the amount of the assignments

D. the number of hours of lectures

19. Degree ________ symbolizes completely unsatisfactory work in the US colleges or universities.

A. B B. C C. D D. E or F

20. Graduate work leading to a master's degree usually requires ________ years' study beyond the bachelor's degree in the United States.

A. two B. three C. four D. five

Ⅱ. Fill in the blanks with proper words or expressions.

1. In 1647, Massachusetts passed a law requiring every town to provide children with ________.

2. The founding fathers of the United States laid down ____________ which still flourish.

3. In America, there is not one but ________ educational systems.

4. Before the Civil War, Americans often asserted that ________ alone had the ________ to determine the extent to which children needed

________.

5. On the state level, educational policy is generally the responsibility of a ________.
6. Most state boards are appointed by ________ or ________, but a few are ________.
7. Local control of education in the Southern states is usually through ________.
8. Most states have ________ for the administration of higher education.
9. State-run universities are financed at least ________ by state and federal grants with students paying the balance in ________.
10. American education is mainly classified into ________, __________, and ________.
11. Elementary and secondary education covers ________ years from age ________ through ________.
12. In spite of the shift in emphasis on the goal of ________ to that of __________, both teachers and students have before them the four sets of general goals, namely ________, ________, ________ and ________.
13. Secondary education in the United States takes place in a variety of ________ and ________ high schools, which can be distinguished as ________, ________ and ________ high schools.
14. It is the ________ of the colleges and universities that decides who shall be taught and for how long, what shall be taught and how, and who shall have the right to teach.
15. A major purpose of the land-grant state universities and the public community colleges is to ________ for the communities they serve.
16. According to their year of study, undergraduate students are called ________, ________, ________ and ________ respectively.
17. During the first two years of study, college students take ________ courses, which are taken as ________ courses for more specialized courses.
18. Midyear exams are given ________ of a term when the subject matter carries over to ________.
19. The number of ________ for a course depends on how many ________

of lectures, class meetings, laboratory work, etc., are offered ________.

20. During the ________ of college, students concentrate most of their courses in one ________, which is known as a major.

Ⅲ. Translate the following into Chinese.

1. the Northwest Ordinance
2. the Morrill Land-Grant College Act
3. compulsory education
4. academic high school
5. the Northwest Territory
6. assistantship
7. community college
8. land-grant university
9. state board of education
10. state superintendent of schools
11. survey course
12. comprehensive high school
13. elective course
14. secondary education
15. colleges and universities

Ⅳ. Match each term in Column A with a time expression in Column B.

	Column A	Column B
1. ____	the Northwest Ordinance	a. 1979
2. ____	the Morrill Land-Grant College Act	b. 1867
3. ____	Harvard College	c. 1787
4. ____	the Department of Education	d. 1636
5. ____	the Office of Education	e. 1862

Ⅴ. Match each term in Column A with all the synonymous expressions in Column B.

	Column A	Column B
1. ____	land-grant universities	a. post-secondary education
2. ____	county	b. private universities
3. ____	higher education	c. state-supported universities

4. ____ independent universities
5. ____ basic education

d. parish
e. colleges and universities
f. state-run universities
g. elementary and secondary education
h. collegiate institutions

Ⅵ. In the five-letter grading system, each letter represents a certain level of achievement. Match each of the five letters in Column A with an expression in Column B that indicates its proper meaning.

Column A	**Column B**
1. ____ A	a. passing
2. ____ B	b. satisfactory
3. ____ C	c. above-average
4. ____ D	d. unsatisfactory
5. ____ E	e. excellent

Ⅶ. Identify each item in Column A with one of the features listed in Column B.

Column A	**Column B**
1. ____ Hawaii	a. the only state that has an elected superintendent but no board
2. ____ New Hampshire	b. where the first great state university in America is located
3. ____ Pennsylvania	c. which has one board member elected from each of the 24 school districts
4. ____ New York State	d. which has complete authority over local schools and administers a single system of education
5. ____ Virginia	e. which only provides schools with 2% of the money needed and the rest 98% comes from local funds
6. ____ Wisconsin	f. which has its citizen school board appointed by the mayor

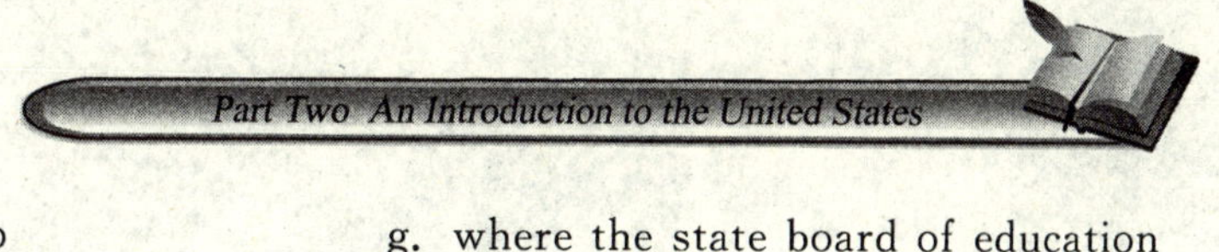

7. ____	Ohio	g.	where the state board of education is chosen by both houses of legislature
8. ____	Chicago	h.	which has the first higher education institution in America—Harvard College
9. ____	Connecticut	i.	where Yale University was founded in 1701
10. ____	Massachusetts	j.	which has a state board of education consisting of two councils, one on higher education and the other on basic education

Key to Exercises

Lesson 11 Geography: The Land

Ⅰ. Choose the best answer and circle the letter before it.

1. B	2. B	3. C	4. A	5. B
6. B	7. D	8. D	9. D	10. B
11. C	12. D	13. B	14. D	15. B
16. C	17. D	18. A	19. A	20. D

Ⅱ. Fill in the following blanks with appropriate words or expressions.

1. 9,631,420
2. Alaska
3. Appalachian Mountain, Mitchell
4. Rocky Mountain, Cascades, Nevada, Coast Mountain
5. Columbia, Colorado
6. Whitney, Death
7. plains
8. Aleutian
9. Michigan
10. Niagara
11. cold, temperate, warm

Ⅲ. Explain the following in English.

1. Alaska is the largest state of the 50 states of America, located in the extreme of Northwestern part of North America and separated from the continental United States by Canada. Alaska was bought by the USA from Russia in 1867. Alaska consists of the mainland and the Aleutian Islands, which form one of the longest volcanic island chains in the world.
2. The Mississippi River is one of the world's great rivers; it was known to American Indians as the "father of waters." Water from

the source of its main branch, the Missouri River, flows about 6,262 kilometers from the northern Rocky Mountains, to the mouth of the Mississippi in the Gulf of Mexico. Its two main tributaries are the Ohio River and the Missouri River. The Mississippi River and its tributaries form an important and vast system of waterways that are connected to the Great Lakes in the north by a canal.

3. The Hudson River flows through New York State from the north to south, with New York City at its mouth. It is linked by canals with the five Great Lakes. The Hudson River serves as a main artery for inland waterway traffic.
4. Gold Rush was one of the greatest mass movements in modern history, in which thousands of people came to California from all over the world to seek their fortunes in the rocks when gold was discovered in San Francisco in 1848. As a result of the Gold Rush, the whole continent of North America was settled within the 19th century.
5. Hawaii is one of the 50 states of America, located in the central Pacific Ocean, approximately 3,200 kilometers away from the mainland of the United States. It was occupied by the American Navy after the Spanish American War of 1898, and was admitted to the Union in 1960. It consists of a long chain of islands, including 8 main islands and over a hundred atolls and uninhabited islets. The island of Hawaii has active volcanoes. Mauna Loa is the world's largest active volcano.
6. The "Motor City" refers to Detroit. The city is located on the Detroit River between Lake Huron and Lake Erie. It is the largest center of the automobile industry in the United States and produces over 90% of all automobiles made in America.
7. The "Space City, USA" is Houston, the largest city in Texas and the sixth largest city in the United States. Houston is the center of the petrochemical industry. With the manned Spacecraft Center, Houston has won the name "Space City, USA."
8. The Appalachian Mountains form the highlands in the eastern part of the United States. It stretches from the St. Lawrence Rive to

the central part of Alabama State, about 2,000 kilometers in length. The northern part of the Appalachian Mountain Range consists of a number of separate mountains, such as the White Mountain, the Green Mountain, and the central part of it consists of several parallel mountain ranges, such as the Blue Ridge, the Allegheny Mountain Range. These highlands are comparatively low, with an average elevation of 800 meters above the sea level.

9. The Cordillera Range is a term given to refer to the mountain ranges in the far west of the United States. It consists of the Rocky Mountains, the Cascades, the Sierra Nevada and the Coast Range.
10. Niagara Falls is a very famous natural scene in the United States. It is located on the US-Canadian boundary between Lake Erie and Lake Ontario. The American Falls is 1,240 meters wide and 49 meters high.

Ⅳ. Match the names of the states in Column A with their major features in Column B.

1. c 2. d 3. b 4. a

Ⅴ. Match the names of the cities in Column A with their features in Column B.

1. c 2. d 3. a 4. b 5. g
6. h 7. e 8. j 9. f 10. i

Lesson 12 Geography: The People

Ⅰ. Choose the best answer and circle the letter before it.

1. B 2. B 3. D 4. A 5. D
6. A 7. B 8. B 9. D 10. C 11. D

Ⅱ. Fill in the following blanks with appropriate words or expressions.

1. European
2. tribes
3. WASPs
4. 50
5. Negro, Africa

6. Emancipation Proclamation
7. Hispanics, Black
8. coolies
9. Japanese, Caucasian, Polynesian
10. oppression, ethnicity
11. 301.139947
12. westward
13. English, Spanish
14. Protestants
15. monopoly, unequal

Ⅲ. Match the names of the ethnic or racial groups with the percentage of the total population they make up at present in the United States.

1. c 2. a 3. d 4. b

Ⅳ. Explain the following in English.

1. Melting pot is metaphorically used to refer to the United States because it is a country of many ethnic groups from different parts of the world, who came to the New World to seek for freedom in politics or religion. They have been dissipating their different ethnic cultures toward some "standard" by living and working together in the "melting pot" of the United States and gradually forming a new nation.
2. The word "WASPs" is the abbreviation of White Anglo-Saxon Protestants. They were early settlers on North America from England, Northern and Western Europe. At present, they constitute the largest and dominant ethnic group in the United States.
3. Ethnicity is different from race. The basis of ethnicity is the country of origin, language spoken and culture that the group of people shared, while the basis of race is the skin color.
4. Population center of gravity refers to that point at which the country would balance if only the weight of the population were considered. The population center of gravity of the United States has kept moving westward ever since 1790 after the establishment of the first Federal government.

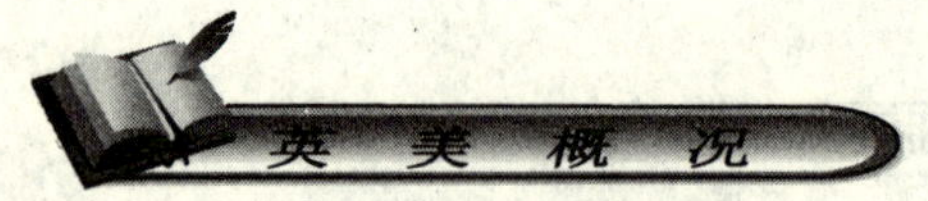

5. Hispanics refers to the people from Latin America, the former Spanish colonies, including Mexican-Americans, Cuban refugees, Puerto Ricans, etc. They speak Spanish language. Today they constitute the second largest ethnic minority in the United States.

Lesson 13 American Economy

Ⅰ. Choose the correct answer and circle the letter before it.

1. B 2. A 3. B 4. C 5. A 6. C
7. A 8. A 9. B 10. A 11. C 12. B
13. A 14. B 15. D 16. D 17. A 18. C

Ⅱ. Fill in the following blanks with proper words or expressions.

1. commercial, industrial, corporate
2. Great Britain
3. the 1870's, rationalized, centralized
4. production, strategies, consumption
5. enormous, diversified, multinational
6. Northeast
7. South
8. mining
9. Automation, computerization
10. central plain
11. corn, wheat, barley, oats, rice
12. Great Lakes, Corn Belt
13. automobile
14. fastest
15. goods, commercial
16. protectionist

Ⅲ. Match the names of the states or regions with their chief agricultural or industrial products.

1. b 2. d 3. a 4. e 5. c

Ⅳ. Explain the following in English.

1. Corporate capitalism or imperialism is the last stage in the development of capitalism, which is characterized by the

emergence of monopoly corporations, high concentration of capital and the disappearance of free competition.

2. ITT is the abbreviation of International Telephone and Telegraph, an American company.
3. IBM is the abbreviation of International Business Machines, an American company.
4. The Corn Belt is a region of Midwest of the United States, south of the Five Great Lakes, extending from Ohio to Arkansas and Nebraska where corn and corn fed livestock are raised.
5. The Wheat Belt is a region in the northern part of the Great Plain of the United States, in the prairie region, including the states of Montana, North Dakota, South Dakota, Nebraska and Kansas, where wheat is grown. The state of Kansas in this region leads the whole country in the production of wheat, followed by N. Dakota, S. Dakota and Oklahoma.

Ⅴ. Translate the following into Chinese.

1. 杜邦化学公司
2. 通用电气公司
3. 通用汽车公司
4. 克里夫兰
5. 巴尔的摩

Lesson 14 Political System: Government

Ⅰ. Choose the best answer and circle the letter before it.

1. D 2. B 3. B 4. A 5. B
6. D 7. B 8. B 9. A 10. C
11. D 12. C 13. D 14. B 15. C 16. B

Ⅱ. Fill in the following blanks with proper words or expressions.

1. federal, separation
2. President
3. Departments
4. veto
5. Senate

6. Congress
7. Secretary of State
8. Attorney General
9. Interior
10. Senate, Representatives
11. laws
12. Vice-President
13. 435
14. committees
15. two-thirds
16. Supreme Court

Ⅲ. Match the names of departments or agencies with their corresponding duties or responsibilities.

1. c 2. d 3. a 4. f 5. g 6. e 7. b

Ⅳ. Explain the following in English.

1. Separation of powers is one of the principles the United States Constitution drawn in 1787 followed. According to this principle, there is a division of powers between the federal government and the state governments. There is also a division of powers among the three branches of the federal government: the legislative branch, the executive branch and the judicial branch. Congress exercises the legislative power, the President, the executive power, and the Supreme Court, the judicial power. They are supposed to be independent of each other, but each checks the other two so that no one can get all the power. This arrangement is called the separation of powers, which calls for "checks and balances."
2. The National Security Council was set up in 1947 to advise the President of the United States on all matters related to national security. The Council is usually made up of the President, Vice-President, the Secretary of State, the Secretary of Defense, the Secretary of the Treasury, the Director of the Office of Emergency Planning, the Director of the CIA, etc. The Council does not make any decision; it makes suggestions to the President concerning the national security.
3. The Central Intelligence Agency was set up in 1947. Its activities have

included collecting information from abroad, instances of subversion, interference, and attempting to control other countries. Its organization, budget and personnel are kept secret.

4. "Pocket veto" is a type of veto power enjoyed by the President of the United States. It is laid down that the President must take action in ten days after he receives the bill passed by Congress. If he holds it for ten days without signing it, the bill also becomes law if congress remains in session. The single exception to this rule is that when Congress adjourns after sending a bill to the President and before the 10-day period has expired, his refusal to take any action then negates the bill. This process is known as the "pocket veto." A bill vetoed this way by the President will not be returned to Congress for further debate and voted once more.
5. Congress of the United States is the legislative branch of the central government. It consists of the Senate and the House of Representatives. It has the power to make any laws that are considered "proper and necessary." There is a division of powers between the two houses. Much of the work is done by their committees. Congress has the power to check the two other branches of government: the executive branch and the judicial branch.
6. The United States Information Agency was set up 1947. It maintains information offices and libraries in most countries, operates the Voice of America and conducts international cultural exchange programs.
7. The Supreme Court of the United States consists of the Chief Justice and eight Justices. It deals with the cases affecting ambassadors, ministers and consuls of foreign countries, and those in which a state is involved. In other cases it acts as a court of final appeal. It has won the power of judicial review ever since 1803.
8. Judicial review is a kind of power that the Supreme Court won for itself in 1803 when John Marshal was the Chief Justice. It is the power to interpret the Constitution and declare a law passed by Congress "unconstitutional" and therefore, null and void, when the case in which the law is involved is put before it. By exercising this power of judicial review, the Supreme Court has actually won the power to say what the

law is and the power to check Congress.

Lesson 15 Political System: State Government and Party Politics

Ⅰ. Choose the correct answer and circle the letter before it.

1. B 2. C 3. A 4. B 5. C
6. B 7. D 8. A 9. B 10. B
11. B 12. C 13. B 14. C 15. B

Ⅱ. Fill in the following blanks with proper words or expressions.

1. three
2. legislature, two
3. governor, popular, National Guard
4. jurisdiction, trial courts, Supreme
5. grand, petit, grand, petit
6. county, village, purpose
7. Federal, Democratic-Republic/Anti-Federal, 19
8. Democratic, Republican
9. four, Presidential, Vice-President platform
10. election campaign, money
11. monopolists
12. delegates
13. platform
14. electors
15. Senators, Representatives, Congress
16. majority
17. electoral
18. House of Representatives, Senate
19. two, ten
20. the Vice-President

Ⅲ. Explain the following in English.

1. The grand jury and the petit jury are two types of jury utilized by the US federal and state courts. The grand jury indicts or refuses to indict the accused persons. If a majority of the grand jury

decides there is sufficient evidence for a trial, the case passes to a court where guilt or innocence is decided by a petit jury, which is usually made up of 12 persons. In most states, the petit jury must reach a unanimous agreement on guilt, or the defendant is acquitted or a mistrial declared.

2. The mayor-council system of city government is the most popular kind of local government. In mayor-council system, the city has an elected mayor as head of the local government and an elected council to help him. Most cities in the US adopt such system.
3. The city-manager type of local government is the second most popular kind of a city government in the United States, in which an elected council hires a professional city manager to administer and watch over the city business, while the elected council keeps the legislative power.
4. The Federal Party is one of the two political parties that emerged immediately after the establishment of the first Federal government in 1789. The Federal Party was headed by Alexander Hamilton, which represented the interests of the commercial capitalists, who were supporters of the Constitution of the United States of America drawn up in 1787 in Philadelphia and were in favor of a strong central government and the development of commerce and industry and tried to maintain friendly relations between the United States and England. The Federal Party became notorious and broke up after the "Second American War of Independence"(1812—1814) in the early 19th century.
5. The Democratic-Republican Party is one of the earliest political parties that were established immediately after the establishment of the first Federal Government in 1789. The Democratic-Republican Party was led by Thomas Jefferson. It represented the interests of southern slave-owners and the middle classes in the North, who were in favor of a week central government, the maintenance of state powers and the development of agriculture. In foreign relations, this party wanted to maintain friendly relations with France. It ceased to exist after the Federal Party broke up.

6. The "Second American War of Independence" was a war fought between the United States and Britain when the United States tried to annex the British colonies in Canada from 1812—1814. In the war, the English took over the capital city Washington and burned down many of its public buildings, including the White House. When the war ended, a peace treaty was signed between the two countries in Paris, in which Britain recognized the independence of the United States, and the United States promised not to invade Canada once more.
7. Popular votes are votes cast by voters for the election of Presidential electors.
8. Electoral votes are votes cast by the Presidential electors for the election of the President and Vice-President. The number of electoral votes a state has is equal to the number of the congressmen the state has in Congress.
9. Party platform of a party is a very general statement of the party's policy for both domestic and foreign affairs. It is usually adopted in the party convention held in July or August of the election year.
10. The Election Day is fixed on the first Tuesday after the first Monday in November in an election year, on which voters in the United States cast ballots for President and Vice President. Some members of Congress and many state and local officials are also elected the same day.

Lesson 16 History: The Early Colonization

Ⅰ. Choose the correct answer and circle the letter before it.

1. C 2. A 3. B 4. B 5. D 6. C
7. C 8. B 9. B 10. A 11. C 12. B

Ⅱ. Fill in the following blanks with proper words or expressions.

1. American Indians, Asia, Bering Strait
2. Marco Polo
3. 1492, India
4. Amerigo Vespucci

5. Brazil, South America, Mexico, St Lawrence, Five Great Lakes
6. Virginia Company of Plymouth, Virginia Company of London
7. Jamestown
8. Puritans, Pilgrims, New England
9. Royal, proprietary, self-governing
10. lumbering, shipping, small farms, plantation, slave

Ⅲ. Match the names of the British colonies in Column A with the corresponding people who founded them in Column B.

1. c 2. a 3. b 4. e 5. d

Ⅳ. Explain the following in English.

1. American Indians were the earliest inhabitants in North and South Americas. They had lived and labored there for thousands of years before the New World was discovered by Christopher Columbus in 1492. It is said that American Indians had come over from Asia about 25, 000 years ago when there was a land bridge that connected Asia and North America. Columbus called them Indians because he mistook the land he discovered for India.
2. Christopher Columbus was an Italian navigator, who believed that he could reach Indian by sailing west across the Atlantic Ocean since the earth was round. He offered his service to the Spanish King and Queen and was given the authority over land he might discover in the name of Spain. Columbus and his men, after two month of sailing west and finally discovered the New World in 1492.
3. Ferdinand Magellan was a Portuguese navigator, who, like Columbus hoped to reach India by sailing west, and in 1519 set out from Spain. He made across the Atlantic Ocean, sailed along the coast of South America and around the southern tip of the continent and on to the broad Pacific Ocean. They reached the Philippines where the natives killed Magellan. At last only one of his ships was able to keep going. It finally sailed around Africa and on to Spain. The voyage took three years and proved that India could be reached by sailing west.
4. Indentured Servants were poor people who would agree to give up

the fruits of their labors to the investors for the first seven, or ten, or even fifteen years to pay for voyage from England to the New World. After that the settlers could enrich themselves.

5. Mayflower Compact was the plan of government signed on the *Mayflower* by 41 English settlers off Cape Cod, on November 11, 1620, before landing and founding their settlement at Plymouth. The Mayflower Compact was a plan for a democratic society on Calvinist lines, and was a model for later colonies; its ideas lie behind the US Constitution of 1789.
6. Jamestown was the first permanent colony set up by the English colonists in North America in 1607. Jamestown soon developed a flourishing economy from its tobacco crop. Later, Jamestown developed into Virginia.
7. New England is the name of a region in northeast USA, consisting of 6 states, Maine, New Hampshire, Vermont, Massachusetts, Rhode Island and Connecticut, where the original settlers were mainly English Puritans. Of the six states, four were once the original British colonies: Massachusetts, Rhode Island, Connecticut and New Hampshire. New England colonies became a center for lumbering, shipping and fishing. New England was the center of the American War of Independence; it has always been the main literary and educational center of the USA, and is also a highly industrialized area. New Englanders are considered to be shrewd and independent: they are known as Yankees, a name first used in the 18th century.
8. Proprietary Colonies were a type of colonies that belonged to a person or a group of persons. For example, Pennsylvania was set up by a group of people from England known as Quakers headed by William Penn in 1682. Georgia was set up in 1733 by Colonel James Oglethorpe to provide homes for poor people from England. Proprietary colonies soon turned into Royal colonies later.
9. Royal Colonies were one type of the British 13 colonies in North America. Royal colonies were those controlled directly by the King of England and the English government.

10. Self-governing colonies were those ruled by the colonists living in them. Only Connecticut and Rhode Island were self-governing colonies.

Lesson 17 History: American Revolution

Ⅰ. Choose the correct answer and circle the letter before it.

1. C 2. B 3. B 4. A 5. D
6. A 7. A 8. D 9. D 10. C
11. B 12. B 13. C 14. C

Ⅱ. Fill in the following blanks with proper words or expressions.

1. English, French, Ohio
2. freedom, taxes
3. reason, agreement, enforcing, reason, altered
4. Benjamin Franklin
5. theoretical, philosophical
6. Mercantilist, markets, manufacturing
7. British
8. economic
9. external
10. representation

Ⅲ. Match the historical events in Column A with the years in which they took place in Column B.

1. d 2. c 3. a 4. b 5. f
6. g 7. h 8. e 9. j 10. i

Ⅳ. Explain the following in English.

1. The French and Indian War was a decisive war fought between the English on the one side and the French and American Indians on the other in the period between 1756 and 1763 in North America, contending for the Ohio Valley. As the result of this war, the French was completely defeated and lost all her land in America and were driven out of India.
2. John Locke was an English materialist philosopher, who furnished the 18th century with a theory about reason. He rejected innate

knowledge, and believed that man's knowledge was acquired from the experience of five senses, from observation and experiment, and from the reflection by the mind. Civil government was instituted by mutual agreement for the purpose of enforcing natural laws. The most important law was that no man should take away the life, liberty, or property of another. A government that failed to protect life, liberty, and property lost its reason for existence and deserved being altered or overthrown by the people it governed.

3. Mercantilist policy was the policy that the British government pursued in the 13 colonies in America to levy more taxes. By practicing such a policy, the British government tried to turn the colonies into the source of raw materials and the market of the manufactured products of the mother country by monopolizing the markets in the colonies and holding back the development of manufacturing there, so as to control everything and keep all profits for the mother country.
4. The Stamp Act was passed by the British Parliament in 1765, which required that a stamp, purchased from the British government, be placed on all legal documents, newspapers and other printed materials. This Act aroused the hostility of the most powerful and articulate groups in the colonial population.
5. The Sugar Act was passed by the British Parliament in 1764 in order to levy more taxes. It provided that all molasses entering the colonies from lands other than the British West Indies would be taxed.
6. Boston Massacre was an incident that took place in Boston in 1770. On March 5, that year, violence broke out in Boston. A group of about fifty Boston citizens were jeering at the British soldiers and tempers ran high. Some of them threw snowballs with stones inside at the British soldiers. As the tension mounted, the soldiers fired at the crowd and killed five men. This incident came to be known as the "Boston Massacre."
7. Boston Tea Party was a historical event in American Revolution. In

1773, the British government passed the Tea Act, which permitted the British East India Company to sell tea directly to its agents in the colonies. This Act made many merchants angrier than ever with the British. On December 16, a group of Boston citizens, who disguised themselves as Indians, boarded three British ships in the harbor and tossed a cargo of tea worth 17,000 pounds overboard. This incident was known as "Boston Tea Party."

8. Sons of Liberty were a revolutionary organization formed by workers, farmers, merchants and revolutionary intellectuals in the thirteen colonies in 1765 for resistance against the Stamp Act passed by the British Parliament. They burnt stamps, made demonstrations and kill or drove away the British tax officers. This organization was called Sons of Liberty. It played a very important part in organizing the thirteen colonies in their fighting against the British rule.
9. The Second Continental Congress was called in May 1775 after the first shot was fired in Lexington and Concord. Representatives from all the thirteen colonies met in Philadelphia to discuss the situation. One of the first decisions it made was to establish a regular army, with George Washington as commander-in-chief. The Second Continental Congress adopted the Declaration of Independence. It played a very important part in leading the Americans in their fight for independence. July 4 later became the National Day of the United States.
10. The Declaration of Independence was drawn up by Thomas Jefferson and was adopted by the Second Continental Congress in 1776. Its main ideas were that all men were created equal and had certain inalienable rights, among which were life, liberty, and the pursuit of happiness; that government got their powers fro[illegible] the consent of those they governed; and that a government th[illegible] did not live up to the purposes for which it was created could [illegible] abolished by the people. The Declaration also listed way[illegible] which the colonists had been mistreated, so as to make [illegible] American Revolution sound reasonable.

11. Committees of Correspondence were one of the revolutionary organizations in the thirteen colonies in North America. It was organized by Samuel Adams in 1772 and made possible the cooperation of colonists all over the thirteen colonies.
12. Bill of Rights referred to the first ten amendments to the Constitution of the United States of America. They were added to the original body of the Constitution in 1791. Among the more important rights guaranteed to the US citizens are freedom of religion, freedom of speech, freedom of the press, the right to assemble and the right to petition for what a citizen may think is needed from the government. Now they are viewed as the original body of the American Constitution.

Lesson 18 History: American Civil War

Ⅰ. Choose the correct answer and circle the letter before it.

1. C 2. D 3. B 4. D 5. C
6. A 7. C 8. A 9. D 10. B

Ⅱ. Fill in the following blanks with proper words or expressions.

1. Louisiana
2. Spain
3. Texas

Oregon

'zarist Russia

10

, textile

lave, high, low

ee, outvoted, political

eecher Stowe

ereignty

e States of America, Jefferson Davis

r

16. Emancipation
17. Richmond, Grant, Appomattox
18. Bourgeois

Ⅲ. Match the following historical events with the corresponding year in which they took place.

1. c 2. b 3. e 4. a 5. d

Ⅳ. Rearrange the following historical events in the order in which they took place.

1. d 2. e 3. b 4. a 5. c

Ⅴ. Explain the following in English.

1. Louisiana Purchase: In 1803, President Thomas Jefferson, by taking advantage of the war in Europe, made Napoleon Ⅰ agree to sell Louisiana Territory for $15 million, at the price of 4 cents per acre. This was a vast region of more than 2.6 million square kilometers, stretching from the Great lakes to the Gulf of Mexico. The Louisiana Purchase doubled the original territory of the United States.
2. Monroe Doctrine was delivered to Congress by President James Monroe in 1823, in which he warned the European powers against any attempt at intervention in Latin American affairs with the aim of keeping the Latin American countries for the United States itself.
3. The Compromise of 1820 was made in 1820 to keep the balance in the Senate when Missouri was to be admitted to the Union as a new state. As a compromise, Missouri was added to the Union as a slave state, and Maine was created and admitted as a free state. The Compromise also prohibited slavery in any other lands in the Louisiana Territory north of the 36°30′ line.
4. The Henry Clay's Compromise of 1850 was made to solve t problem of California when it was to be admitted to the Unior 1850: whether California would be a slave state or a free state Henry Clay's Compromise, California became a free state, wh the new territories of Utah and New Mexico the citizens w

decide for themselves on the issue of slavery, and a new, more strict Fugitive Slave Act was passed by Congress, which gave slave-owners the right to search and seize runaway slaves in any free states.

5. The Kansas-Nebraska Act was passed by the US Congress in 1854, which extended the idea of "popular sovereignty." The land it referred to had been closed to slavery by the Missouri Compromise of 1820. The passage of the Kansas-Nebraska Act meant the Missouri Compromise of 1820 was in effect repealed.
6. Popular sovereignty was a doctrine advocated by the moderates in 1850s in the US, proposing respect for the American tradition of self-government and grant of permission to the people who actually settled in a territory to decide the issue of slavery for themselves.
7. The Confederate States of America consisted of states that had seceded from the Union. It was formed in February 1861. They elected Jefferson Davis President and took Richmond as their capital.
8. The Emancipation Proclamation was issued by President A. Lincoln in on September 22, 1862, which would liberated all slaves of the seceded states that refused to return to the Union before the Proclamation went into effect on January 1, 1863. It was one of the most important measures taken by Lincoln's Administration in 1862 in order to change the situation of the Civil War.

The Homestead Act was one of the measures taken by Lincoln's ...dministration in May 1862 to change the situation of the Civil ... Under the Homestead Act the land problem was solved in ...erests of the small farmers.

...gers referred to the Northerners who took the advantage of ...tability in the reconstruction of Southern states and went ...e profits for themselves by controlling the Blacks and the ...nents.

Lesson 19 History: US Imperialism

Ⅰ. Choose the correct answer and circle the letter before it.

1. C 2. A 3. D 4. B 5. B
6. B 7. A 8. A 9. A 10. D

Ⅱ. Fill in the following blanks with proper words or expressions.

1. 1894
2. competitive, monopoly
3. meat-packing
4. 86
5. Latin America
6. 1889
7. Cuba, Cuba, Puerto Rico, Guam
8. Columbia
9. *Wangxia*
10. *Tientsin*
11. Open Door
12. 1917
13. seas, League
14. Pearl
15. Cold, containment, contention
16. 72, 1979

Ⅲ. Explain the following in English.

1. "Blacklists": During the 1880's and 1890's, workers in America began to form unions on a large scale. The capitalists tried to sabotage the unions by enlisting the union workers on "blacklist," which would be sent to other companies in the industry with a warning not to hire them.
2. "Yellow dog" contracts: In the late 19th century, along the development of workers' unions, capitalists in America forced workers to sign contracts pledging not to join unions so as to sabotage the unions. Such contracts are called "yellow dog"

contract.

3. A. F of L is the abbreviated form of the American Federation of Labor, which was organized in the 1880's.
4. CIO is the short form for the Congress of Industrial Organization, which was formed by combination of a group of unions in the 1930's. In 1955, A. F. of L and the CIO merged to form a single national union.
5. Closed shop can be used to refer to an agreement that requires the employer to hire only union members, or such a plant, or shop.
6. Haymarket martyrs refer to those who died at Chicago's Haymarket on May 1, 1886 when the police fired at workers who went on simultaneous strikes in Chicago, Washington, D. C., New York and other large cities.
7. The Spanish-American War was a war launched by the United States against Spain in 1898 when an American battleship, the Maine, was blown up in Havana Harbor with a loss of 260 lives. The war broke out in April, lasted for only 70 days and ended with the US as victor. A peace treaty was signed, under which Spain was forced to cede her former colonies Cuba, Puerto Rico, Guam and the Philippines to the United States.
8. The New Deal is a name for the measures taken by President Franklin D. Roosevelt in 1933 in his efforts to save the economic situation in the great depression. The New Deal measures had two principal purposes. Internally, through a huge increase in government expenditure to create employment by launching large-scale public works, to raise the sagging farm prices by destroying crops and reducing agricultural production. Externally, the United States adopted a "Good Neighbor Policy" toward Latin American countries and established diplomatic relations with the Soviet Union. Efforts were made to consolidate the old market abroad and to conquer the new ones.
9. Truman Doctrine was initiated by President Truman in 1947, which promised economic and military aid to any nation threatened by an outside power, in an attempt to check the spread of Communism.

10. Marshal Plan, like Truman Doctrine, was directed towards the aim at checking Communism after the end of World War Ⅱ by offering economic aid to Western European countries for their post-war reconstruction.

Lesson 20 American Education

Ⅰ. Choose the correct answer and circle the letter before it.

1. A 2. B 3. A 4. C 5. D
6. C 7. D 8. B 9. D 10. C
11. C 12. A 13. A 14. C 15. B
16. D 17. A 18. D 19. D 20. A

Ⅱ. Fill in the blanks with proper words or expressions.

1. Schools and schoolmasters
2. principles and institutions of education
3. 50
4. parents, right and responsibility, formal schooling
5. state board of citizens
6. the state legislature, governor, elected
7. counties
8. separate university boards
9. two-thirds, the form of tuition and other fees
10. elementary, secondary, higher
11. 12, 6, 18
12. a sense of responsibility, autonomous individuals, academic, vocational, social, personal
13. junior, senior, vocational, technical, academic
14. faculty
15. provide services
16. freshmen, sophomores, juniors, seniors
17. survey, introductory
18. at the end, the next semester
19. credits, hours, each week
20. the third and fourth years, subject

Ⅲ. Translate the following into Chinese.

1. 西北条例
2. 莫里尔关于划拨土地兴办大学的法案
3. 强制性教育
4. 非职业中学
5. 西北领土
6. 研究生助教奖学金
7. 社区学院
8. 由联邦政府划拨土地兴建的大学
9. 州教育委员会
10. 州教育主管
11. 概况课程
12. 综合中学
13. 选修课程
14. 中等教育
15. 学院和大学

Ⅳ. Match each term in Column A with a time expression in Column B.

1. c　　2. e　　3. d　　4. a　　5. b

Ⅴ. Match each term in Column A with all the synonymous expressions in Column B.

1. c　　2. d　　3. a　　4. b　　5. g

Ⅵ. In the five-letter grading system, each letter represents a certain level of achievement. Match each of the five letters in Column A with an expression in Column B that indicates its proper meaning.

1. e　　2. c　　3. b　　4. a　　5. d

Ⅶ. Identify each item in Column A with one of the features listed in Column B.

1. d　　2. e　　3. j　　4. g　　5. b
6. a　　7. c　　8. f　　9. i　　10. h

APPENDIX Ⅰ

Ⅰ. Outstanding Events in English History

2,500—7th century B. C.	Iberians
7th century B. C. —5th century A. D.	Celts
55—54 B. C.	Julius Caesar explored England.
43—50 A. D.	Claudius conquered England.
43—410 A. D.	Roman Britain
Mid-5th century	Anglo-Saxon Conquest
597 A. D.	Augustine landed in Kent.
The late 8th century	Danish Invasion
878	Alfred defeated Danes.
Oct. 14, 1066	the Battle of Hastings
Dec. 25, 1066	William was crowned King of England.
1086	Doomsday Book
1215	The Magna Carta was signed.
1265	Simon de Montfort summoned the first parliament.
1337—1453	the Hundred Years' War
1348—1350	Black Death
1381	Wat Tyler's Uprising
1455—1485	Wars of the Roses
1485—1603	the House of Tudor
1529—1536	the Reformation
1535	the union with Wales
1549	the peasant uprising led by Kett
1588	The English defeated the Spanish Armada.
1640—1653	the "Long Parliament"

1642—1646	the First Civil War in Britain
1648	the Second Civil war
1649	Charles Ⅰ was beheaded in January; the Commonwealth was founded.
1653—1658	Cromwell became Protector of the Commonwealth.
1660	the Restoration of the Stuart
1679	the formation of the first political parties: the Tories and the Whigs
1688	the "Glorious Revolution"
1707	Scotland united with England.
1756—1763	the Seven Years' War
The 1760's	the establishment of British colonies in N. America, India and West Indies
The 1760's—1840's	the Industrial Revolution in Britain
1769	James Watt made steam engine.
1801	the British annexation of Ireland
1805	the Battle of Trafalgar: Nelson destroyed the French Navy.
1814	Stephenson built steam locomotive.
1815	the Battle of Waterloo: Allies under Wellington defeated Napoleon.
1819	Peterloo Massacre
1837—1848	Chartism
1840	the Opium War
1842	the Treaty of Nanking
1864	the First International was founded in London.
1875	The British government controlled the Suez.
1899—1902	the Anglo-Boer War
1906	the Labor Party was formed.
1914—1918	the First World War
1929	the world economic crisis
1938	Munich Agreement
1939	Britain declared war on Germany.

1972	Britain established diplomatic relations with China at the ambassadorial rank.
1979	Mrs. Thatcher was elected Prime Minister of Britain.
1987	Mrs. Thatcher was re-elected.
1990	John Major won the election.
1997	Hong Kong returned to China.

Ⅱ. The List of Kings of England

1. Saxon Kings (871—1066) 撒克逊国王

Alfred the Great 阿尔弗雷德大帝	871—900
Edward Elder 老爱德华	900—924
Athelstan 埃塞尔斯坦	924—940
Edgar 爱德加	959—975
Ethelred 爱塞雷德	979—1016
Canute (Danish) 卡纽特(丹麦)	1016—1036
Edward the Confessor 信教者爱德华	1042—1066
Harold Ⅱ 哈罗德二世	1066

2. House of Normandy (1066—1154) 诺曼底王朝

William Ⅰ the Conqueror 征服者威廉一世	1066—1087
William Ⅱ 威廉二世	1087—1100
Henry Ⅰ 亨利一世	1100—1135
Stephen 斯蒂芬	1135—1154

3. House of Plantagenet (1154—1399) 金雀花王朝

Henry Ⅱ 亨利二世	1154—1189
Richard Ⅰ 理查一世	1189—1199
John 约翰	1199—1216
Henry Ⅲ 亨利三世	1216—1272
Edward Ⅰ 埃德华一世	1272—1307
Edward Ⅱ 埃德华二世	1307—1327
Edward Ⅲ 爱德华三世	1327—1377
Richard Ⅱ 理查二世	1377—1399

4. House of Lancaster (1399—1461)兰开斯特王朝

Henry Ⅳ 亨利四世	1399—1413
Henry Ⅴ 亨利五世	1413—1422

Henry Ⅵ 亨利六世 1422—1461

5. House of York (1461—1485)约克王朝

Edward Ⅳ 爱德华四世 1461—1483

Edward Ⅴ 爱德华五世 1483

Rickard Ⅲ 理查三世 1483—1485

6. House of Tudor (1485—1603)都铎王朝

Henry Ⅶ 亨利七世 1485—1509

Henry Ⅷ 亨利八世 1509—1547

Edward Ⅵ 爱德华六世 1547—1553

Mary Ⅰ 玛丽一世 1553—1558

Elizabeth Ⅰ 伊丽莎白一世 1558—1603

7. House of Stuart (1603—1714)斯图亚特王朝

James Ⅰ 詹姆士一世 1603—1625

Charles Ⅰ 查理一世 1625—1649

Oliver Cromwell 奥利弗·克伦威尔 1653—1658

Richard Cromwell 理查德·克伦威尔 1658—1659

Charles Ⅱ 查理二世 1660—1685

James Ⅱ 詹姆士二世 1685—1688

William Ⅲ and Mary Ⅱ 威廉三世和玛丽二世 1689—1702

Anne 安妮 1702—1714

8. House of Hanover (1714—1910) 汉诺威王朝

George Ⅰ 乔治一世 1714—1727

George Ⅱ 乔治二世 1727—1760

George Ⅲ 乔治三世 1760—1820

George Ⅳ 乔治四世 1820—1830

William Ⅳ 威廉四世 1830—1837

Victoria 维多利亚 1837—1901

Edward Ⅶ 爱德华七世 1901—1910

9. House of Windsor (1910—present) 温莎王朝

George Ⅴ 乔治五世 1910—1936

Edward Ⅷ 爱德华八世 1936

George Ⅵ 乔治六世 1936—1952

Elizabeth Ⅱ 伊丽莎白二世 1952—present

Ⅲ. Counties of Great Britain

1. Avon (A)
2. Antrim (AN)
3. Armagh (AR)
4. Borders (B)
5. Bedford (BD)
6. Berkshire (BE)
7. Buckinghamshire (BK)
8. Central (C)
9. Cambridgeshire (CA)
10. Cheshire (CA)
11. Clyde (CL)
12. Cornwall (CO)
13. Cumbria (CU)
14. Cleveland (CV)
15. Durham (D)
16. Derbyshire(DE)
17. Dumfries & Galloway (DG)
18. Down (DO)
19. Dorset (DR)
20. Devon (DV)
21. Dyfed (DY)
22. Essex (E)
23. E. Sussex (ES)
24. Fife (F)
25. Fermanagh (FE)
26. Grampian (G)
27. Glouchester (GC)
28. Greater London (GL)
29. Greater Manchester (GM)
30. Gwent (GT)
31. Gwynedd (GW)
32. Highland (H)
33. Hampshire (HA)
34. Hertford (HT)
35. Humberside (HU)
36. Hereford & Worcester (HW)
37. Isle of Wight (IOW)
38. Kent (K)
39. Lothian (L)
40. Lancashire (LA)
41. Londonderry (LD)
42. Leicestershire (LE)
43. Lincoln (LI)
44. Merseyside (M)
45. Mid Glamorgan (MG)
46. Northumberland (N)
47. Norfolk (NF)
48. Nottinghamshire (NO)
49. Northampton (NT)
50. N. Yorkshire (NY)
51. Orkney (O)
52. Oxfordshire (OX)
53. Powys (P)
54. Strathclyde (S)
55. Salop (SA)
56. S. Glamorgan (SG)
57. Shetland (SM)
58. Somerset (SO)
59. Surrey (SR)
60. Staffordshire (ST)
61. Suffolk (SU)
62. S. Yorkshire (SY)
63. Tayside (T)
64. Tyne & Wear (TW)
65. Tyrone (TY)
66. Warwick (W)

67. W. Glamorgan (WG)
68. Western Isles (WI)
69. W. Midlands (WM)
70. W. Sussex (WS)
71. Wiltshire (WT)
72. W. Yorkshire (WY)

Ⅳ. Territories of Great Britain

Anguilla 安圭拉岛

Bermuda 百慕大群岛

British Antarctic Territory 南极属地

British India Ocean Territory 印度洋属地

British Virgin Islands 英属维尔京群岛

Cayman Islands 开曼群岛

Falkland Islands 富克兰群岛

Gibraltar 直布罗陀

Montserrat Island 蒙特塞拉岛

Pitcairn Islands 皮特凯恩群岛

St. Helena and Dependencies (Ascension, Tristan da Cunha) 圣赫勒拿岛及其附属岛屿(阿森松岛、特里斯坦·达库尼亚岛)

Turks and Caicos Islands 特克斯和凯科斯群岛

Ⅴ. British Commonwealth of Nations

COUNTRY	YEAR JOINED
In Africa	
Botswana	1966
British Indian Ocean Territory	1965
Gambia	1965
Ghana	1957
Kenya	1963
Lesotho	1966
Malawi	1964
Mauritius	1968
Namibia	1990
Nigeria	1960
St. Helena	1931
Seychelles	1976
Sierra Leone	1961
Swaziland	1968

Tanzania	1961
Uganda	1962
Zambia	1964
Zimbabwe	1980
In the Americas	
Anguilla	1931
Antigua and Barbuda	1981
Bahamas	1973
Barbados	1966
Belize	1982
Bermuda	1931
British Virgin Islands	1931
Canada	1931
Cayman Islands	1931
Dominica	1978
Falklands Islands	1931
Grenada	1974
Guyana	1966
Jamaica	1962
Montserrat	1931
St. Christopher-Nevis	1983
St. Lucia	1979
St. Vincent and the Grenadines	1979
Trinidad and Tobago	1962
Turks and Caicos Islands	1931
Dependencies	
Ross Dependency	1931
In Asia	
Bangladesh	1972
Brunei	1984
India	1947
Malaysia	1957
Maldives	1982
Pakistan	1947

Singapore	1965
Sri Lanka	1948
In Austral-Asia and Pacific	
Australia	1931
Cook Islands	1931
Norfolk Island	1931
Kiribati	1979
Nauru	1968
New Zealand	1931
Niue	1931
Papua New Guinea	1975
Pitcairn Islands	1931
Solomon Islands	1978
Tokelau	1931
Tonga	1970
Tuvalu	1978
Vanuatu	1980
In Europe	
Channel Islands	1931
Cyprus	1961
Gibraltar	1931
Malta	1964
Isle of Man	
United Kingdom	1931

APPENDIX Ⅱ

Ⅰ. Fifty States of the United States

1. New England States

Massachusetts*	(1788)	马萨诸塞
New Hampshire*	(1788)	新罕布什尔
Connecticut*	(1788)	康涅狄格
Rhode Island*	(1790)	罗德岛
Vermont	(1791)	佛蒙特
Maine	(1820)	缅因

2. Middle Atlantic Coast States

Delaware*	(1787)	特拉华
Pennsylvania*	(1788)	宾夕法尼亚
New Jersey*	(1787)	新泽西
New York*	(1788)	纽约
Maryland*	(1788)	马里兰
West Virginia	(1863)	西弗吉尼亚

3. Middle Western States

Ohio	(1803)	俄亥俄
Indiana	(1816)	印第安纳
Illinois	(1818)	伊利诺伊
Missouri	(1821)	密苏里
Michigan	(1837)	密执安
Iowa	(1846)	艾奥瓦
Wisconsin	(1848)	威斯康星
Minnesota	(1858)	明尼苏达
Kansas	(1861)	堪萨斯
Nebraska	(1867)	内布拉斯加
North Dakota	(1889)	北达科他

South Dakota	(1889)	南达科他
4. Southern States		
South Carolina*	(1788)	南卡罗来纳
North Carolina*	(1789)	北卡罗来纳
Georgia*	(1788)	佐治亚
Kentucky	(1792)	肯塔基
Tennessee	(1796)	田纳西
Louisiana	(1812)	路易斯安娜
Mississippi	(1817)	密西西比
Alabama	(1819)	阿拉巴马
Arkansas	(1836)	阿肯色
Florida	(1845)	佛罗里达
Texas	(1845)	得克萨斯
Oklahoma	(1907)	俄克拉何马
Virginia*	(1788)	弗吉尼亚
5. Mountain States		
Nevada	(1864)	内华达
Colorado	(1876)	科罗拉多
Montana	(1889)	蒙大拿
Wyoming	(1890)	怀俄明
Idaho	(1890)	爱达荷
Utah	(1896)	犹他
New Mexico	(1912)	新墨西哥
Arizona	(1912)	亚利桑那
California	(1850)	加利福尼亚
Oregon	(1859)	俄勒冈
Washington	(1889)	华盛顿
6. Overseas States		
Alaska	(1959)	阿拉斯加
Hawaii	(1959)	夏威夷

"*" indicates the original thirteen states.

Ⅱ. The Ten Great Interest Groups in the United States

1. Rockefeller Interest Group 洛克菲勒财团
2. Morgan Interest Group 摩根财团

3. Bank of America Interest Group 加利福尼亚财团
4. First National City Bank Interest Group 第一花旗银行财团
5. Chicago Interest Group 芝加哥财团
6. Mellon Interest Group 梅隆财团
7. Du Pont Interest Group 杜邦财团
8. Texas Interest Group 得克萨斯财团
9. Boston Interest Group 波士顿财团
10. Cleveland Interest Group 克里夫兰财团

Ⅲ. Outstanding Events in American History

1492	October 12, Christopher Columbus landed on Salvador Island.
1607	the setting up of Jamestown
1620	The First group of Puritans arrived in America.
1756—1763	the French and Indian War
1770	Boston Massacre
1773	Boston Tea Party
1774	The First Continental Congress was called on September 5 in Philadelphia, Pennsylvania.
1775	First shots of American War of Independence were fired at Lexington, Massachusetts, on April 19.
1775	The Second Continental Congress was called.
1776	July 4, the thirteen colonies signed the Declaration of Independence from England.
1776	December 25, the battle of Trenton was fought.
1777	October 17, Americans won a victory at Saratoga.
1781	October 19, the English army under general Cornwallis surrendered.
1786	Daniel Shays led an armed uprising in Massachusetts.
1787	the Constitutional Convention
1789	George Washington was elected first

President.

1801	December 1, Federal capital moved to Washington, D.C. from temporary quarters in Philadelphia.
1803	Louisiana Purchase
1819	The United States bought Florida from Spain.
1823	Monroe Doctrine
1828	the formation of the Democratic Party
1846—1848	the Mexican-US war
1854	the formation of the Republican Party
1860	Abraham Lincoln was elected the 16th President.
1861	First guns were fired in war over question of southern states' right to secede.
1862	September 22, President Lincoln issued Emancipation Proclamation granting freedom to slaves in southern states.
1865	April 9, the Civil War ended with the surrender of Confederate States. April 14, President Lincoln was shot dead while attending theater in Washington.
1867	Territory of Alaska was purchased from Czarist Russia.
1879	Thomas A. Edison invented first electric lamp.
1898	the Spanish-American War
1917	April 6, the United States entered World War I.
1941	December 7th, the Japanese attached Pearl Harbor.
1958	January 31, the United States sent up the first satellite, Explorer I.
1966	Unmanned Surveyor I spacecraft successfully landed on the moon.
1968	Richard Nixon was elected 37th President.
1972	President Nixon visited China.
1979	January 1, full diplomatic relations were established between the United States and the People's Republic of China.
1980	Ronald Reagan was elected 40th President.
1988	George Bush was elected 41st President.

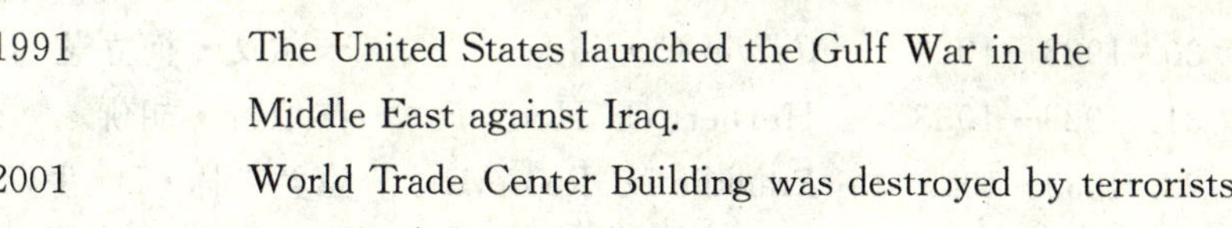

1991	The United States launched the Gulf War in the Middle East against Iraq.
2001	World Trade Center Building was destroyed by terrorists
2003	Iraq War/ the Second Gulf War

Ⅳ. The List of Presidents of the United States

1. 1789—1797	George Washington	乔治・华盛顿
2. 1797—1801	John Adams	约翰・亚当斯
3. 1801—1809	Thomas Jefferson	托马斯・杰斐逊
4. 1809—1817	James Madison	詹姆斯・麦迪逊
5. 1817—1825	James Monroe	詹姆斯・门罗
6. 1825—1829	John Q. Adams	约翰・Q・亚当斯
7. 1829—1837	Andrew Jackson	安德鲁・杰克逊
8. 1837—1841	Martin Van Buren	马丁・范布伦
9. 1841	William H. Harrison	威廉・H・哈里森
10. 1841—1845	John Tyler	约翰・泰勒
11. 1845—1849	James K. Polk	詹姆斯・K・波尔克
12. 1849—1850	Zachary Taylor	扎卡里・泰勒
13. 1850—1853	Millard Fillmore	米勒德・菲尔莫尔
14. 1853—1857	Franklin Pierce	弗兰克林・皮尔斯
15. 1857—1861	James C. Buchanan	詹姆斯・C・布坎南
16. 1861—1865	Abraham Lincoln	阿伯拉罕・林肯
17. 1865—1869	Andrew Johnson	安德鲁・约翰逊
18. 1869—1877	Ulysses S. Grant	尤利塞斯・S・格兰特
19. 1877—1881	Rutherford B. Hays	拉瑟富德・B・海斯
20. 1881	James A. Garfield	詹姆斯・A・加菲尔德
21. 1881—1885	Chester A. Arthur	切斯特・A・阿瑟
22. 1885—1889	Grover Cleveland	格罗弗・克利夫兰
23. 1889—1893	Benjamin Harrison	本杰明・哈里森
24. 1893—1897	Grover Cleveland	格罗弗・克利夫兰
25. 1897—1901	William McKinley	威廉・麦金莱
26. 1901—1909	Theodore Roosevelt	西奥多・罗斯福
27. 1909—1913	William H. Taft	威廉・H・塔夫脱
28. 1913—1921	Woodrow Wilson	伍德罗・威尔逊
29. 1921—1923	Warren G. Harding	沃伦・G ・哈丁

30. 1923—1929	Calvin Coolidge	卡尔文·柯立芝
31. 1929—1933	Herbert C. Hoover	赫伯特·胡佛
32. 1933—1945	Franklin D. Roosevelt	富兰克林·D·罗斯福
33. 1945—1953	Harry S. Truman	哈里·S·杜鲁门
34. 1953—1961	Dwight D. Eisenhower	德怀特·D·艾森豪威尔
35. 1961—1963	John F. Kennedy	约翰·F·肯尼迪
36. 1963—1969	Lyndon B. Johnson	林顿·B·约翰逊
37. 1969—1974	Richard M. Nixon	理查德·M·尼克松
38. 1974—1977	Gerald R. Food	杰拉尔德·R·福特
39. 1977—1981	Jimmy Carter	吉米·卡特
40. 1981—1989	Ronald Reagan	罗纳德·里根
41. 1989—1993	George Bush	乔治·布什
42. 1993—2001	Bill Clinton	比尔·克林顿
43. 2001—present	George W. Bush	乔治·W·布什

Bibliography

1. Anthony Paul, *A Guide to the English-Speaking World*, Longman, 1975.
2. Central Office of Information (London), *Britain in Brief*, 1972.
3. Ernest S. Griffith, *The American System of Government*, Frederick A. Praeger, New York, 1954.
4. John M. Blum, Edmund S. Morgan et al., *The National Experience* (Fifth Edition), Harcourt Brace Jovanovich, Inc., New York, 1981.
5. John Nist, *A Structural History of English*, St. Martin's Press, Inc., 1966.
6. Luther S. Luedtke, *Making America*, Forum Series, United States Information Agency, 1987.
7. M. D. Munro Machenzie and L. J. Westwood, *Background to Britain*, The Macmillan Press Ltd., 1983.
8. Peter Bromhead, *Life in Modern America*, Longman, 1977.
9. Richard Musman, *Background to the USA*, Macmillan Publishers Ltd., 1995.
10. 安徽师范大学外语系:《英语语言与文化》,安徽大学出版社 1998 年版。
11. 陈治刚、张承谟:《英美概况》(新编本),上海外语教育出版社 1994 年版。
12. 董乐山:《英汉美国社会知识小词典》,新华出版社 1984 年版。
13. 范存忠:《英国史提纲》,四川人民出版社 1982 年版。
14. 梁实秋:《远东英汉大辞典》,远东图书公司 1977 年版。
15. 美国大使馆文化处:《美国政府简介》,1981 年版。
16. 美国大使馆文化处:《美国历史简介》,1982 年版。
17. 《世界现代史》编写组:《世界现代史》(1917～1954),山东人民出版社 1981 年版。

18. 汪尧田、陈治刚:《英美概况》，上海外语教育出版社 1984 年版。
19. 辛华:《英语国家姓名译名手册》，商务印书馆 1965 年版。
20. 许鲁之:《新编英美概况》，青岛海洋大学出版社 1995 年版。
21. 于志远:《英语国家概况》,外语教学与研究出版社 2000 年版。
22. 中国地名委员会:《外国地名译名手册》，商务印书馆 1983 年版。
23. 朱永涛:《英美文化基础教程》，外语教学与研究出版社 1991 年版。
24. 朱永涛:《英语国家社会与文化入门》(上、下册)，高等教育出版社 2002 年版。